CHURCH GONE WILD

A CALL TO RENEWAL AND RESTORATION

BISHOP AL CHEEKS

FAITH RESOLUTE PUBLISHING – an imprint of Sandton Goldfield Publishing

Church Gone Wild
Copyright © 2024 by Bishop Al Cheeks

Requests for information should be addressed to:
ChurchGoneWild@FaithResolute.com
Faith Resolute Publishing, 30 N Gould Street, Suite 25665, Sheridan, Wyoming 82801

Faith Resolute titles are available for bulk purchases intended for educational, business, fundraising, or sales promotional purposes. For inquiries, kindly contact BulkOrders@FaithResolute.com.

ISBN: 978-1-963628-56-2

Any internet addresses (websites, blogs, social media accounts, etc.) and telephone numbers provided in this book are offered for informational purposes only. They do not constitute an endorsement or warranty by Faith Resolute Publishing. Faith Resolute Publishing neither verifies nor warrants the accuracy, completeness, or quality of the content contained within these websites, blogs, social media accounts, and contact numbers during the lifespan of this book.

All rights reserved. No part of this publication may be reproduced, distributed, or transmitted in any form or by any means, including photocopying, recording, or other electronic or mechanical methods, without the prior written permission of the publisher, except in the case of brief quotations embodied in critical reviews and certain other noncommercial uses permitted by copyright law.

For permissions requests, please contact Faith Resolute Publishing at Permissions@FaithResolute.com.

Table of Contents

Introduction vii
Section 1: The Historical Roots of Drift 1
   Chapter 1: Early Church vs. Modern Church 2
   Chapter 2: The Rise of Cultural Christianity 9
   Chapter 3: Pivotal Moments in Church History 16
   Chapter 4: Warning from Scripture on the Danger of Doctrinal Drift 24
   Chapter 5: Contemporary Examples 31
Section 2: The Pursuit of Popularity 39
   Chapter 6: Seeking Approval 40
   Chapter 7: Media and Technology Influence 48
   Chapter 8: Consequences of Compromise 55
   Chapter 9: Scriptural Admonition on Standing Firm in Faith. 62
   Chapter 10: Turning Back 69
Section 3: Financial Gain over Spiritual Riches 75
   Chapter 11: The Prosperity Gospel 76
   Chapter 12: Money and Ministry 83
   Chapter 13: Accountability in Stewardship 89
   Chapter 14: Scriptural Guidance on Managing Church Finances 96
   Chapter 15: Restoring Right Priorities 103
Section 4: Leadership Compromise 109
   Chapter 16: Character over Charisma 110
   Chapter 17: Accountability Failures 116

Chapter 18: Biblical Leadership Models 123

Chapter 19: Scriptural Warning on the Responsibilities of Church Leaders 130

Chapter 20: Reforming Church Leadership 137

Section 5: Doctrine Dilution 144

Chapter 21: Watered-Down Teachings................................. 145

Chapter 22: Impact on Congregational Depth 152

Chapter 23: Calling for Doctrinal Purity............................... 159

Chapter 24: Scriptural Insight on the Dangers of Diluted Doctrine.. 165

Chapter 25: Reviving Sound Doctrine 171

Section 6: Social Justice vs. Scriptural Justice 177

Chapter 26: Modern Social Movements and the Gospel 178

Chapter 27: The Role of the Church in Society 185

Chapter 28: Scriptural Examples of Justice 191

Chapter 29: Dangers of Political Entanglement.................. 198

Chapter 30: Emphasizing Biblical Justice 204

Section 7: Worship Trends and True Worship 211

Chapter 31: Entertainment over Worship............................ 212

Chapter 32: The Purpose of Worship 219

Chapter 33: Scriptural Foundations for Worship 226

Chapter 34: Correcting Course 232

Chapter 35: Case Studies of Authentic Worship 238

Section 8: Church Community vs. Individualism.................... 245

Chapter 36: The Rise of Individualistic Christianity 246

Chapter 37: Biblical Community Life 252

Chapter 38: Restoring Community 259
Chapter 39: Scriptural Encouragement to Build a Strong Church Community.. 265
Chapter 40: Success Stories 272
Section 9: The Influence of Culture on Church 280
Chapter 41: Cultural Trends vs. Eternal Truths..................... 281
Chapter 42: Scriptural Integrity 288
Chapter 43: Strategies for Resistance 294
Chapter 44: Scriptural Guidance on Cultural Influence........ 301
Chapter 45: Balancing Engagement and Separation............ 308
Section 10: The Call to Holiness 314
Chapter 46: Understanding Biblical Holiness....................... 315
Chapter 47: Practical Holiness.. 321
Chapter 48: The Challenges of Holiness in Modern Society 327
Chapter 49: Scriptural Exhortation to Pursue Holiness 334
Chapter 50: Fostering a Culture of Holiness......................... 341
Section 11: The Prophetic Warning of Separation.................... 347
Chapter 51: The Biblical Basis for Separation...................... 348
Chapter 52: The Necessity of Separation for Renewal 354
Chapter 53: Prophetic Voices in Scripture 360
Chapter 54: Scriptural Warning About Separation................ 367
Chapter 55: Heeding the Call.. 373
Section 12: The Road to Renewal... 379
Chapter 56: Steps to Spiritual Renewal 380
Chapter 57: Revival Histories 386

Chapter 58: Role of Prayer and Repentance 393

Chapter 59: Scriptural Promise of Divine Restoration 399

Chapter 60: Envisioning the Future Church 405

Amen and Beyond 414

A Prayer for You 418

About The Author 422

Introduction

In the tumultuous seas of modern society, where the currents of cultural acceptance and financial reward threaten to carry us away, it is imperative to recall the anchor of our faith: the sound, unalterable doctrine of Scripture. As we open the pages of "Church Gone Wild: A Call to Renewal and Restoration," we find ourselves confronting a stark reality—a reality where many of our cherished institutions, our churches, have drifted far from their biblical moorings. This drift is not merely a deviation; it is a departure that has left many believers yearning for the pure spiritual milk of the Word, as emphasized in 1 Peter 2:2, which urges us to long for this pure milk that we may grow up into salvation.

It seems with each passing day, the church's identity is increasingly marred by the quest for cultural relevancy and material wealth, overshadowing its divine commission. In Matthew 28:19-20, Christ commissioned us to go and make disciples of all nations, baptizing them and teaching them to observe all that He commanded. This foundational mandate calls for spiritual depth and doctrinal purity, yet, how often does this sacred call get drowned out by the noise of modernity and the applause of the masses?

This departure from doctrinal soundness to a more culturally accommodating gospel is alarming. It echoes the prophetic warning of 2 Timothy 4:3, where Paul foretells a time when people will not endure sound teaching, but, having itching ears, they will accumulate for themselves teachers to suit their own passions. This prophecy seems all too real today as we witness a church landscape that increasingly bends towards entertainment and self-satisfaction, neglecting the harder truths of Scripture.

Consider the subtle yet profound impact of this shift. The essence of worship, the depth of scriptural engagement, the commitment to community and discipleship—all these pillars of church life are compromised when the primary aim shifts from glorifying God to pleasing man. Galatians 1:10 challenges us with a pivotal question: "For am I now seeking the approval of man, or of God? Or am I trying to please man? If I were still trying to please man, I would not be a servant of Christ." This question is not merely rhetorical; it demands deep self-examination and realignment with our true purpose.

In the quest for acceptance, many churches have embraced a form of godliness but deny its power, as warned in 2 Timothy 3:5. This form of godliness manifests in a polished exterior, a church that is outwardly vibrant and successful but often lacks spiritual vitality and genuine transformation. The danger here is not just in the superficiality but in the gradual erosion of biblical truth that accompanies the pursuit of outward success.

The consequences of this drift are not trivial; they are spiritually catastrophic. When churches stray from the anchor of biblical truth, they not only endanger their own spiritual health but also that of their congregants. Hebrews 2:1 implores us to pay much closer attention to what we have heard, lest we drift away from it. This admonition is not just for the individual believer but is critically applicable to the collective journey of our church communities.

Yet, amidst this sobering landscape, there is a clarion call—a prophetic, urgent call to renewal and restoration. It is a call that resonates with the promise of revival, a return to our first love, as Christ implores the church in Ephesus in Revelation 2:4-5. This call to renewal is not just about reclaiming lost ground; it is about advancing the kingdom with renewed vigor and undefiled purity.

This call is deeply rooted in the character of God, who is unchanging despite the fluctuating trends of culture. James 1:17 reminds us that every good gift and every perfect gift is from above, coming down from the Father of lights, with whom there is no variation or shadow due to change. Our pursuit, therefore, must align with His unchanging nature, seeking not to conform to the world but to be transformed by the renewal of our mind, as Romans 12:2 so powerfully instructs.

The urgency of this renewal cannot be overstated. As the world grows darker, the church is meant to shine brighter, a city set on a hill that cannot be hidden, as Matthew 5:14 describes. However, this shining forth is not through superficial means but through a deep, abiding commitment to the truths of Scripture, lived out in love and obedience.

This book is a prophetic warning but also a heartfelt invitation. It invites us back to the heart of worship, to the foundational truths of our faith, to the passionate pursuit of God's presence and His righteousness. It calls for a bold rejection of the patterns of this world, urging us to embrace the transformative power of the Holy Spirit, as described in Titus 3:5, which speaks of the renewal of the Holy Spirit generously poured out through Jesus Christ our Savior.

As we embark on this journey together through the pages of this book, let us approach with a spirit of humility and expectation. Let us be like the Bereans, who received the word with all eagerness, examining the Scriptures daily to see if these things were so (Acts 17:11). Let this not be merely an academic exercise but a transformative experience that realigns our hearts, our churches, and our mission with the unerring truth of God's Word.

In doing so, we are not merely preserving a heritage; we are actively participating in the kingdom work, laying up treasures in heaven where neither moth nor rust destroys, and where thieves do not break in and steal, as Matthew 6:20 promises. This is the eternal investment that no economic downturn can deplete, no cultural shift can devalue.

Therefore, let this introduction serve as both a sobering reflection and an inspiring call to action. As we turn each page, may we be stirred not by fear or nostalgia but by a resolute commitment to the call of Christ, to walk in His ways, to uphold His truths, and to advance His kingdom with purity, passion, and perseverance.

Section 1: The Historical Roots of Drift

Chapter 1: Early Church vs. Modern Church

In the vibrant tapestry of early Christianity, the church was marked by an unwavering commitment to apostolic doctrine, communal living, and fervent prayer. This nascent community, emerging in the shadow of Christ's resurrection, thrived under the nurturing guidance of the Holy Spirit. The book of Acts paints a vivid picture of their daily walk: "And they continued steadfastly in the apostles' doctrine and fellowship, and in breaking of bread, and in prayers" (Acts 2:42). Their simplicity and purity of faith enabled them to navigate through persecution and societal disdain with a focus that was distinctly heavenward. This focus is a stark contrast to the complex and often convoluted practices of many modern congregations.

Today, numerous churches, especially in culturally affluent areas, appear to have drifted from these foundational pillars into arenas that would seem foreign to early Christians. The modern church often emphasizes growth metrics, social media influence, and cultural relevance, sometimes at the expense of doctrinal purity and depth. This pursuit of broad appeal can lead to a dilution of the potent truths that once defined the church's identity. Paul's words to Timothy in 1 Timothy 6:5 warn of such a time when men would consider "gain is godliness," prompting leaders to intertwine commercial success with spiritual health—a concept largely alien to the first followers of Christ.

Reflecting on this, the transformation from an intimate, community-focused entity to a performance-driven model raises profound concerns. In the early church, leaders like Peter and John

CHAPTER 1: EARLY CHURCH VS. MODERN CHURCH

were more concerned with preaching in the streets and healing the sick than with how their sermons might be received on a broader stage. They were emboldened by the Holy Spirit, as Acts 4:31 recounts, "And when they had prayed, the place was shaken where they were assembled together; and they were all filled with the Holy Ghost, and they spake the word of God with boldness." The contrast with today's approach, where the fear of offending can muzzle the church's prophetic voice, is alarming.

The early church's engagement with society was transformative because it flowed from their identity in Christ rather than from a strategy to enhance church attendance. They understood the weight of Jesus' instruction in Matthew 5:13-14, where He calls His followers "the salt of the earth" and "the light of the world." Their influence on society was a natural overflow of their commitment to live out Christ's teachings, irrespective of societal accolades or acceptance. This raises a crucial question: does the modern church still prioritize influencing the world through spiritual authenticity, or has it shifted to adapting itself to the expectations of the world to maintain relevance?

Moreover, the governance of the early church was based on spiritual discernment and a close adherence to the guidance of the Holy Spirit. This is exemplified by the selection of deacons in Acts 6:3, "Wherefore, brethren, look ye out among you seven men of honest report, full of the Holy Ghost and wisdom, whom we may appoint over this business." Modern church leadership, while often well-meaning, sometimes leans heavily on business models and corporate strategies. This can lead to a preference for leaders who are more skilled in management than in spiritual matters, potentially sidelining the crucial requirement of divine guidance.

The essence of worship in the early church also starkly contrasts with today's practices. They gathered in homes, sharing meals and their lives, their worship marked by a profound simplicity and authenticity. As Paul mentions in 1 Corinthians 14:26, "How is it then, brethren? when ye come together, every one of you hath a psalm, hath a doctrine, hath a tongue, hath a revelation, hath an interpretation. Let all things be done unto edifying." This model of mutual edification is far removed from the spectator-oriented services prevalent in many of today's churches, where the congregation passively receives rather than actively participates.

The commitment to doctrinal purity was paramount in the early church, and deviation from this was met with swift correction. Consider how Paul addressed the Galatians when they were tempted to turn to a different gospel (Galatians 1:6-8). He expressed astonishment that they were so quickly deserting the one who called them in the grace of Christ. This proactive stance against doctrinal drift safeguarded the church's theological integrity. In contrast, today's church often struggles with presenting a unified stance on scriptural truths, leading to confusion and a lack of solid teaching that can equip believers to stand firm in their faith.

The early church's approach to community and sharing was radical and countercultural. Acts 4:32-35 describes a community where believers were of one heart and soul, and none said that any of the things that belonged to him was his own, but they had everything in common. This spirit of generosity and unity is something that

CHAPTER 1: EARLY CHURCH VS. MODERN CHURCH

many modern churches aspire to yet often find challenging to implement in a culture that prizes individualism and personal success.

In reflecting on these contrasts, it becomes clear that the call to return to the roots of our faith is both urgent and necessary. The church must reevaluate its priorities, methods, and practices, aligning them more closely with those of the early church, whose members walked closely with God and impacted their world profoundly. Just as Revelation 2:5 admonishes, "Remember therefore from whence thou art fallen, and repent, and do the first works; or else I will come unto thee quickly, and will remove thy candlestick out of his place, except thou repent." The path to renewal lies in this heartfelt return to our first love, driven by a desire to embody the purity and power of the early Christian church.

The early believers were known for their unyielding faith and the miraculous signs that followed them. Mark 16:17-18 declares, "And these signs shall follow them that believe; In my name shall they cast out devils; they shall speak with new tongues; They shall take up serpents; and if they drink any deadly thing, it shall not hurt them; they shall lay hands on the sick, and they shall recover." This was not just theoretical but a lived reality. The faith of the early church was palpable, leading to the conversion of many and the spread of the gospel with a fervor that transformed the known world.

The issue we face today is the temptation to replace the miraculous with the mundane, the divine with the pragmatic. The early church did not shy away from the supernatural; it was their norm.

However, many modern churches have become uncomfortable with the unexplainable and have instead leaned on human reasoning and natural solutions. This shift has significant implications for how we perceive God's power and presence in our midst. Hebrews 13:8 reminds us, "Jesus Christ the same yesterday, and to day, and for ever." The power that fueled the early church is still available, yet our expectations have diminished.

Furthermore, the early church's persecution forged a resilient faith, as Peter writes in 1 Peter 4:12-13, "Beloved, think it not strange concerning the fiery trial which is to try you, as though some strange thing happened unto you: But rejoice, inasmuch as ye are partakers of Christ's sufferings; that, when his glory shall be revealed, ye may be glad also with exceeding joy." Their willingness to suffer for their faith made them stronger and more unified. Today, the absence of persecution in many parts of the world has led to a complacency that weakens the church's resolve and commitment to Christ's teachings.

Another significant aspect is the way the early church handled conflicts and disputes. They prioritized reconciliation and unity, often going to great lengths to maintain peace among believers. Matthew 18:15-17 provides a clear directive on handling disputes, emphasizing restoration over division. Modern churches often struggle with this, as conflicts can lead to splits and factions. The early church's example of addressing issues head-on, with a spirit of humility and a desire for unity, is a practice we need to reclaim.

The early church's evangelistic zeal was also unparalleled. They took the Great Commission seriously, as seen in Acts 1:8, "But ye shall receive power, after that the Holy Ghost is come upon you:

CHAPTER 1: EARLY CHURCH VS. MODERN CHURCH

and ye shall be witnesses unto me both in Jerusalem, and in all Judaea, and in Samaria, and unto the uttermost part of the earth." Their mission was clear, and their commitment unwavering. This contrasts sharply with the modern church's often sporadic and programmatic approach to evangelism, which can lack the personal passion and urgency that drove the early believers.

Moreover, the role of women in the early church, while reflective of cultural norms, still saw significant contributions from women who were deeply involved in ministry. Figures like Priscilla, Phoebe, and Lydia played crucial roles, as seen in Acts and Paul's epistles. This inclusivity within the bounds of scriptural teachings provided a rich diversity in ministry. Today, the church can learn from this balance, ensuring that all members are encouraged to use their gifts in service to God while adhering to biblical principles.

The spiritual disciplines of the early church—prayer, fasting, and scripture meditation—were foundational to their faith and practice. Acts 13:2-3 describes how they "ministered to the Lord, and fasted, the Holy Ghost said, Separate me Barnabas and Saul for the work whereunto I have called them. And when they had fasted and prayed, and laid their hands on them, they sent them away." These practices connected them deeply to God's will and empowered their ministry. In contrast, the modern church's engagement with these disciplines can sometimes be superficial, treated as optional rather than essential.

Ultimately, the early church's success lay in their absolute dependence on the Holy Spirit. They understood that apart from Him, they could do nothing. John 15:5, where Jesus says, "I am the vine, ye are the branches: He that abideth in me, and I in him, the same bringeth forth much fruit: for without me ye can do nothing," was a lived reality for them. This reliance on divine guidance and empowerment is something we must recapture if we are to see a true revival and renewal in our time.

In conclusion, examining the early church provides us with a clear mirror to reflect upon our current practices and priorities. The differences are stark, but they also offer a roadmap for returning to a faith that is powerful, pure, and transformative. We must heed the call to return to our first love, to the practices and principles that defined the early followers of Christ. As we do, we can trust that God will honor our commitment with His presence and power, renewing His church to be a light in the world once more.

Chapter 2: The Rise of Cultural Christianity

As we delve deeper into the historical roots of the drift in modern churches, we encounter a significant shift—a rise in what we might call "Cultural Christianity." This phenomenon is not merely a change in the style of worship or pastoral delivery; it represents a foundational shift toward aligning the church's practices and beliefs with the prevailing cultural norms rather than the immutable Word of God. The Apostle Paul warned the Colossians, "Beware lest any man spoil you through philosophy and vain deceit, after the tradition of men, after the rudiments of the world, and not after Christ" (Colossians 2:8). This admonition remains ever relevant as we observe today's churches increasingly embracing cultural approval over biblical truth.

In exploring this trend, it's essential to understand the subtlety with which cultural influences have permeated the church. Initially, these influences appeared benign—simple changes to make the church more "accessible" or "relevant" to a broader audience. Yet, as we've seen, these seemingly harmless adjustments often lead to significant doctrinal compromises. Churches, in an effort to remain culturally relevant, have gradually drifted away from preaching the challenging truths of the gospel, favoring instead a message that aligns more comfortably with societal norms. The scripture reminds us, "For the time will come when they will not endure sound doctrine; but after their own lusts shall they heap to themselves teachers, having itching ears" (2 Timothy 4:3). This prophecy stunningly encapsulates the current scenario many congregations face.

Moreover, as churches seek to cater to a culture that values feelings over facts, emotional experiences are often emphasized at the expense of doctrinal depth. Worship services are increasingly designed to evoke emotional responses rather than to facilitate genuine encounters with the divine through the rigorous study of Scripture. Jesus Himself pointed out the necessity of basing our lives on solid, scriptural foundations when He said, "Therefore whosoever heareth these sayings of mine, and doeth them, I will liken him unto a wise man, which built his house upon a rock" (Matthew 7:24). The rock here symbolizes the enduring truth of Christ's teachings, not the shifting sands of cultural trends and popular opinion.

This drift into cultural Christianity not only affects the content of sermons and the style of worship but also extends into the church's broader engagement with the world. Many modern churches have become indistinguishable from the world, using the same marketing strategies, business models, and even political tactics, forgetting the Apostle James's sobering reminder: "Ye adulterers and adulteresses, know ye not that the friendship of the world is enmity with God? whosoever therefore will be a friend of the world is the enemy of God" (James 4:4). This scripture warns against the dangers of aligning too closely with worldly methods and mindsets, urging a separation that preserves the church's sanctity and distinctiveness.

One might wonder, then, how to counteract this trend. The first step is to recognize that our allegiance lies with Christ, not with

CHAPTER 2: THE RISE OF CULTURAL CHRISTIANITY

the world. The church must recommit to the unchanging truths of the gospel, even if they counter cultural norms. This commitment requires courage, especially in a society that often shuns absolute truths. But as believers, we are called to be set apart, illuminated by the light of God's Word in a world dimmed by relativism. The Lord Himself assures us of the strength to do so, saying, "I can do all things through Christ which strengtheneth me" (Philippians 4:13). With this divine empowerment, we can resist the pull of cultural conformity and stand firm in our faith.

Moreover, pastors and church leaders play a critical role in this process. They are tasked not only with preaching the truth but with living it authentically before their congregations. Leadership in the church should reflect the servant leadership modeled by Christ, not the hierarchical, power-driven models so common in the corporate world. In the book of Peter, we find a directive for leaders: "Feed the flock of God which is among you, taking the oversight thereof, not by constraint, but willingly; not for filthy lucre, but of a ready mind" (1 Peter 5:2). This scripture highlights the selfless, humble approach required of those who lead God's people.

In confronting cultural Christianity, we must also renew our commitment to discipleship and biblical literacy. A church well-grounded in scripture is less likely to drift into cultural complacency. This grounding in the Word equips believers to discern truth from error, essential in an era marked by spiritual deception. As it is written, "Sanctify them through thy truth: thy word is truth" (John 17:17). True sanctification and transformation come from an unwavering commitment to the truths found in God's Word, not the fleeting doctrines of human invention.

The rise of cultural Christianity has also led to a significant shift in how churches approach their mission and vision. Instead of focusing on the Great Commission—"Go ye therefore, and teach all nations, baptizing them in the name of the Father, and of the Son, and of the Holy Ghost" (Matthew 28:19)—many churches now prioritize programs and initiatives designed to enhance their public image and societal standing. This shift often results in a diluted message that emphasizes good works over the transformative power of the gospel. While community service and social justice are integral to the Christian faith, they should never overshadow the core message of salvation through Jesus Christ.

This emphasis on cultural acceptance often leads to the marginalization of key biblical doctrines. Teachings on sin, repentance, and the need for a Savior are frequently downplayed or ignored altogether in favor of messages that promote self-help and personal improvement. The Apostle Paul addressed this issue in his letter to the Galatians: "I marvel that ye are so soon removed from him that called you into the grace of Christ unto another gospel: Which is not another; but there be some that trouble you, and would pervert the gospel of Christ" (Galatians 1:6-7). This perversion of the gospel creates a form of Christianity that is palatable to the masses but lacks the power to transform lives.

As we consider the implications of cultural Christianity, it is vital to acknowledge the role of media and technology in shaping church practices and beliefs. While these tools can be used to spread the gospel and reach a broader audience, they can also contribute to the commodification of faith. Churches that prioritize online presence and social media engagement may find themselves

CHAPTER 2: THE RISE OF CULTURAL CHRISTIANITY

tailoring their messages to attract likes and shares rather than faithfully proclaiming God's Word. This trend is reminiscent of the warning in 2 Timothy 3:5, where Paul speaks of those "having a form of godliness, but denying the power thereof."

The allure of cultural Christianity is further compounded by the pressures of numerical growth and financial stability. Many churches equate success with the size of their congregations and the health of their budgets. This mindset can lead to a compromise of biblical standards in favor of strategies that attract more attendees and increase revenue. Jesus addressed this issue directly, cautioning His followers about the dangers of wealth and materialism: "No man can serve two masters: for either he will hate the one, and love the other; or else he will hold to the one, and despise the other. Ye cannot serve God and mammon" (Matthew 6:24).

In this context, it is crucial for churches to examine their priorities and realign them with the teachings of Christ. This process involves a return to the foundational principles of the faith and a rejection of the temptation to conform to worldly standards. As the Apostle Paul exhorted the Romans, "And be not conformed to this world: but be ye transformed by the renewing of your mind, that ye may prove what is that good, and acceptable, and perfect, will of God" (Romans 12:2). This transformation requires a deliberate effort to resist cultural influences and maintain a focus on spiritual growth and maturity.

Churches must also foster an environment that encourages genuine worship and heartfelt devotion. In many cases, worship services have become performances designed to entertain rather than opportunities for believers to encounter God. The psalmist declares, "O come, let us worship and bow down: let us kneel before the LORD our maker" (Psalm 95:6). True worship is an act of surrender and reverence, not a spectacle for human approval. By prioritizing authentic worship, churches can create a space where God's presence is truly felt and experienced.

Another aspect of cultural Christianity is the tendency to prioritize individualism over community. In a society that values personal autonomy and self-expression, the biblical concept of the church as a body of believers united in Christ can be overshadowed. The Apostle Paul emphasized the importance of unity and interdependence within the church: "For as we have many members in one body, and all members have not the same office: So we, being many, are one body in Christ, and every one members one of another" (Romans 12:4-5). By fostering a sense of community and mutual support, churches can counteract the isolating effects of cultural individualism.

In addressing the rise of cultural Christianity, it is also essential to consider the prophetic role of the church. Throughout history, the church has served as a voice for truth and justice, calling society to repentance and righteousness. This prophetic mandate requires courage and conviction, especially in a culture that often rejects absolute truths. As the prophet Isaiah declared, "Cry aloud, spare not, lift up thy voice like a trumpet, and shew my people their transgression, and the house of Jacob their sins" (Isaiah 58:1). By embracing this prophetic calling, the church can stand as a beacon of hope and truth in a world marred by moral confusion.

CHAPTER 2: THE RISE OF CULTURAL CHRISTIANITY

In conclusion, the rise of cultural Christianity poses a significant challenge to the modern church. Yet, it also offers an opportunity for renewal and revival. By recognizing the subtle ways in which cultural influences have shaped church practices and beliefs, believers can take deliberate steps to realign with the truths of God's Word. This process involves a commitment to sound doctrine, authentic worship, and genuine community. It requires a rejection of worldly standards and a return to the foundational principles of the faith. As the church embraces its prophetic role and recommits to the transformative power of the gospel, it can serve as a powerful witness to the world, shining the light of Christ in the darkness.

Chapter 3: Pivotal Moments in Church History

The history of the church is a tapestry woven with moments of profound faith and periods of troubling drift. Each era has left its mark, shaping the church's path and, at times, leading it astray from its foundational truths. Understanding these pivotal moments is crucial if we are to heed God's call for renewal and restoration today. One such defining moment occurred when Emperor Constantine embraced Christianity in the early fourth century. His conversion and subsequent endorsement of Christianity as the state religion fundamentally transformed the church. No longer a persecuted minority, the church found itself intertwined with political power. While this alignment brought an end to widespread persecution and facilitated the spread of the gospel, it also introduced new challenges. As Paul admonished in 2 Corinthians 6:14, "Be ye not unequally yoked together with unbelievers: for what fellowship hath righteousness with unrighteousness? and what communion hath light with darkness?" This union with the state often led to compromises that diluted the church's spiritual purity.

During the medieval period, the church's ascent to power continued unabated. The rise of the papacy saw the church accruing immense wealth and political influence, but with this power came a shift in focus. The spiritual mission of the church was overshadowed by temporal concerns. Practices such as the sale of indulgences emerged, leading many to believe they could buy their way into heaven. This stark deviation from the gospel's

CHAPTER 3: PIVOTAL MOMENTS IN CHURCH HISTORY

message of salvation by grace alone was a direct affront to Ephesians 2:8-9, which reminds us, "For by grace are ye saved through faith; and that not of yourselves: it is the gift of God: Not of works, lest any man should boast." The church's drift into materialism and corruption during this time set the stage for the profound disquiet that would lead to the Reformation.

The Reformation, ignited by figures like Martin Luther and John Calvin, was indeed a watershed moment in church history. These reformers stood boldly against the prevailing ecclesiastical norms, calling for a return to the scriptures as the sole authority for Christian life and practice. Luther's act of nailing his 95 Theses to the door of the Wittenberg Church was a prophetic declaration, echoing the boldness of Old Testament prophets like Jeremiah, who declared God's word to a wayward Israel. Luther's cry for reform, "Scripture alone," resonated deeply, reminding the faithful of Acts 17:11, where the Bereans were commended because they "received the word with all readiness of mind, and searched the scriptures daily, whether those things were so." This return to scriptural authority was a clarion call for the church to purify itself from the accumulated traditions that had no basis in the Word of God.

However, the aftermath of the Reformation also illustrates the human tendency to fracture. Protestantism, initially a unified movement calling for reform, soon splintered into numerous denominations. Each group sought to adhere to scriptural truth as they understood it, yet the proliferation of interpretations led to an ever-widening array of beliefs and practices. This fragmentation serves as a stark reminder of Paul's exhortation to the Corinthians about the dangers of division within the body of Christ, "Now I beseech you, brethren, by the name of our Lord Jesus Christ, that ye all speak the same thing, and that there be no divisions among you; but that ye be perfectly joined together in the same mind and in the same judgment" (1 Corinthians 1:10). The desire for doctrinal purity, while noble, often led to an unintended scattering of the faithful.

In the centuries that followed, the church faced the challenges of the Enlightenment and the rise of secularism. The Enlightenment's emphasis on reason and scientific inquiry posed significant questions to the church's teachings. Many church leaders struggled to reconcile faith with the new scientific worldview. This period saw a drift toward rationalism, where faith was sometimes subordinated to reason. Yet, amidst these challenges, voices like that of John Wesley emerged, advocating for a faith that engaged both the heart and the mind. Wesley's Methodist movement emphasized personal holiness and social action, reminding the church of its call to be a transformative presence in the world. His commitment to a lived faith was reminiscent of James 2:17, which states, "Even so faith, if it hath not works, is dead, being alone."

The 19th and 20th centuries brought about the rise of the evangelical movement, marking another pivotal period in church history. This movement emphasized personal faith, evangelism, and a return to the authority of the scriptures. It sparked a revival of grassroots Christianity, reminiscent of the early church's vibrancy. The fervor for missions and spreading the gospel echoed the spirit of the Apostles as described in Acts, particularly in Paul's missionary journeys. However, this era also saw the emergence of

CHAPTER 3: PIVOTAL MOMENTS IN CHURCH HISTORY

the prosperity gospel, which preached that material wealth and physical health were signs of God's favor. This message, appealing as it was, stood in stark contrast to the biblical teaching on suffering and discipleship. As Jesus reminded His followers in Matthew 16:24, "If any man will come after me, let him deny himself, and take up his cross, and follow me." The prosperity gospel's focus on earthly rewards often overshadowed the call to self-denial and sacrificial living.

Today, we stand at a crossroads where the church must critically evaluate its historical drifts and the current influences shaping its course. The commercialization of the gospel in some modern mega-churches raises pressing questions about the purity of the church's witness. As believers, we must heed the cautionary words found in Matthew 7:15, "Beware of false prophets, which come to you in sheep's clothing, but inwardly they are ravening wolves." This warning is vital as we consider the seductive allure of modernity that can, at times, lead to a dilution of the gospel's transformative power. The church's engagement with culture is essential, yet it must be done without compromising the integrity of its message. We are called to be "the salt of the earth" (Matthew 5:13), preserving the truth of the gospel even as we engage with a changing world.

Reflecting on these historical shifts, it becomes evident that each era brought both challenges and opportunities for growth. The church's journey is a testament to God's enduring faithfulness, despite human frailty and missteps. The call for today's church is to remember and return to the fervent, unadulterated pursuit of Christ's teachings. Just as Revelation 2:5 urges, "Remember therefore from whence thou art fallen, and repent, and do the first works; or else I will come unto thee quickly, and will remove thy candlestick out of his place, except thou repent." This scriptural mandate to repent and return to our first love is as relevant now as ever.

In contemplating the road ahead, we must anchor ourselves in the wisdom of scripture and the guiding presence of the Holy Spirit. The journey towards renewal is not merely about reforming structures or updating practices but about a deep, heart-level transformation that rekindles the church's original passion and purpose. The prophetic call to renewal is not just about avoiding past mistakes but about moving forward with a renewed commitment to embody the love, truth, and power of the gospel in a world that desperately needs it.

The journey of the church through history is marked by cycles of decline and renewal. The Great Awakening in the 18th century, led by figures like Jonathan Edwards and George Whitefield, was a powerful reminder of God's ability to revive His people. These revivals were characterized by intense preaching, deep conviction of sin, and a renewed commitment to holy living. They echoed the call of Isaiah 57:15, "For thus saith the high and lofty One that inhabiteth eternity, whose name is Holy; I dwell in the high and holy place, with him also that is of a contrite and humble spirit, to revive the spirit of the humble, and to revive the heart of the contrite ones."

As we look to the future, the lessons of the past should guide us. The church must remain vigilant, constantly measuring its practices and teachings against the standard of God's Word. The

CHAPTER 3: PIVOTAL MOMENTS IN CHURCH HISTORY

temptation to conform to societal norms and cultural trends will always be present, but we are called to a higher standard. Romans 12:2 exhorts us, "And be not conformed to this world: but be ye transformed by the renewing of your mind, that ye may prove what is that good, and acceptable, and perfect, will of God." Our commitment to this transformation process is vital if we are to be effective witnesses in a world that is often hostile to the gospel.

The story of the church is one of both human frailty and divine sovereignty. God has consistently raised up leaders and movements to call His people back to Himself. The prophetic voices throughout history, from the Old Testament prophets to modern-day reformers, have served as reminders of God's unchanging standards and His relentless pursuit of His people. As Amos 3:7 declares, "Surely the Lord God will do nothing, but he revealeth his secret unto his servants the prophets." These prophetic voices are a gift to the church, guiding and correcting it when it strays.

The task before us is daunting, but it is also filled with promise. The same God who has guided the church through centuries of turmoil and triumph is still at work today. Our part is to remain faithful, to listen to His voice, and to respond with obedience and humility. The church's future depends on our willingness to embrace God's call to renewal and restoration fully. As we do, we can trust in His promise found in Isaiah 43:19, "Behold, I will do a new thing; now it shall spring forth; shall ye not know it? I will even make a way in the wilderness, and rivers in the desert." God is ready to do a new thing in our midst, if we are prepared to follow Him wholeheartedly.

In this pursuit of renewal, prayer must be our foundation. Throughout history, every significant movement of God has been preceded by prayer. The early church devoted themselves to prayer, as seen in Acts 1:14, "These all continued with one accord in prayer and supplication, with the women, and Mary the mother of Jesus, and with his brethren." This devotion to prayer is a model for us today. It is in the place of prayer that we align our hearts with God's will, receive His guidance, and are empowered by His Spirit.

Let us also remember that renewal is not solely an individual endeavor but a corporate one. The church, as the body of Christ, must move together in unity and purpose. Ephesians 4:3 urges us to "endeavor to keep the unity of the Spirit in the bond of peace." This unity is essential if we are to fulfill our mission and impact the world for Christ. It requires humility, forgiveness, and a commitment to love one another as Christ has loved us.

As we embrace this call to renewal, let us do so with hope and expectation. God's promises are sure, and His plans for His church are glorious. The journey may be challenging, and the obstacles great, but we can take heart in knowing that we serve a God who is able to do "exceeding abundantly above all that we ask or think, according to the power that worketh in us" (Ephesians 3:20). Our confidence is in Him, and our hope is anchored in His unchanging Word.

In conclusion, the pivotal moments in church history serve as both warnings and encouragements. They remind us of the dangers of drifting from sound doctrine and the necessity of returning to our first love. They also testify to God's faithfulness and His power to renew and restore. As we stand on the precipice of a new era, let us heed the lessons of the past, remain grounded in scripture, and pursue the fullness of God's calling for His church. The journey ahead is filled with promise, for we know that "He which hath begun a good work in you will perform it until the day of Jesus Christ" (Philippians 1:6).

Chapter 4: Warning from Scripture on the Danger of Doctrinal Drift

In "Church Gone Wild: A Call to Renewal and Restoration," we confront a sobering reality: the church has drifted far from its foundational moorings. As we navigate the historical roots of this drift, it's imperative to heed the timeless warnings that scripture provides. Jeremiah 6:16 commands, "Thus saith the LORD, Stand ye in the ways, and see, and ask for the old paths, where is the good way, and walk therein, and ye shall find rest for your souls." This is not just a nostalgic longing for the past but a divine directive to reclaim the steadfast principles that have been the bedrock of our faith.

When we reflect on the early church, we see a community deeply committed to doctrine, prayer, and mutual care. They were undeterred by societal pressures and were characterized by a profound dedication to the Gospel. Acts 2:42 describes how "they continued steadfastly in the apostles' doctrine and fellowship, and in breaking of bread, and in prayers." This early church model was not focused on cultural acceptance or financial gain but on spiritual authenticity and devotion to Christ. It's a stark contrast to many modern churches that seem more invested in popularity and profit than in scriptural fidelity.

The allure of modernity is seductive, promising growth and relevance. Yet, in our quest to be culturally relevant, we often sacrifice the very essence of our faith. Paul's warning in Galatians 1:10 is particularly pertinent: "For do I now persuade men, or God?

CHAPTER 4: WARNING FROM SCRIPTURE ON THE DANGER OF DOCTRINAL DRIFT

or do I seek to please men? for if I yet pleased men, I should not be the servant of Christ." This verse challenges us to examine our motives. Are we seeking to please God or to gain the approval of the world? The church's mandate is to stand firm in the unchanging word of God, not to conform to the ever-shifting standards of society.

This drift from doctrinal purity has profound implications. When we dilute the Gospel to make it more palatable, we undermine its power and effectiveness. Paul's prophecy in 2 Timothy 4:3-4 speaks to our time: "For the time will come when they will not endure sound doctrine; but after their own lusts shall they heap to themselves teachers, having itching ears; And they shall turn away their ears from the truth, and shall be turned unto fables." This is a prophetic warning about the dangers of abandoning sound doctrine for messages that merely entertain or comfort.

Returning to the old paths requires a courageous stand against the current trends. It means prioritizing scripture over societal applause and divine approval over fleeting popularity. This journey back is not for the faint-hearted. Jesus reminds us in John 4:24 that true worshipers must worship the Father in spirit and in truth. This return to true worship is about rekindling the original fire that ignited the early church's explosive growth—a fire fueled by the undiluted preaching of the Gospel and a community united in its mission to serve and save.

Every believer has a role to play in this restoration. James 1:22 exhorts us to be "doers of the word, and not hearers only, deceiving your own selves." Our faith must be active and engaged. It is not enough to merely listen to sermons or read scripture; we must live out these truths in our daily lives. This practical application is the true test of our commitment to God's ways. The early church thrived because its members were deeply involved in each other's lives, holding one another accountable and supporting each other in their walk with Christ.

As we commit to walking in the old paths, we must remember the promise in Isaiah 58:11, which assures us that "the LORD shall guide thee continually, and satisfy thy soul in drought, and make fat thy bones: and thou shalt be like a watered garden, and like a spring of water, whose waters fail not." This divine guidance is not just for our spiritual journey but encompasses all aspects of our lives. It reassures us that even in times of spiritual drought, God's provision is sufficient.

Walking in the old paths does not mean retreating into a past era; rather, it is about engaging with a living tradition that bridges our rich history with the present. Psalm 119:105 declares, "Thy word is a lamp unto my feet, and a light unto my path." This verse highlights the guiding power of scripture, which illuminates our way even in the darkest times. As we navigate the complexities of modern life, we must rely on the unchanging word of God to guide our steps.

In returning to these old paths, we are not merely preserving the legacy of the early church; we are participating in the renewal and refreshing that God is calling us toward. This is a divine invitation to return to the purity and power of the Gospel. Matthew 7:13-14 warns us about the narrow gate that leads to life and the broad way that leads to destruction. This analogy is crucial as it underscores

CHAPTER 4: WARNING FROM SCRIPTURE ON THE DANGER OF DOCTRINAL DRIFT

the necessity of choosing the path less traveled, the one that leads to spiritual renewal and true life in Christ.

The modern church often faces the temptation to embrace trends and practices that promise growth but compromise core beliefs. The warning in Colossians 2:8 is clear: "Beware lest any man spoil you through philosophy and vain deceit, after the tradition of men, after the rudiments of the world, and not after Christ." This scripture calls us to vigilance, ensuring that our teachings and practices remain grounded in Christ and not in the transient philosophies of the age.

This call to vigilance extends to our personal lives as well. Proverbs 4:23 admonishes us to "Keep thy heart with all diligence; for out of it are the issues of life." Our personal commitment to Christ and His teachings directly impacts the health of the church. When individual believers prioritize their relationship with God and His word, the collective body of Christ is strengthened.

The church must also address the issue of leadership. Leaders who prioritize charisma over character often lead congregations astray. Titus 1:7-9 outlines the qualifications for church leaders, emphasizing integrity, faithfulness, and sound doctrine. Leaders must model the behavior and commitment they wish to see in their congregations. The failure to do so can lead to a breakdown in trust and a weakening of the church's witness.

Reforming church leadership is not an easy task, but it is essential for the health of the body. Leaders must be held accountable to biblical standards, and congregations must support them in this endeavor. Hebrews 13:17 reminds us to "Obey them that have the rule over you, and submit yourselves: for they watch for your souls, as they that must give account." This relationship between leaders and members is crucial for maintaining a church that is aligned with God's will.

The broader issue at hand is the church's relationship with the world. Romans 12:2 instructs us, "And be not conformed to this world: but be ye transformed by the renewing of your mind, that ye may prove what is that good, and acceptable, and perfect, will of God." Conformity to the world leads to spiritual compromise. The church must maintain a distinct identity, rooted in the truth of the Gospel.

This distinct identity is not about isolation but about engagement with a clear purpose. The church is called to be in the world but not of it. John 17:15-16 captures Jesus' prayer for His disciples: "I pray not that thou shouldest take them out of the world, but that thou shouldest keep them from the evil. They are not of the world, even as I am not of the world." This delicate balance requires wisdom and discernment.

Engagement with the world also involves addressing social issues from a biblical perspective. The church must not shy away from issues of justice and mercy. Micah 6:8 states, "He hath shewed thee, O man, what is good; and what doth the LORD require of thee, but to do justly, and to love mercy, and to walk humbly with thy God?" This scripture calls us to action, ensuring that our faith is demonstrated through our deeds.

However, the pursuit of social justice must not overshadow the core mission of the church, which is to preach the Gospel and make disciples. Mark 16:15 charges us, "Go ye into all the world, and preach the gospel to every creature." This mission remains

CHAPTER 4: WARNING FROM SCRIPTURE ON THE DANGER OF DOCTRINAL DRIFT

paramount. Social action and Gospel proclamation are not mutually exclusive but must be integrated in a way that remains faithful to scripture.

The journey back to the old paths is also a journey of personal and corporate repentance. 2 Chronicles 7:14 offers a powerful promise: "If my people, which are called by my name, shall humble themselves, and pray, and seek my face, and turn from their wicked ways; then will I hear from heaven, and will forgive their sin, and will heal their land." This verse encapsulates the heart of our call to renewal. It begins with humility, prayer, and repentance.

As we embrace this call, we must do so with the assurance that God is faithful to His promises. He desires to heal and restore His church. Joel 2:25-26 offers hope: "And I will restore to you the years that the locust hath eaten… And ye shall eat in plenty, and be satisfied, and praise the name of the LORD your God, that hath dealt wondrously with you." Restoration is God's desire for His people.

In this process of restoration, the role of prayer cannot be overstated. James 5:16 encourages us, "The effectual fervent prayer of a righteous man availeth much." Prayer is the lifeline that connects us to God's power and wisdom. It is through prayer that we seek guidance, strength, and renewal.

In conclusion, the warnings from scripture are not merely historical footnotes but are deeply relevant to the contemporary church. They call us back to a place of purity, power, and purpose. The path may be challenging, but it is the path that leads to life. As we heed these warnings and embrace the call to renewal, we align ourselves with God's will and position the church to be a powerful witness in a world desperately in need of truth and hope. Let us return to the old paths with determination and faith, trusting that God will guide and sustain us in this crucial journey.

Chapter 5: Contemporary Examples

As we observe the state of contemporary churches, it becomes evident that many have strayed from the foundational tenets of biblical doctrine, often reflecting the world more than the Word. This shift is not merely a subtle change but a profound drift that has led to significant deviations in practice and belief. One of the most striking examples of this drift is the transformation of worship services into entertainment spectacles. Churches today often focus on creating an experience that appeals to the senses, employing elaborate lighting, powerful sound systems, and professional-grade performances. While there is nothing inherently wrong with using technology to enhance worship, the danger lies in prioritizing entertainment over genuine spiritual engagement. This trend aligns with Paul's warning in 2 Timothy 4:3-4, "For the time will come when they will not endure sound doctrine; but after their own lusts shall they heap to themselves teachers, having itching ears; And they shall turn away their ears from the truth, and shall be turned unto fables." The emphasis on creating a feel-good experience can lead congregations away from the truth of the gospel, focusing more on emotional highs than on the transformative power of the Word.

Another example of this drift is the trend among churches to align their messages with popular societal ideologies. In an effort to remain relevant and culturally accepted, some churches have diluted the gospel's radical calls to repentance and transformation. This shift towards a more inclusive and less confrontational gospel might seem compassionate, but it often compromises the integrity of the message. Jesus never shied away from speaking the truth, even when it was unpopular. In John 6:66, we read, "From that time many of his disciples went back, and walked no more with him." This verse illustrates that truth often divides even as it defines. When churches prioritize cultural acceptance over scriptural fidelity, they risk losing the transformative power of the gospel that calls us to a higher standard.

Financial prosperity doctrines also exemplify the drift from sound doctrine. Prosperity teaching, which links God's blessing with material success, appeals to the human desire for financial security and abundance. While God does promise to provide for His children, the focus on wealth as a sign of spiritual favor mimics the materialism of the surrounding culture more than the teachings of Christ, who said in Matthew 6:24, "No man can serve two masters... Ye cannot serve God and mammon." This scriptural reminder calls us to a higher purpose beyond earthly wealth. The danger of prosperity teaching is that it can create a transactional view of faith, where the primary focus is on what we can get from God rather than how we can serve Him.

Leadership within the church also reflects this drift. Instead of leaders who exhibit the humility and servant-heartedness of Christ, some modern church leaders pursue power and celebrity. They focus on building their personal brands rather than shepherding their flocks with integrity. Paul's words to the Ephesian elders in Acts 20:28, "Take heed therefore unto yourselves, and to all the

CHAPTER 5: CONTEMPORARY EXAMPLES

flock, over the which the Holy Ghost hath made you overseers, to feed the church of God, which he hath purchased with his own blood," underscore the profound responsibility of church leaders. This scriptural mandate highlights the calling to guide and protect the spiritual well-being of the congregation, a stark contrast to the celebrity culture that has infiltrated many modern churches.

The dilution of doctrine extends into how churches handle biblical teachings on sin and repentance. In a bid to be more inclusive and less "judgmental," there's a noticeable trend where messages about sin and the need for repentance are conspicuously absent. This is in direct opposition to Acts 17:30, where Paul declares, "And the times of this ignorance God winked at; but now commandeth all men everywhere to repent." The omission of such fundamental doctrines not only weakens the church's spiritual health but also robs individuals of the deep, transforming encounter with the grace of God that comes through true repentance. When churches fail to preach the full counsel of God, they deny their congregations the opportunity to experience genuine transformation.

Social justice issues have also become a focal point in many churches, sometimes at the expense of gospel proclamation. While social justice is deeply rooted in biblical principles, it should not replace the preaching of the gospel but rather accompany it. The Great Commission, outlined in Matthew 28:19-20, commands us to make disciples of all nations, teaching them to observe all that Jesus has commanded. This directive makes it clear that social transformation should flow from heart transformation, which can only come through encountering the gospel. When churches prioritize social justice over gospel proclamation, they risk addressing symptoms rather than the root cause of societal issues, which is the fallen nature of humanity.

Community life within churches has also changed. In many modern congregations, the deep, interconnected community life prescribed in Acts 2:42-47 has given way to a more superficial, program-driven model of church engagement. This scriptural passage describes the early Christians devoting themselves to the apostles' teaching and to fellowship, to the breaking of bread and to prayer. The strong sense of community and mutual support seen in the early church is often replaced by transient relationships and minimal commitment, reflecting more of our individualistic society than the interdependent community model set forth in the New Testament. This shift towards individualism can lead to a weakened sense of belonging and accountability within the church.

The prophetic voice of the church has also been muted in many circles. In an age where political correctness and fear of backlash reign, many churches remain silent on controversial issues, preferring neutrality to the risk of confrontation. This is far removed from the bold, uncompromising stance of prophets like Elijah, who declared God's truth to a wayward Israel in 1 Kings 18:21, "And Elijah came unto all the people, and said, How long halt ye between two opinions? if the LORD be God, follow him: but if Baal, then follow him." The reluctance to take a definitive stand on moral and spiritual issues showcases a concerning shift from the church's call to be a "light of the world" as Jesus instructed in Matthew 5:14. This retreat from prophetic boldness not only diminishes the church's witness but also fails to provide the moral clarity that society desperately needs.

As these contemporary examples illustrate, the drift from sound doctrine is not merely a theoretical concern but a tangible reality impacting churches across the globe. The call for renewal and restoration is urgent, beckoning us back to the uncompromising truth of the Scriptures. It is a call to rediscover our first love, to realign with the foundational teachings of our faith, and to embody the transformative power of the gospel in a world that desperately needs it. The drift has not happened overnight; it is the result of subtle compromises and gradual shifts in focus and priority. However, the remedy is a return to the basics of our faith, a recommitment to the principles that have sustained the church through centuries.

In this era of cultural and technological change, it is essential for the church to remain anchored in the unchanging truth of God's Word. Hebrews 13:8 reminds us, "Jesus Christ the same yesterday, and today, and forever." This verse underscores the constancy of Christ and His teachings, which should be the bedrock of our faith and practice. As the world around us continues to evolve, the church must resist the temptation to conform to every new trend and instead hold fast to the timeless truths of Scripture. This steadfastness will not only preserve the integrity of the church but also ensure that it remains a true light in a dark world.

The examples of drift in contemporary churches serve as a sobering reminder of the importance of vigilance and discernment. In 1 Peter 5:8, we are admonished, "Be sober, be vigilant; because your adversary the devil, as a roaring lion, walketh about, seeking whom he may devour." This call to vigilance is crucial in an age where spiritual compromise can easily creep in unnoticed. By staying alert and grounded in the Word, we can guard against the subtle shifts that lead to doctrinal drift and ensure that our churches remain true to their biblical mandate.

It is also vital for individual believers to take responsibility for their spiritual growth and maturity. Ephesians 4:14-15 encourages us, "That we henceforth be no more children, tossed to and fro, and carried about with every wind of doctrine, by the sleight of men, and cunning craftiness, whereby they lie in wait to deceive; But speaking the truth in love, may grow up into him in all things, which is the head, even Christ." This passage highlights the importance of doctrinal stability and spiritual growth, which are essential for resisting the winds of false teaching and remaining steadfast in the faith.

Churches must also prioritize the development of strong, biblically grounded leadership. In 1 Timothy 3:1-7, Paul outlines the qualifications for church leaders, emphasizing qualities such as blamelessness, temperance, and sound doctrine. These qualifications are not optional but essential for ensuring that

CHAPTER 5: CONTEMPORARY EXAMPLES

church leaders are equipped to guide their congregations faithfully. By investing in the spiritual and doctrinal development of leaders, churches can create a foundation of integrity and faithfulness that will support the entire congregation.

Finally, the church must remember its prophetic calling. In a world filled with confusion and moral ambiguity, the church is called to be a voice of truth and righteousness. Isaiah 58:1 exhorts, "Cry aloud, spare not, lift up thy voice like a trumpet, and show my people their transgression, and the house of Jacob their sins." This prophetic mandate requires courage and conviction, as it often involves speaking uncomfortable truths. However, it is through this bold proclamation that the church can fulfill its role as a moral and spiritual guide for the world.

In conclusion, the contemporary examples of drift from sound doctrine serve as a powerful reminder of the need for renewal and restoration within the church. By returning to the foundational truths of Scripture, prioritizing spiritual integrity, and embracing our

prophetic calling, we can realign with God's purposes and ensure that the church remains a faithful witness to the gospel. The call to renewal is not just for church leaders but for every believer, as we collectively seek to embody the transformative power of the gospel in a world that desperately needs it. As we heed this call, let us be encouraged by the promise of 2 Chronicles 7:14, "If my people, which are called by my name, shall humble themselves, and pray, and seek my face, and turn from their wicked ways; then will I hear from heaven, and will forgive their sin, and will heal their land." This promise of divine intervention and healing offers hope and motivation for the journey ahead.

Section 2: The Pursuit of Popularity

Chapter 6: Seeking Approval

In our quest for relevance, many churches have embarked on a journey that subtly, yet significantly, deviates from the unchanging Word of God to a gospel shaped by the whims of culture. This shift often stems from a desire to be accepted and celebrated in the public square, yet Galatians 1:10 challenges us profoundly: "For do I now persuade men, or God? or do I seek to please men? for if I yet pleased men, I should not be the servant of Christ." As we navigate these turbulent waters, we must ask ourselves whether our actions are directed towards pleasing God or garnering the fleeting applause of men.

The seduction of popularity can be compelling. Churches, in an effort to fill pews and appear 'successful,' may adopt the latest trends, diluting the potency of their messages to avoid offending attendees. But remember, Christ did not call us to be popular; He called us to be faithful. In John 15:18, Jesus reminds us, "If the world hate you, ye know that it hated me before it hated you." This is not a call to seek controversy for its own sake but rather a solemn reminder that our message will naturally challenge the sinful patterns of this world.

It's crucial to consider the long-term impacts of seeking approval from society rather than from God. When churches shift their focus from biblical truths to societal trends, they risk losing their prophetic voice, becoming echo chambers of the prevailing culture rather than beacons of divine truth. As Romans 12:2 implores us, "And be not conformed to this world: but be ye transformed by the renewing of your mind, that ye may prove what is that good, and

CHAPTER 6: SEEKING APPROVAL

acceptable, and perfect, will of God." Our mission is transformation, not conformity.

How then can we resist the allure of popularity? It begins with a steadfast commitment to the Gospel's truth, a truth that comforts the afflicted but also afflicts the comfortable. This balance is vital, as 2 Timothy 4:2 instructs us to "Preach the word; be instant in season, out of season; reprove, rebuke, exhort with all longsuffering and doctrine." The true measure of our ministry is not quantified by our popularity but by our adherence to the Scriptures and the transformation it brings about in people's lives.

Moreover, church leaders must foster environments where biblical literacy and spiritual maturity are prioritized. Only through deep, consistent engagement with the Bible can congregations be equipped to discern and resist the superficial allure of cultural approval. We must return to the Acts 2 model of fellowship, where believers devoted themselves to the apostles' teaching and to fellowship, to the breaking of bread and to prayer. Such a foundation will not crumble under the pressure of popular opinion but will stand firm in the face of societal shifts.

In promoting this depth of scriptural engagement, we recall the wise admonition found in Joshua 1:8, "This book of the law shall not depart out of thy mouth; but thou shalt meditate therein day and night, that thou mayest observe to do according to all that is written therein: for then thou shalt make thy way prosperous, and then thou shalt have good success." Success in God's kingdom is defined by obedience to His Word, not by the metrics of worldly acclaim.

As we encourage our congregations to embrace this countercultural stance, we must also model it. Leaders are called to be examples to the flock, as stated in 1 Peter 5:3, "Neither as being lords over God's heritage, but being examples to the flock." By living lives that reflect a genuine commitment to Christ above all else, leaders can inspire their congregations to do the same, fostering a culture that values divine approval over human endorsement.

Engaging with culture is not inherently wrong; indeed, Jesus Himself engaged thoughtfully with the societal norms of His time. However, He never compromised His message to gain acceptance or evade conflict. Our engagement should similarly be thoughtful and intentional, always aligning with scriptural truths and aiming to bring light to the dark corners of societal norms, as Ephesians 5:11 instructs, "And have no fellowship with the unfruitful works of darkness, but rather reprove them."

Ultimately, the church must remember its divine mandate to be salt and light in the world, as described in Matthew 5:13-16. Salt preserves and prevents decay; light dispels darkness. By reclaiming our identity as keepers of the Gospel, we resist the decay of truth and shine forth the light of Christ into a world marred by confusion and despair.

In closing, let us take heart and be courageous, not swayed by the winds of popularity but anchored in the eternal truth of Scripture. As we do so, we will fulfill our God-given mandate, and indeed, as James 4:4 reminds us, "Ye adulterers and adulteresses, know ye not that the friendship of the world is enmity with God? whosoever therefore will be a friend of the world is the enemy of God." May

CHAPTER 6: SEEKING APPROVAL

we choose wisely, with eternal perspectives shaping our earthly engagements, ensuring our actions resonate with God's will, even if it means standing alone against the tide of popular opinion.

In our modern age, the church faces unprecedented pressure to conform to societal expectations. Social media platforms, public opinion polls, and cultural trends can exert a powerful influence, often swaying even the most steadfast believers. Yet, we must remember the words of Proverbs 29:25, "The fear of man bringeth a snare: but whoso putteth his trust in the LORD shall be safe." The safety and security we seek cannot be found in the approval of man but in the unwavering trust we place in God.

Consider the story of Shadrach, Meshach, and Abednego in Daniel 3. Faced with the king's decree to bow down to the golden image, they stood firm in their faith, refusing to conform despite the threat of a fiery furnace. Their response in Daniel 3:16-18 is a powerful testimony of unwavering faith: "O Nebuchadnezzar, we are not careful to answer thee in this matter. If it be so, our God whom we serve is able to deliver us from the burning fiery furnace, and he will deliver us out of thine hand, O king. But if not, be it known unto thee, O king, that we will not serve thy gods, nor worship the golden image which thou hast set up." This kind of resolute faith is what the church needs today.

The pursuit of popularity often leads to the erosion of core values and principles. When churches focus more on filling seats than filling hearts, the true essence of the Gospel can be lost. The Apostle Paul warned of this in 2 Timothy 4:3-4, "For the time will come when they will not endure sound doctrine; but after their own lusts shall they heap to themselves teachers, having itching ears;

And they shall turn away their ears from the truth, and shall be turned unto fables." It is a sobering reminder that the allure of pleasing the masses can lead to a departure from sound teaching.

Moreover, the quest for approval can create a climate where difficult truths are avoided. The fear of offending or alienating can lead to a watered-down gospel that lacks the transformative power of the Holy Spirit. Jesus Himself did not shy away from speaking hard truths. In John 6, after delivering a challenging teaching, many of His disciples turned back and no longer followed Him. Yet, Jesus did not soften His message to retain followers. John 6:67-68 records, "Then said Jesus unto the twelve, Will ye also go away? Then Simon Peter answered him, Lord, to whom shall we go? thou hast the words of eternal life." This bold proclamation highlights the eternal significance of Christ's teachings, even when they are difficult to accept.

In navigating these challenges, it is essential for churches to foster a culture of deep spiritual maturity and discernment. This requires a commitment to teaching and living out the full counsel of God, not just the parts that are palatable to contemporary tastes. Hebrews 5:14 emphasizes the importance of maturity, stating, "But strong meat belongeth to them that are of full age, even those who by reason of use have their senses exercised to discern both good and evil." This depth of discernment is crucial for standing firm in the face of societal pressures.

Church leaders play a pivotal role in this process. They must lead by example, demonstrating a life devoted to Christ and His teachings above all else. The Apostle Paul's words to the Corinthians in 1 Corinthians 11:1, "Be ye followers of me, even as

I also am of Christ," underscore the importance of modeling Christ-like behavior. When leaders prioritize God's approval over human praise, they set a powerful precedent for their congregations.

Furthermore, churches must prioritize prayer as a foundational practice. Prayer aligns our hearts with God's will, providing the strength and guidance needed to resist the pressures of conformity. Philippians 4:6-7 encourages us, "Be careful for nothing; but in every thing by prayer and supplication with thanksgiving let your requests be made known unto God. And the peace of God, which passeth all understanding, shall keep your hearts and minds through Christ Jesus." This divine peace guards our hearts against the anxieties and fears that drive us to seek human approval.

The church's mission is not to blend in with the world but to stand out as a beacon of truth and love. Jesus calls us to be "the light of the world" in Matthew 5:14-16, "Ye are the light of the world. A city that is set on an hill cannot be hid. Neither do men light a candle, and put it under a bushel, but on a candlestick; and it giveth light unto all that are in the house. Let your light so shine before men, that they may see your good works, and glorify your Father which is in heaven." Our good works, rooted in the truth of the Gospel, are meant to point others to God, not to ourselves.

In our pursuit of divine approval, we must also remember the importance of humility. James 4:10 teaches, "Humble yourselves in the sight of the Lord, and he shall lift you up." True humility acknowledges our dependence on God and prioritizes His glory over our own. It is through this posture of humility that we can effectively serve and lead others in the path of righteousness.

As we navigate the complexities of seeking approval in a culture that often opposes biblical values, let us hold fast to the truth of Scripture. Colossians 3:23-24 exhorts us, "And whatsoever ye do, do it heartily, as to the Lord, and not unto men; Knowing that of the Lord ye shall receive the reward of the inheritance: for ye serve the Lord Christ." Our ultimate reward comes from the Lord, not from the accolades of man. This eternal perspective empowers us to stand firm in our faith, even when it is unpopular or misunderstood.

The call to seek God's approval above all else is not an easy one. It requires courage, conviction, and an unwavering commitment to the truth of the Gospel. Yet, it is a call that comes with the promise of eternal reward and the assurance of God's presence with us. Hebrews 13:5-6 provides this comfort, "Let your conversation be without covetousness; and be content with such things as ye have: for he hath said, I will never leave thee, nor forsake thee. So that we may boldly say, The Lord is my helper, and I will not fear what man shall do unto me." With this assurance, we can face the challenges of seeking God's approval with confidence and hope.

In conclusion, the pursuit of popularity must never overshadow our commitment to Christ and His teachings. As we strive to be faithful servants, let us remember the words of Jesus in Matthew 7:13-14, "Enter ye in at the strait gate: for wide is the gate, and broad is the way, that leadeth to destruction, and many there be which go in thereat: Because strait is the gate, and narrow is the way, which leadeth unto life, and few there be that find it." The narrow path may be challenging, but it leads to eternal life. Let us, therefore, commit ourselves to this path, seeking God's approval above all else, and trusting in His grace to guide us every step of the way.

Chapter 7: Media and Technology Influence

In the ever-evolving landscape of the 21st century, the church finds itself standing at a critical intersection shaped profoundly by the forces of media and technology. As these platforms evolve, they not only redefine the method of gospel delivery but also subtly shift the message itself. This transformation is not merely a trend but a deep-seated change that has permeated the fabric of church operations and outreach. The Apostle Paul's wisdom in Romans 12:2 is especially pertinent here: "And be not conformed to this world: but be ye transformed by the renewing of your mind, that ye may prove what is that good, and acceptable, and perfect, will of God." As we navigate the digital noise, we must strive to preserve the purity and power of the Gospel amidst the clamoring for clicks and views.

The digital age offers unprecedented opportunities for spreading the Word of God, enabling churches to reach previously inaccessible corners of the globe, thus fulfilling the Great Commission as stated in Matthew 28:19: "Go ye therefore, and teach all nations." However, with this great power comes great responsibility. The critical question is not whether we use these tools, but how we use them. Are we diluting the profound truths of Christianity to make them more palatable for a digital audience, or are we using these platforms to genuinely enrich and deepen the faith of our followers?

Maintaining this balance is delicate. On one hand, technology can enhance our understanding and engagement with scripture, providing dynamic new ways to explore the Bible and Christian

CHAPTER 7: MEDIA AND TECHNOLOGY INFLUENCE

teachings. On the other, there's a growing trend toward crafting messages that are not only user-friendly but also entertaining. This shift toward entertainment changes the focus from worship and reverence to a consumer-oriented approach, where the value of the message is judged by its viral potential rather than its spiritual impact.

Consider the implications of this shift. As church services are streamed online and sermons are posted on social media, the metrics of likes, shares, and comments can start to dictate content. This scenario can lead to the compromise of sermon depth for broader appeal. Jesus' words in John 15:19 remind us, "If ye were of the world, the world would love his own: but because ye are not of the world, but I have chosen you out of the world, therefore the world hateth you." Our message, inherently countercultural, calls us not to seek the world's approval but to challenge it, compelling us to deepen our engagement with the faithful rather than merely expanding our digital reach.

Moreover, the personalization of digital experiences further complicates this landscape. Algorithms tailor content to individual preferences, potentially isolating us in echo chambers where challenging teachings are smoothed over or omitted entirely. This approach runs counter to the biblical model of community and accountability, where we are encouraged to "iron sharpeneth iron" (Proverbs 27:17). The church must therefore be vigilant, ensuring that its use of digital tools fosters genuine community and confrontation with the whole truth of God's Word, not just the comforting parts.

The speed at which information is disseminated can sometimes outpace our capacity for reflection and prayerful consideration. In the rush to stay relevant, we risk reacting rather than responding thoughtfully to current events or cultural shifts. James 1:19 advises, "Wherefore, my beloved brethren, let every man be swift to hear, slow to speak, slow to wrath." This scripture guides our engagement with technology, urging us to use these powerful tools to listen and learn first, then to speak with wisdom and grace that reflects our deep commitment to Christ.

Teaching discernment is crucial in an age where anyone can publish their opinions as facts. It is not enough to passively consume; we must actively engage, question, and seek the truth in alignment with Philippians 1:9-10, "And this I pray, that your love may abound yet more and more in knowledge and in all judgment; That ye may approve things that are excellent; that ye may be sincere and without offence till the day of Christ." Encouraging critical thinking within our congregations is vital, fostering a community that is not easily swayed by the fleeting trends of the digital age.

The personal touch remains irreplaceable in our eagerness to embrace the digital. While technology connects us in many ways, it cannot replicate the profound human need for face-to-face fellowship and pastoral care. The church must balance its online presence with real-world relationships, ensuring that our embrace of technology never replaces the warm, personal interaction that fosters genuine spiritual growth and community. Hebrews 10:25 exhorts us, "Not forsaking the assembling of ourselves together, as the manner of some is; but exhorting one another: and so much the

CHAPTER 7: MEDIA AND TECHNOLOGY INFLUENCE

more, as ye see the day approaching." This verse highlights the irreplaceable value of coming together in physical fellowship.

We must also be mindful of the potential for digital platforms to foster a culture of comparison and envy. Social media often showcases the highlights of people's lives, creating unrealistic expectations and leading to feelings of inadequacy among viewers. Galatians 6:4-5 advises, "But let every man prove his own work, and then shall he have rejoicing in himself alone, and not in another. For every man shall bear his own burden." This scripture encourages us to focus on our own spiritual journey and growth, rather than comparing ourselves to others.

The use of technology in the church also presents an opportunity for distraction. With constant notifications and the lure of instant gratification, our attention spans are shrinking. This can affect our ability to engage deeply with God's Word and to cultivate a disciplined prayer life. Psalm 46:10 reminds us, "Be still, and know that I am God: I will be exalted among the heathen, I will be exalted in the earth." This call to stillness is a powerful antidote to the distractions of the digital age, urging us to create space for quiet reflection and communion with God.

Furthermore, the pursuit of popularity through digital means can lead to the temptation of self-promotion. In a world where personal branding is often emphasized, church leaders must guard against the desire for personal acclaim. John 3:30 encapsulates the right attitude, "He must increase, but I must decrease." This humility is crucial in ensuring that our digital presence points people to Christ, rather than to ourselves.

In navigating the digital age, it is essential to remain anchored in the unchanging truth of God's Word. The Bible offers timeless wisdom that transcends the latest technological advancements. 2 Timothy 3:16-17 affirms, "All scripture is given by inspiration of God, and is profitable for doctrine, for reproof, for correction, for instruction in righteousness: That the man of God may be perfect, thoroughly furnished unto all good works." By grounding our digital engagement in scripture, we ensure that our message remains pure and powerful.

As we reflect on the influence of media and technology, it is clear that these tools are double-edged swords. They have the potential to amplify our outreach and to engage with a global audience in ways previously unimaginable. However, they also carry risks that require careful, prayerful management. Colossians 3:17 reminds us, "And whatsoever ye do in word or deed, do all in the name of the Lord Jesus, giving thanks to God and the Father by him." This scripture calls us to approach our digital endeavors with a heart of gratitude and a commitment to glorify God in all that we do.

Our ultimate goal should not be to mold the Gospel to fit the tools we use, but to mold the tools to fit the Gospel. This perspective helps us harness the full potential of media and technology while standing firm in the faith once delivered to the saints, as Jude 1:3 exhorts us to "earnestly contend for the faith which was once delivered unto the saints." This is our call to action in the digital age, to use every tool at our disposal to faithfully convey the unchanging message of Christ's love and redemption.

Prayerful discernment is key as we navigate this complex landscape. By seeking God's wisdom and guidance, we can use

CHAPTER 7: MEDIA AND TECHNOLOGY INFLUENCE

media and technology to advance His kingdom while preserving the integrity of the Gospel message. James 1:5 encourages us, "If any of you lack wisdom, let him ask of God, that giveth to all men liberally, and upbraideth not; and it shall be given him." Let us continually seek this divine wisdom as we engage with the digital world.

As we move forward, let our digital footprints lead others not merely to our churches but through the narrow gate that leads to life eternal. Matthew 7:14 reminds us, "Because strait is the gate, and narrow is the way, which leadeth unto life, and few there be that find it." This scripture underscores the importance of guiding our digital audience towards a deeper, more meaningful relationship with Christ.

In conclusion, while the media and technology landscape offers vast opportunities for outreach and engagement, it also presents significant challenges that require careful, prayerful management. We are stewards of a mighty digital arsenal in the service of the Lord, tasked not with changing the message to fit the medium, but with using the medium to faithfully convey the unchanging message of Christ's love and redemption. By staying rooted in scripture and guided by the Holy Spirit, we can navigate this terrain with wisdom and grace, ensuring that our digital presence amplifies the Gospel rather than dilutes it.

Let us embrace the tools of our age with discernment and intentionality, always seeking to glorify God and advance His kingdom. Our mission remains the same: to make disciples of all nations, teaching them to observe all things that Christ has commanded us. May our digital endeavors reflect this mission, shining the light of Christ into every corner of the digital world.

Chapter 8: Consequences of Compromise

In the relentless pursuit of popularity, many churches today have compromised the very essence of their calling, gradually veering away from the uncompromising truth of the Gospel. This trend towards seeking acceptance in the eyes of the world has profound and often devastating spiritual consequences. It is reminiscent of Paul's stern admonition to the Galatians, "For do I now persuade men, or God? or do I seek to please men? for if I yet pleased men, I should not be the servant of Christ" (Galatians 1:10). The quest for human approval rather than divine approval places the church on a precarious path, one that leads to a dilution of its spiritual authority and integrity.

Initially, the steps towards compromise might seem insignificant. Adjusting a sermon to make it less confrontational, incorporating secular elements into worship to attract a larger audience, or avoiding topics that might be deemed controversial can all seem like harmless strategies. Yet, Jesus warned His disciples about the leaven of the Pharisees and Sadducees, equating their doctrine to yeast that, once introduced, spreads throughout the dough (Matthew 16:12). In the same way, even small compromises can infiltrate and eventually transform the entire belief system of a church, leading it away from the truth of God's Word.

One of the most profound dangers of compromising to achieve popularity is the loss of the church's prophetic voice. Throughout history, the church has served as a counter-cultural force, challenging societal norms and calling people to repentance and righteousness. However, a church that mirrors the world in its values and practices loses its distinctiveness and, consequently, its ability to effect meaningful change. In the book of Revelation, Christ's message to the church at Ephesus is a sobering reminder: "Remember therefore from whence thou art fallen, and repent, and do the first works" (Revelation 2:5). This call to repentance highlights the necessity of returning to the foundational works and truths that once characterized the church.

Furthermore, when churches align themselves too closely with the transient ideals of society, they sacrifice their legacy of eternal impact for the sake of immediate gratification. This pursuit of popularity often leads to a neglect of genuine discipleship, with churches more focused on filling seats than nurturing souls. The writer of Hebrews admonishes believers to move beyond elementary teachings towards maturity (Hebrews 6:1). This call to maturity is not just for individual growth but is essential for the collective strength and witness of the church.

The mission of the church, as commissioned by Jesus, is to make disciples of all nations, teaching them to obey everything He commanded (Matthew 28:19-20). However, a message that has been diluted to appeal to the masses often lacks the depth and conviction necessary for true discipleship. It becomes challenging to disciple others effectively when the foundational truths of the faith are either ignored or softened to avoid offending. A compromised message results in compromised disciples, who may lack the strength and resilience to stand firm in their faith.

Internal conflict and division within the church are other significant consequences of doctrinal compromise. When churches prioritize popularity over truth, they often find themselves divided

CHAPTER 8: CONSEQUENCES OF COMPROMISE

over essential beliefs and practices. Paul's appeal to the Corinthians is particularly relevant: "I appeal to you, brothers and sisters, in the name of our Lord Jesus Christ, that all of you agree with one another in what you say and that there be no divisions among you, but that you be perfectly united in mind and thought" (1 Corinthians 1:10). Unity in the church is grounded in adherence to the truth, and without it, the church's testimony is weakened.

Compromise also desensitizes congregations to the nuances and power of biblical truth, leading to a form of godliness but denying its power (2 Timothy 3:5). This form of godliness, characterized by outward rituals and appearances, fails to bring about the deep, heart-level transformation that true Christianity demands. Individuals who are exposed to a watered-down gospel may find themselves ill-equipped to face life's challenges with genuine faith and dependence on God. This superficial approach to faith leaves believers vulnerable and spiritually anemic.

A return to biblical fidelity is essential for the renewal and restoration of the church. This return is not about adopting a more conservative stance for the sake of tradition, but about realigning with the transformative power of the Gospel, which transcends cultural shifts and trends. Jesus' teaching on being the salt of the earth and the light of the world (Matthew 5:13-14) underscores the church's role in preserving truth and illuminating the darkness with the hope of Christ. When the church compromises, it loses its saltiness and its light grows dim, failing to fulfill its God-given mandate.

Restoring biblical fidelity requires courage and conviction. It demands that church leaders and congregants choose the harder path of obedience over convenience. Joshua's challenge to the Israelites is still relevant: "Choose you this day whom ye will serve; whether the gods which your fathers served that were on the other side of the flood, or the gods of the Amorites, in whose land ye dwell: but as for me and my house, we will serve the LORD" (Joshua 24:15). This decisive choice is foundational for the spiritual renewal of the church and the healing of our communities.

In addition to doctrinal soundness, the pursuit of popularity often leads churches to compromise on ethical and moral standards. Leaders may be tempted to overlook or downplay sin to avoid alienating members or losing financial support. This tendency is starkly contrasted by the biblical mandate for holiness: "But as he which hath called you is holy, so be ye holy in all manner of conversation" (1 Peter 1:15). Holiness is not optional for believers; it is a command that reflects the nature of God and the transformative work of the Holy Spirit within us.

The compromise also manifests in worship practices, where the focus shifts from glorifying God to entertaining the congregation. This trend towards performance-oriented worship can distract from the true purpose of worship, which is to honor and encounter the living God. Jesus' words to the Samaritan woman at the well serve as a timeless reminder: "God is a Spirit: and they that worship him must worship him in spirit and in truth" (John 4:24). True worship is not about the style or the spectacle; it is about the heart's posture before God.

Moreover, the pursuit of popularity can lead churches to engage in social and political causes in ways that compromise their primary mission. While the church is called to be a prophetic voice in

CHAPTER 8: CONSEQUENCES OF COMPROMISE

society, this must be done without losing sight of the Gospel's central message. Jesus' teaching in Matthew 6:33 is clear: "But seek ye first the kingdom of God, and his righteousness; and all these things shall be added unto you." The church's involvement in social justice must be rooted in and driven by the pursuit of God's kingdom and righteousness.

The consequences of compromise extend to the church's influence in the broader culture. A church that blends in with the world rather than standing out as a beacon of truth and hope loses its ability to draw people to Christ. Paul's exhortation to the Romans is a clarion call for the church today: "And be not conformed to this world: but be ye transformed by the renewing of your mind, that ye may prove what is that good, and acceptable, and perfect, will of God" (Romans 12:2). Transformation, not conformity, is the hallmark of a vibrant and impactful church.

Ultimately, the path to renewal and restoration begins with repentance. The church must acknowledge where it has compromised and seek God's forgiveness and guidance to return to the path of righteousness. The promise of 2 Chronicles 7:14 offers hope and a blueprint for this renewal: "If my people, which are called by my name, shall humble themselves, and pray, and seek my face, and turn from their wicked ways; then will I hear from heaven, and will forgive their sin, and will heal their land." Humility, prayer, and repentance are the keys to unlocking God's healing and restoration.

In the midst of these challenges, there is a call to perseverance and faithfulness. The journey towards renewal is not easy, and it requires steadfastness in the face of opposition and difficulty. The apostle Paul's words to Timothy resonate with timeless relevance: "But continue thou in the things which thou hast learned and hast been assured of, knowing of whom thou hast learned them" (2 Timothy 3:14). Continuity in sound doctrine and practice is essential for maintaining the integrity and effectiveness of the church's witness.

As we reflect on the consequences of compromise, let us be spurred into action, not out of fear or condemnation, but out of a deep love for what the church is called to represent: the living body of Christ on earth. Each decision to uphold truth, each act of repentance, and each step towards biblical fidelity contributes to the renewal and restoration of the church. We are called to be stewards of the Gospel, faithfully proclaiming its truths in word and deed, regardless of the cost.

In this light, the church must re-evaluate its methods and messages, ensuring that everything aligns with the uncompromising truth of God's Word. This re-evaluation is not merely an exercise in nostalgia or tradition; it is a necessary step towards reclaiming the power and presence of God in our midst. As Jesus said, "Ye shall know the truth, and the truth shall make you free" (John 8:32). Freedom comes not from compromise but from a steadfast commitment to the truth.

The journey towards renewal is one of transformation, both individually and corporately. It involves a return to the basics of faith, prayer, worship, and discipleship. It requires a community of believers who are willing to stand firm in their convictions, even when it is unpopular or counter-cultural. Together, we can reclaim the church's prophetic voice and its role as a beacon of hope and truth in a world that desperately needs both.

Let us, therefore, commit ourselves to this journey with unwavering faith and determination. The road may be challenging, but the rewards are eternal. As we realign our lives and our churches with the truth of the Gospel, we will witness a powerful move of God that brings about transformation, healing, and revival. This is the promise and the hope that lies before us if we choose to heed the call and reject the compromises that threaten to undermine our faith.

Chapter 9: Scriptural Admonition on Standing Firm in Faith

In today's era, where the digital footprint of a church often speaks louder than its spiritual depth, it's crucial to remember whom we serve. The Apostle Paul's admonition to the Galatians resonates powerfully, especially in our current context: "For do I now persuade men, or God? Or do I seek to please men? For if I yet pleased men, I should not be the servant of Christ" (Galatians 1:10). This scripture is a stark reminder that our primary allegiance is to God, not to the shifting sands of cultural approval or disapproval. It's a call to resist the seductive allure of popularity, which can divert us from the foundational truths of the gospel.

The church's engagement with the world should be transformative, not conformative. When we prioritize public approval over divine truth, we dilute our message and weaken our witness. The pursuit of popularity can lead us into compromising situations, where the clarity of the gospel is muddied to fit into the acceptable norms of society. However, Christ never sought the approval of the masses at the expense of truth. He spoke with authority that stemmed from His relationship with the Father, not from the accolades of His followers or detractors.

Consider the early church leaders who faced intense scrutiny and persecution, yet never wavered in their mission to proclaim the gospel. They did not water down their messages to make them more palatable to the cultural elites or the ruling powers. Instead, they boldly proclaimed the truth, fully aware of the potential

CHAPTER 9: SCRIPTURAL ADMONITION ON STANDING FIRM IN FAITH

consequences. They understood something crucial: the truth of the gospel has the power to offend, to divide, and to unsettle—but also to heal, to save, and to transform.

In our ministries, how often are we tempted to echo what the crowd wants to hear rather than what they need to hear? The truth is, shaping our messages for likes, shares, or societal acceptance can be a subtle but slippery slope. It can start innocently but can eventually lead us away from the tough truths of scripture and into a place where the gospel is merely another commodity to be marketed.

We must be vigilant. The words of James caution us: "Pure religion and undefiled before God and the Father is this, To visit the fatherless and widows in their affliction, and to keep himself unspotted from the world" (James 1:27). This scriptural directive does not merely call for acts of charity but commands us to remain unpolluted by the world's values. Our actions and our church's practices must reflect this dual commitment to service and sanctity, showcasing a faith that is both active and unadulterated.

The quest for popularity can be intoxicating. It's a subtle brew that, once sipped, can be difficult to refuse. As church leaders and believers, our challenge is to ensure that our actions and decisions are motivated by a desire to serve God rather than to receive human accolades. This is not a passive resistance but an active, daily decision to align our lives and our ministries with the Word of God and not the word of the crowd.

We must continually ask ourselves: Are we more concerned with the number of attendees on Sunday or the spiritual depth of those attendees? Are we seeking conversions that are genuine and rooted in a true understanding of the gospel, or are we merely collecting decisions for Christ that are shallow and not disciple-focused? This introspection is necessary if we are to maintain the purity and power of our mission.

In times of cultural shift and moral fluidity, the temptation to adapt the gospel to fit the prevailing winds of doctrine is high. Yet, we are called to be steadfast, immovable, always abounding in the work of the Lord, knowing that our labor is not in vain in the Lord (1 Corinthians 15:58). This steadfastness comes from a deep-rooted belief in the eternal truth of God's Word, which transcends time and culture.

The call to return to scriptural fidelity is urgent and clear. We must re-anchor our faith in the truths of the Bible, resisting the drift towards a gospel reshaped by cultural currents. It's about finding our voice—a voice that echoes the prophets and apostles, who despite opposition, declared God's truth boldly and without compromise.

As we navigate these challenging waters, let us cling to the assurance that our labor in the Lord is not in vain. Let us take heart in the promise of God's Word, which is sharper than any two-edged sword, capable of penetrating even to dividing soul and spirit, joints and marrow; it judges the thoughts and attitudes of the heart (Hebrews 4:12). With such a powerful tool at our disposal, how can we settle for anything less than its full, unadulterated proclamation?

We must also remember the cost of discipleship. Jesus did not call us to a life of ease but to a life of sacrifice and sometimes, even suffering for His name's sake. He warned, "If the world hate you,

CHAPTER 9: SCRIPTURAL ADMONITION ON STANDING FIRM IN FAITH

ye know that it hated me before it hated you" (John 15:18). Our aim should be to follow Christ, even if it means walking a path that is unpopular and fraught with challenges.

There is a growing trend where the gospel is tailored to avoid offending anyone, but the truth of the matter is that the gospel is inherently offensive to those who are perishing. Paul stated, "For the preaching of the cross is to them that perish foolishness; but unto us which are saved it is the power of God" (1 Corinthians 1:18). We must not shy away from preaching the full counsel of God, even when it is counter-cultural.

We must be wary of the influence of secular ideologies infiltrating our teaching. There is a delicate balance between engaging with the world and being influenced by it. Paul reminds us in Romans 12:2, "And be not conformed to this world: but be ye transformed by the renewing of your mind, that ye may prove what is that good, and acceptable, and perfect, will of God." Our transformation should be a testament to the transformative power of the gospel, not a reflection of worldly values.

The allure of success, measured by worldly standards, is another trap that we must avoid. True success in ministry is not about the size of our congregation or the scope of our influence but about our faithfulness to God's call. "Moreover it is required in stewards, that a man be found faithful" (1 Corinthians 4:2). Our faithfulness to the gospel message must take precedence over all other measures of success.

This faithfulness often requires a willingness to stand alone. Jeremiah, the weeping prophet, stood alone in his generation to deliver God's message, despite the opposition he faced. His faithfulness to God's word is a powerful example for us today. "Therefore thus saith the LORD; If thou return, then will I bring thee again, and thou shalt stand before me: and if thou take forth the precious from the vile, thou shalt be as my mouth: let them return unto thee; but return not thou unto them" (Jeremiah 15:19).

In our pursuit of popularity, we must not forget that we are called to be salt and light in the world. Jesus said, "Ye are the salt of the earth: but if the salt have lost his savour, wherewith shall it be salted? it is thenceforth good for nothing, but to be cast out, and to be trodden under foot of men" (Matthew 5:13). Our distinctiveness as followers of Christ should not be compromised for the sake of acceptance.

The church is called to be a city set on a hill, shining the light of Christ in a dark world. This light should not be hidden under a bushel but should shine brightly for all to see. "Let your light so shine before men, that they may see your good works, and glorify your Father which is in heaven" (Matthew 5:16). Our good works and our unwavering commitment to truth should point others to God.

We must also remember that our battle is not against flesh and blood but against spiritual forces of evil in the heavenly realms. Paul exhorts us to "put on the whole armour of God, that ye may be able to stand against the wiles of the devil" (Ephesians 6:11). This spiritual armor is essential if we are to withstand the pressures to conform and remain faithful to our calling.

The pursuit of popularity can lead to a dangerous path of compromise, where the lines between right and wrong become blurred. We must hold fast to the truth of God's Word, which is the

CHAPTER 9: SCRIPTURAL ADMONITION ON STANDING FIRM IN FAITH

anchor for our souls. The Psalmist declared, "Thy word is a lamp unto my feet, and a light unto my path" (Psalm 119:105). This divine guidance is critical in navigating the complexities of modern ministry.

It is time for a renewed commitment to the gospel, a return to the foundational truths that have sustained the church through the ages. This commitment requires courage, conviction, and an unwavering trust in God's promises. We are called to be faithful stewards of the mysteries of God, proclaiming the truth with boldness and clarity.

In this journey, we must also cultivate a deep love for the truth. Paul warned the Thessalonians about the danger of not loving the truth: "And with all deceivableness of unrighteousness in them that perish; because they received not the love of the truth, that they might be saved" (2 Thessalonians 2:10). Our love for the truth should drive us to uphold it, even in the face of opposition.

As we reflect on our motives and actions, let us be mindful of Paul's exhortation to Timothy: "Preach the word; be instant in season, out of season; reprove, rebuke, exhort with all longsuffering and doctrine" (2 Timothy 4:2). This charge emphasizes the importance of steadfastness and perseverance in proclaiming the gospel, regardless of the season or the audience.

Our ultimate goal should be to please God and fulfill His purpose for our lives and ministries. The applause of men is fleeting, but the approval of God is eternal. Let us strive to hear those precious words from our Lord: "Well done, thou good and faithful servant" (Matthew 25:21). This commendation should be our highest aspiration, driving us to serve with integrity and faithfulness.

In conclusion, let us recommit ourselves to the unchanging truths of scripture, resisting the pull of popularity and the temptation to compromise. Our calling is a sacred trust, and we must guard it with diligence and devotion. May we be found faithful in our generation, proclaiming the gospel with clarity, conviction, and courage. As we do so, we can trust that God will honor His Word and use our faithfulness to advance His kingdom and glorify His name.

Chapter 10: Turning Back

The journey of turning back to God's original design for the church is both challenging and essential. In our quest for popularity and acceptance, many churches have drifted from their foundational principles. This chapter calls for a heartfelt return to the truths that once defined us. Our modern pursuit of relevance has led to compromises that dilute the Gospel's power. As Paul admonished the Galatians, "Am I now trying to win the approval of human beings, or of God? Or am I trying to please people? If I were still trying to please people, I would not be a servant of Christ" (Galatians 1:10). This piercing question should resonate deeply within us, prompting a reevaluation of our ministry motives.

The allure of cultural acceptance often leads churches to soften their message, aiming to attract rather than transform. Yet, the essence of the Gospel is transformation, not attraction. Jesus warned about the dangers of a compromised faith, saying, "No one can serve two masters. Either you will hate the one and love the other, or you will be devoted to the one and despise the other" (Matthew 6:24). Our allegiance must be clear and unwavering. Serving Christ means upholding His teachings even when they contradict popular opinion. The challenge is to stand firm in a culture that pressures us to conform.

Turning back to God involves a deep, introspective examination of our church practices and personal lives. We must ask ourselves whether our actions and decisions align with God's Word. The church in Ephesus received a sobering message in Revelation: "Yet

I hold this against you: You have forsaken the love you had at first. Consider how far you have fallen! Repent and do the things you did at first" (Revelation 2:4-5). This call to repentance is a reminder that returning to our first love for Christ is crucial. It's about rekindling the passion and commitment that initially drew us to Him.

Prayer is the cornerstone of this return. Through prayer, we connect with God, seek His guidance, and gain the strength needed to make necessary changes. James emphasized the power of prayer, stating, "The prayer of a righteous person is powerful and effective" (James 5:16). In our prayer closets, we can ask God to reveal the areas where we have strayed and to give us the courage to realign our paths. Prayer not only transforms situations but also transforms hearts. It re-centers us on God's will and prepares us to walk in His ways.

Recommitting to biblical teaching is another vital step. Paul's charge to Timothy was clear: "Preach the word; be prepared in season and out of season; correct, rebuke and encourage—with great patience and careful instruction" (2 Timothy 4:2). Sound doctrine is the bedrock of a thriving church. It equips believers to discern truth from falsehood and to live out their faith authentically. Returning to robust, scripture-based teaching strengthens the church body and fosters a deeper understanding of God's will.

Discipleship must also take center stage in our efforts to turn back. Peter urged believers to "grow in the grace and knowledge of our Lord and Savior Jesus Christ" (2 Peter 3:18). True discipleship involves nurturing believers to mature in their faith, helping them to become more like Christ. This growth is not just for personal edification but for the edification of the entire church. As individuals grow, the church becomes stronger and more resilient against the pressures of conformity.

Addressing and correcting errors within our church practices is a necessary but often difficult task. It requires courage and a commitment to truth. Proverbs teaches us, "Faithful are the wounds of a friend; profuse are the kisses of an enemy" (Proverbs 27:6). Constructive criticism, though sometimes painful, is essential for growth. Leaders must be willing to confront issues head-on, even when it's uncomfortable. This honesty paves the way for genuine repentance and restoration.

Worship is another area that demands our attention. In many churches, worship has shifted from a heartfelt expression of reverence to a form of entertainment. Jesus highlighted the essence of true worship when He said, "God is spirit, and his worshipers must worship in the Spirit and in truth" (John 4:24). Authentic worship focuses on God, not on human performance. It's about offering our hearts in adoration and surrender, creating an atmosphere where God's presence is honored and welcomed.

Community is integral to the church's identity. However, the rise of individualism has eroded the sense of community within many congregations. Hebrews encourages us, "And let us consider how we may spur one another on toward love and good deeds, not giving up meeting together, as some are in the habit of doing, but encouraging one another" (Hebrews 10:24-25). Building strong, supportive communities requires intentional effort. It involves fostering relationships that encourage accountability, support, and spiritual growth.

Cultural influences often seep into the church subtly, leading to a gradual shift away from biblical principles. Paul's warning in Romans is pertinent: "Do not conform to the pattern of this world, but be transformed by the renewing of your mind. Then you will be able to test and approve what God's will is—his good, pleasing and perfect will" (Romans 12:2). Renewal of the mind through scripture helps us to resist these influences and remain true to God's calling.

Holiness is a calling that should characterize the life of every believer and the church as a whole. Peter's exhortation, "But just as he who called you is holy, so be holy in all you do; for it is written: 'Be holy, because I am holy'" (1 Peter 1:15-16), is a clear mandate. Holiness involves setting ourselves apart for God's purposes, living in a manner that reflects His character. This pursuit of holiness must be evident in our conduct, decisions, and priorities.

The prophetic call to separation is a theme that runs throughout scripture. Jesus' parable of the wheat and the tares in Matthew 13 underscores the necessity of separation: "Let both grow together until the harvest. At that time I will tell the harvesters: First collect the weeds and tie them in bundles to be burned; then gather the wheat and bring it into my barn" (Matthew 13:30). God is calling His church to distinguish itself from the world, to be in the world but not of it. This separation is crucial for maintaining our spiritual integrity and effectiveness.

CHAPTER 10: TURNING BACK

Turning back also involves a commitment to ongoing renewal and reformation. It's not a one-time event but a continuous process. Paul's encouragement in 2 Corinthians serves as a reminder: "Therefore we do not lose heart. Though outwardly we are wasting away, yet inwardly we are being renewed day by day" (2 Corinthians 4:16). This daily renewal strengthens our resolve and keeps us aligned with God's will.

The future of a church that turns back to God is one of vibrant spiritual health and powerful witness. Imagine a church where the Word of God is preached with authority, where prayer is a priority, and where worship is a genuine encounter with God's presence. Such a church will stand out in a world that desperately needs the hope and truth of the Gospel. Jesus' words in John 15:5 remind us of the source of our strength: "I am the vine; you are the branches. If you remain in me and I in you, you will bear much fruit; apart from me you can do nothing." Remaining connected to Christ is essential for bearing fruit that lasts.

As we turn back, let's not forget the promise of God's grace and mercy. He is always ready to forgive and restore. Joel 2:13 encourages us, "Rend your heart and not your garments. Return to the Lord your God, for he is gracious and compassionate, slow to anger and abounding in love, and he relents from sending calamity." God's heart is for His church to return to Him wholeheartedly. His desire is for our restoration and renewal.

Turning back also means embracing humility. James 4:10 exhorts us, "Humble yourselves before the Lord, and he will lift you up." Humility allows us to recognize our need for God's guidance and to submit to His leading. It opens the door for God to work in and through us, restoring what has been lost and setting us on a path of righteousness.

In conclusion, the call to turn back is a call to return to the essence of our faith. It's a call to realign with God's purposes, to recommit to His Word, and to restore authentic worship and community. It's a call to separate from worldly influences and to pursue holiness. This journey requires courage, humility, and a deep dependence on God. As we respond to this call, we can trust that God will honor our efforts and lead us into a season of renewal and fruitfulness. Let us heed the prophetic warning and turn back to the Lord with all our hearts, knowing that His grace is sufficient and His love is everlasting.

Section 3: Financial Gain over Spiritual Riches

Chapter 11: The Prosperity Gospel

In today's church, the allure of the prosperity gospel has woven itself deeply into the fabric of many congregations. This theology, which equates God's blessing with financial gain, fundamentally misinterprets the essence of divine provision and misleads many into valuing temporal wealth over eternal riches. In the words of Paul to Timothy, "For the love of money is the root of all evil: which while some coveted after, they have erred from the faith, and pierced themselves through with many sorrows" (1 Timothy 6:10). This scripture warns of the dangers associated with a preoccupation with wealth, pointing out that such pursuits can lead to a devastating departure from the faith.

The Prosperity Gospel's central claim—that God rewards increased faith with financial blessings—raises serious concerns about the true nature of faith and God's intentions for His followers. Faith, biblically portrayed, is not a tool to secure material wealth but a profound trust in God's provision and timing. Jesus Himself taught us to seek first the kingdom of God and His righteousness, and all these things shall be added unto you (Matthew 6:33). Here, the promise of provision follows the pursuit of spiritual riches, not the other way around.

Moreover, the emphasis on wealth can distort the Christian message of sacrifice and service. The early church exemplified a community that shared everything in common, ensuring no one was in need. Acts 4:34-35 describes a community where "Neither was there any among them that lacked: for as many as were possessors of lands or houses sold them, and brought the prices of the things that were sold, And laid them down at the apostles' feet: and distribution was made unto every man according as he had need." This act of selflessness is in stark contrast to the self-serving messages often propagated under the guise of prosperity teaching.

The narrative that God bestows financial blessings as a reward for faith can lead to harmful disillusionment when believers face poverty or financial hardship. This disillusionment often stems from a misunderstanding of scriptures like Malachi 3:10, which talks about God opening the windows of heaven for tithers. However, the "blessings" referred to are not limited to material wealth but encompass the full spectrum of God's provisions, which include peace, protection, and spiritual abundance.

In response to these challenges, we must call for a return to the gospel that Jesus preached—one of humility, generosity, and trust in God's provision. The true gospel calls us to a life marked not by accumulating wealth but by giving liberally and loving abundantly. 2 Corinthians 8:9 reminds us of the generosity of Christ: "For ye know the grace of our Lord Jesus Christ, that, though he was rich, yet for your sakes he became poor, that ye through his poverty might be rich." Here, richness is defined not in financial terms but in spiritual abundance.

Teaching about financial stewardship in the church should be rooted in the principle of wise management and generosity, rather than the pursuit of wealth. We must remember the words of Jesus in Luke 12:15, where He cautioned, "Take heed, and beware of covetousness: for a man's life consisteth not in the abundance of the things which he possesseth." This directive calls us to a life where our possessions do not define our worth or our relationship with God.

Furthermore, it is vital to realign our church's focus towards the needs of the community and the world, reflecting Christ's teachings on caring for the least of these. James 1:27 describes pure religion as one that cares for orphans and widows in their distress and keeps oneself unstained by the world. This scripture challenges the prosperity gospel's emphasis on personal gain, urging a shift towards communal and selfless living.

The seductive nature of the prosperity gospel lies in its ability to tap into our deepest desires for security and success. It promises a tangible, immediate payoff for faith, which can be very appealing in our results-oriented culture. But true faith is not about manipulating God into providing for our material wants; it is about trusting Him to meet our needs according to His will and purpose. Philippians 4:19 assures us, "But my God shall supply all your need according to his riches in glory by Christ Jesus." This scripture emphasizes that God's provision is according to His riches and glory, not our materialistic expectations.

Many churches today have unfortunately adopted business models that prioritize growth and revenue over spiritual depth and discipleship. This shift can often lead to a focus on fundraising and financial prosperity as measures of success. But the true measure of a church's health is found in its faithfulness to the gospel and its impact on the lives of its members and community. Jesus warned in Matthew 6:24, "Ye cannot serve God and mammon." This clear admonition calls us to choose whom we will serve—God or wealth.

CHAPTER 11: THE PROSPERITY GOSPEL

The proliferation of the prosperity gospel has also led to a dangerous form of spiritual elitism, where wealth is seen as a sign of God's favor and poverty as a sign of His disfavor. This notion is completely antithetical to the teachings of Jesus, who blessed the poor in spirit and warned the rich of the dangers of wealth. Luke 6:20-24 contrasts these blessings and woes, showing that God's kingdom operates on a different value system than the world's. "Blessed be ye poor: for yours is the kingdom of God... But woe unto you that are rich! for ye have received your consolation."

In practical terms, embracing the true gospel over the prosperity gospel means living lives marked by contentment and generosity. Paul's testimony in Philippians 4:11-12 offers a profound insight into Christian contentment: "I have learned, in whatsoever state I am, therewith to be content. I know both how to be abased, and I know how to abound: every where and in all things I am instructed both to be full and to be hungry, both to abound and to suffer need." This contentment comes from understanding that our true wealth is in Christ and that our circumstances do not define our spiritual riches.

Generosity is a hallmark of the Christian faith, and it stands in stark contrast to the hoarding mentality promoted by the prosperity gospel. Jesus taught in Luke 6:38, "Give, and it shall be given unto you; good measure, pressed down, and shaken together, and running over, shall men give into your bosom." This promise is not about financial gain but about the blessings that come from a generous heart. Our giving should reflect the love and sacrifice of Christ, who gave everything for us.

As leaders and members of the church, we must model this generosity and teach it as a core principle of discipleship. We are called to be stewards of God's resources, using them to further His kingdom and care for those in need. The parable of the talents in Matthew 25:14-30 illustrates the importance of faithful stewardship, showing that we are accountable for how we use the resources God has entrusted to us. "Well done, thou good and faithful servant: thou hast been faithful over a few things, I will make thee ruler over many things: enter thou into the joy of thy lord."

This shift from a prosperity mindset to one of stewardship and generosity requires a renewed commitment to teaching and living out the full counsel of God's Word. It means confronting the distortions of the prosperity gospel with the truth of Scripture, which calls us to a life of sacrifice, service, and trust in God's provision. We must emphasize the eternal over the temporal, the spiritual over the material.

Our churches should be places where the true gospel is preached and lived out, where members are equipped to grow in their faith and serve their communities. This transformation begins with a return to the core teachings of Jesus, who said, "If any man will come after me, let him deny himself, and take up his cross daily, and follow me" (Luke 9:23). Following Christ means embracing His call to self-denial and service, not seeking personal gain.

In addressing the prosperity gospel, it is also essential to acknowledge the legitimate needs and desires of believers. God does care about our physical and material well-being, and He does bless His people in various ways. However, these blessings should

CHAPTER 11: THE PROSPERITY GOSPEL

not be the primary focus of our faith or the goal of our spiritual pursuits. As Paul wrote in 1 Timothy 6:17-19, "Charge them that are rich in this world, that they be not highminded, nor trust in uncertain riches, but in the living God, who giveth us richly all things to enjoy; That they do good, that they be rich in good works, ready to distribute, willing to communicate; Laying up in store for themselves a good foundation against the time to come, that they may lay hold on eternal life."

Ultimately, the call to reject the prosperity gospel is a call to rediscover the true riches of the Christian faith. It is a call to live lives that reflect the character and priorities of Christ, who "though he was rich, yet for your sakes he became poor, that ye through his poverty might be rich" (2 Corinthians 8:9). This richness is not measured in dollars and cents but in the depth of our relationship with God and the impact of our lives on others.

As we navigate the complexities of living out our faith in a materialistic world, let us keep our eyes fixed on Jesus, "the author and finisher of our faith" (Hebrews 12:2). Let us seek first His kingdom and His righteousness, trusting that all other things will be added unto us according to His perfect will. In doing so, we will find true contentment and joy, rooted not in the fleeting treasures of this world but in the eternal riches of God's kingdom.

In conclusion, as we confront the distortions of the prosperity gospel, let us return to the core of our faith, where Christ is the treasure and His Kingdom our greatest reward. "But seek ye first the kingdom of God, and his righteousness; and all these things shall be added unto you" (Matthew 6:33). With this as our guide, we can navigate through the temptations of materialism and anchor our hearts in the everlasting riches of God's kingdom.

Chapter 12: Money and Ministry

The modern church faces a profound challenge that threatens to erode its spiritual foundation: the pursuit of financial gain over spiritual riches. As Paul admonished Timothy, "For the love of money is the root of all evil: which while some coveted after, they have erred from the faith, and pierced themselves through with many sorrows" (1 Timothy 6:10). This scripture isn't merely a caution; it is a profound revelation of the dangers that lie in the love of money. Ministries today must vigilantly guard against the seduction of monetary success, which can mislead even the most devout.

In many churches, financial discussions and fundraising efforts dominate more than the dissemination of the Word. While resources are necessary for any organization, including churches, a line must be drawn. Jesus pointed out that it is impossible to serve both God and mammon (Matthew 6:24). When financial pursuits begin to dictate church activities more than spiritual guidance, the church inadvertently shifts its worship from the Creator to the creation. This dangerous pivot can lead to spiritual bankruptcy.

The essence of ministry should always focus on spiritual growth and nurturing souls, with finances playing a supporting role, not the leading one. Churches must revisit their primary call to feed the flock the bread of life, not just to seek ways of filling their coffers. The early church in Acts was noted for its generosity and sharing of resources so that none among them lacked anything (Acts 4:34-35). This model highlights a community united by spiritual goals rather than financial gain, a stark contrast to some modern church scenarios where financial success is sometimes celebrated more than spiritual victories.

The handling of finances within a ministry must be marked by utmost integrity and transparency. The apostle Paul set a standard when he spoke about the handling of the generous donations for the church in Jerusalem: "Providing for honest things, not only in the sight of the Lord, but also in the sight of men" (2 Corinthians 8:21). It's crucial for churches to adopt financial practices that are beyond reproach, ensuring that every penny given and spent is accounted for in a manner that honors God and builds trust with the congregation.

Addressing the issue of financial focus in ministry also requires a return to preaching and teaching about the dangers of materialism. John warns us not to love the world or the things in the world, for if anyone loves the world, the love of the Father is not in him (1 John 2:15). By realigning the church's teachings to focus on eternal, not earthly, treasures, leaders can help congregants develop a healthier relationship with money, viewing it as a tool for God's work and not an end in itself.

The quest for financial security can lead some to compromise their moral and ethical standards, but the Gospel offers a starkly different approach. Consider the story of the widow's offering in Mark 12:41-44. Here, Jesus commends the widow for her small, yet significant contribution, which was all she had. Her trust wasn't in the security of wealth but in the providence of God. This lesson is invaluable for today's church: the measure of giving is not in the amount but the heart behind it.

CHAPTER 12: MONEY AND MINISTRY

This principle should extend to how churches approach fundraising and tithing messages. Instead of high-pressure tactics or guilt-inducing sermons, leaders should encourage a spirit of cheerful giving, as noted in 2 Corinthians 9:7: "Every man according as he purposeth in his heart, so let him give; not grudgingly, or of necessity: for God loveth a cheerful giver." It's about fostering a culture of generosity that flows from a deep understanding of God's generosity towards us.

In many instances, the problem is not the possession of wealth but the attitude towards it. The church at Laodicea was rebuked by Christ for their self-sufficiency, claiming they were rich and in need of nothing, while being spiritually wretched, miserable, poor, blind, and naked (Revelation 3:17). This stark contrast serves as a powerful reminder that true riches lie in our relationship with Christ, not in our material possessions.

Leaders must examine their motives when it comes to financial growth. Are the funds being raised to further the mission of Christ, or are they being accumulated to build personal empires and reputations? Jesus said, "Lay not up for yourselves treasures upon earth, where moth and rust doth corrupt, and where thieves break through and steal: But lay up for yourselves treasures in heaven" (Matthew 6:19-20). The focus must always be on heavenly investments rather than earthly accumulations.

Furthermore, there needs to be a clear distinction between faith-based financial stewardship and secular business practices. While it is wise to manage church resources prudently, the church should not adopt a corporate mindset that prioritizes profit over people. Jesus drove out the money changers from the temple, declaring,

"My house shall be called the house of prayer; but ye have made it a den of thieves" (Matthew 21:13). This act underscores the sanctity of the church and the need to keep it free from the corrupting influence of greed.

Churches must also educate their members on the biblical principles of giving. Paul's letters are filled with teachings on the importance of supporting the ministry and the poor, always emphasizing the heart behind the giving. In Philippians 4:19, Paul reassures the Philippians that "my God shall supply all your need according to his riches in glory by Christ Jesus." This promise is rooted in their generosity towards his ministry, showing that God honors those who give with a sincere heart.

Another vital aspect of this discussion is the role of the church in addressing social and economic inequalities. The early church was known for its communal living and support for the needy. Acts 2:44-45 describes how "all that believed were together, and had all things common; And sold their possessions and goods, and parted them to all men, as every man had need." This model challenges modern churches to use their resources not just for internal growth but for the betterment of the wider community.

The misuse of funds and financial mismanagement can lead to scandals that damage the church's witness. Transparency and accountability are crucial in preventing such issues. Paul's practice of involving multiple people in the handling of the collection for the saints (2 Corinthians 8:18-20) is an excellent example of how to maintain integrity in financial matters. Churches should implement similar practices to safeguard against misuse and ensure that funds are used appropriately.

CHAPTER 12: MONEY AND MINISTRY

The spiritual health of a church can often be gauged by its attitude towards money. Jesus' parable of the rich fool in Luke 12:16-21 serves as a sobering reminder of the futility of hoarding wealth without being rich towards God. The rich fool's focus on accumulating more for himself ultimately led to his downfall. This parable calls churches to introspect on their financial priorities and realign them with God's kingdom purposes.

Ministries that prioritize spiritual richness over financial gain often find that God provides for their needs in miraculous ways. The feeding of the five thousand (John 6:1-14) illustrates how God can multiply the little we have when we trust Him completely. Jesus took five barley loaves and two small fishes, gave thanks, and distributed them to the multitude, with twelve baskets of leftovers collected afterward. This miracle shows that God's provision is not limited by our resources but by our faith and willingness to serve.

Church leaders must lead by example, demonstrating a lifestyle of generosity and faith in God's provision. Paul could boldly declare, "I have coveted no man's silver, or gold, or apparel" (Acts 20:33) because he lived a life free from the love of money. His contentment and reliance on God's provision set a powerful example for others to follow. Leaders who model such integrity inspire their congregations to adopt similar attitudes.

Furthermore, churches should invest in programs that foster financial literacy and stewardship among their members. Teaching biblical principles of money management can help congregants avoid the pitfalls of debt and financial stress, enabling them to give more generously. Proverbs 22:7 warns that "the borrower is servant to the lender," highlighting the bondage that debt can create. Equipping believers with the knowledge to manage their finances wisely aligns with the church's mission to promote holistic well-being.

In conclusion, the relationship between money and ministry must be carefully managed to ensure that the church remains focused on its spiritual mission. Financial resources should be seen as tools for advancing God's kingdom, not ends in themselves. By adhering to biblical principles of generosity, integrity, and faith, churches can avoid the pitfalls of materialism and maintain their spiritual vitality. As Jesus reminded us, "Seek ye first the kingdom of God, and his righteousness; and all these things shall be added unto you" (Matthew 6:33). This promise assures us that when our priorities are aligned with God's will, He will take care of our needs, enabling us to fulfill our divine calling with integrity and purpose.

Chapter 13: Accountability in Stewardship

In the bustling landscape of modern ministry, where churches often resemble corporations more than congregations, the profound need for accountability in stewardship has never been more pressing. As followers of Christ, we are called to manage not just the spiritual assets of the church but the financial ones with an integrity that reflects our heavenly stewardship. The Apostle Paul, in his first letter to the Corinthians, reminds us, "Moreover it is required in stewards, that a man be found faithful" (1 Corinthians 4:2). This directive establishes a clear benchmark for our conduct, emphasizing faithfulness as the cornerstone of stewardship.

In many contemporary churches, however, this biblical mandate seems blurred by the allure of financial gain. The influx of generous tithes and offerings, if not carefully managed, can lead to temptations that steer us away from our primary mission—to serve and glorify God. It's crucial that church leaders create a transparent system where finances are handled with utmost honesty and openness. This transparency not only builds trust within the community but also honors the scriptural principle found in Luke 16:10, where Jesus teaches, "He that is faithful in that which is least is faithful also in much: and he that is unjust in the least is unjust also in much."

To embody this transparency, churches must implement regular financial audits conducted by independent, qualified auditors. Such practices ensure that every dollar given in faith by the congregation is accounted for and used in alignment with the church's mission and God's broader kingdom purposes. These audits serve as a practical application of Proverbs 27:23, which urges us to "Be thou diligent to know the state of thy flocks, and look well to thy herds." Just as a shepherd watches over his flock, so must church leaders vigilantly oversee the resources entrusted to them, ensuring they are utilized wisely and effectively.

Accountability in stewardship also involves clear communication about financial matters to the church body. Regularly sharing financial statements and updates not only demonstrates an adherence to biblical standards but also engages the entire church in the stewardship process. This practice aligns with Acts 4:34-35, where the early church leaders distributed to each as anyone had need, ensuring there was not a needy person among them. By being transparent about the church's financial health, leaders can foster a community that is united and committed to supporting one another, reflecting the unity and generosity of the early church.

Financial integrity extends beyond mere transparency; it requires a heart aligned with God's purposes. The danger of financial compromise often begins not with the act of mismanagement, but with a heart that has strayed from God. Matthew 6:21 declares, "For where your treasure is, there will your heart be also." Church leaders must continually examine their motives, ensuring that their financial decisions promote spiritual growth and community support, rather than personal gain or organizational expansion at the cost of spiritual depth.

When financial misconduct occurs, it is imperative that it be addressed swiftly and justly, with corrective measures and, if necessary, restoration processes put into place. This approach not only adheres to biblical commands but also restores faith and trust within the church community. As Galatians 6:1 advises, "Brethren, if a man be overtaken in a fault, ye which are spiritual, restore such an one in the spirit of meekness; considering thyself, lest thou also be tempted." Restoration not only reconciles the one who has faltered but also heals the entire body, demonstrating the redemptive power of grace and the seriousness with which we take our stewardship responsibilities.

It is also critical for church leaders to foster an environment where accountability is not just a response to error but a proactive measure. Implementing checks and balances, where no single individual holds unchecked power over church finances, can prevent many potential issues. This approach is reflective of Ecclesiastes 4:12, which tells us that a cord of three strands is not quickly broken. By instituting multiple layers of oversight, churches can safeguard their ministries against financial mishaps and moral failures, ensuring their strength and integrity.

In this era of prosperity teaching, where wealth is often wrongly equated with divine favor, it is essential to return to the biblical understanding that our true riches are in Christ. Paul's words to Timothy are starkly relevant today: "But godliness with contentment is great gain" (1 Timothy 6:6). This perspective shifts the focus from accumulating wealth to fostering spiritual depth, encouraging leaders and congregations alike to prioritize eternal investments over temporal gains.

Another aspect of accountability in stewardship involves educating the congregation on biblical principles of giving and financial management. Leaders must teach that giving is an act of worship and obedience, not a means to gain material blessings. Jesus Himself highlighted the heart behind giving in Mark 12:43-44, commending the poor widow who gave out of her poverty, saying, "Verily I say unto you, That this poor widow hath cast more in, than all they which have cast into the treasury." This example shows that the value of a gift is measured not by its amount but by the sacrifice and intention behind it.

Churches should also encourage a culture of generosity that goes beyond tithes and offerings. Acts of kindness, support for missions, and community outreach are vital components of stewardship that reflect God's love. Paul reminds us in 2 Corinthians 9:7, "Every man according as he purposeth in his heart, so let him give; not grudgingly, or of necessity: for God loveth a cheerful giver." By promoting a generous spirit, churches can inspire their members to contribute to God's work joyfully and willingly, ensuring that their giving is a true reflection of their faith.

To support this culture of generosity, church leaders must lead by example. Their lives should exemplify the principles of stewardship they preach, demonstrating humility, integrity, and selflessness. Peter exhorts leaders in 1 Peter 5:2-3, "Feed the flock of God which is among you, taking the oversight thereof, not by constraint, but willingly; not for filthy lucre, but of a ready mind; Neither as being lords over God's heritage, but being ensamples to the flock." By living out these values, leaders can earn the respect and trust of their congregation, motivating them to follow suit.

Another critical element in fostering accountability is the establishment of clear, ethical guidelines for the use of church funds. This includes setting budgets, prioritizing expenditures, and

CHAPTER 13: ACCOUNTABILITY IN STEWARDSHIP

ensuring that all financial decisions align with the church's mission and biblical principles. Proverbs 16:3 advises, "Commit thy works unto the LORD, and thy thoughts shall be established." By committing their financial plans to God, church leaders can seek divine guidance and wisdom in their stewardship, ensuring that their actions honor Him.

In addition to ethical guidelines, churches must create opportunities for congregational input and oversight. This could involve forming finance committees or holding open forums where members can ask questions and provide feedback on financial matters. Such practices foster a sense of ownership and responsibility within the church body, encouraging members to stay engaged and supportive. James 1:5 assures us, "If any of you lack wisdom, let him ask of God, that giveth to all men liberally, and upbraideth not; and it shall be given him." Seeking collective wisdom and input can lead to more sound and God-honoring financial practices.

Addressing the broader issue of accountability in stewardship, it is essential to recognize the role of prayer and spiritual discernment in financial decisions. Church leaders must regularly seek God's guidance through prayer, asking for wisdom and clarity in managing resources. Philippians 4:6-7 encourages us, "Be careful for nothing; but in every thing by prayer and supplication with thanksgiving let your requests be made known unto God. And the peace of God, which passeth all understanding, shall keep your hearts and minds through Christ Jesus." By prioritizing prayer, leaders can align their financial decisions with God's will, ensuring that their stewardship is guided by His wisdom and peace.

Furthermore, fostering a culture of accountability requires ongoing education and training for church leaders and staff. Workshops, seminars, and courses on financial management and ethical practices can equip them with the necessary skills and knowledge to handle church finances responsibly. Paul's exhortation to Timothy in 2 Timothy 2:15, "Study to show thyself approved unto God, a workman that needeth not to be ashamed, rightly dividing the word of truth," applies here. Just as they are to be diligent in handling the Word, so must they be diligent in managing the church's resources.

In dealing with the issue of financial integrity, it is also important to cultivate an attitude of gratitude and humility among church leaders and members. Recognizing that all we have comes from God should inspire us to handle His resources with the utmost care and respect. Psalm 24:1 declares, "The earth is the LORD'S, and the fullness thereof; the world, and they that dwell therein." This acknowledgment reminds us that we are merely stewards of God's creation, entrusted with the responsibility to use His gifts wisely and faithfully.

Moreover, churches must be vigilant in safeguarding against conflicts of interest and ensuring that personal gain does not influence financial decisions. Transparency in transactions, clear policies, and regular reviews can help maintain integrity. Proverbs 11:1 warns, "A false balance is abomination to the LORD: but a just weight is his delight." Upholding fairness and justice in financial dealings is paramount in honoring God and maintaining the church's credibility.

Ultimately, the goal of accountability in stewardship is to ensure that the church remains focused on its divine mission—spreading the Gospel and serving the community. Financial resources should be viewed as tools for ministry, not as ends in themselves. Jesus' directive in Matthew 28:19-20, the Great Commission, should be the driving force behind all financial decisions. By keeping this mission at the forefront, churches can avoid the pitfalls of financial mismanagement and remain faithful to their calling.

As we reflect on the importance of accountability in stewardship, let us remember that it is not just about managing money but about honoring God with every aspect of our lives. Colossians 3:23-24 urges us, "And whatsoever ye do, do it heartily, as to the Lord, and not unto men; Knowing that of the Lord ye shall receive the reward of the inheritance: for ye serve the Lord Christ." This scripture encapsulates the heart of stewardship—serving God with all our resources, talents, and efforts, knowing that our ultimate reward comes from Him.

In conclusion, accountability in stewardship is a vital component of a healthy, thriving church. By adhering to biblical principles, fostering transparency, and maintaining a heart aligned with God's purposes, church leaders can ensure that their financial practices honor God and support His work. Let us commit to being faithful stewards, managing the resources entrusted to us with integrity, wisdom, and a deep sense of responsibility. In doing so, we not only build trust within our congregations but also reflect the character of Christ to the world, advancing His kingdom and glorifying His name.

Chapter 14: Scriptural Guidance on Managing Church Finances

In today's rapidly advancing society, where the pursuit of financial gain seems to overshadow almost every other ambition, even the church is not immune to the seductive lure of wealth. As believers, we must vigilantly guard against the temptation to elevate financial success as the benchmark of spiritual blessing. Paul's solemn warning to Timothy resonates with profound urgency now more than ever: "For the love of money is the root of all evil: which while some coveted after, they have erred from the faith, and pierced themselves through with many sorrows" (1 Timothy 6:10). This scripture is not merely an admonition but a prophetic insight into the debilitating spiritual decay that can ensue when wealth becomes an idol in our lives and our ministries.

The church's primary mission is to serve, to shepherd, to teach, and to heal, reflecting Christ's love and humility in every action. When financial gain becomes a focal point, it subtly shifts the church's foundational principles. It begins with small compromises, perhaps in the messages delivered from the pulpit, which increasingly focus on prosperity as a sign of God's favor rather than the virtues of sacrifice, humility, and service. The narrative subtly shifts, and the congregation begins to equate financial blessings with divine approval, neglecting the Beatitudes, which blessed the poor in spirit, the meek, and those who hunger and thirst for righteousness.

CHAPTER 14: SCRIPTURAL GUIDANCE ON MANAGING CHURCH FINANCES

Consider the early church, which operated under the guidance of the Holy Spirit, sharing all they had so that no one among them was in need. Acts 4:34-35 tells us, "Neither was there any among them that lacked: for as many as were possessors of lands or houses sold them, and brought the prices of the things that were sold, And laid them down at the apostles' feet: and distribution was made unto every man according as he had need." This spirit of generosity and communal support starkly contrasts with today's oft-emphasized prosperity gospel, which sometimes glorifies wealth accumulation as the primary evidence of God's favor, thereby distorting the gospel's essence and mission.

Moreover, the relentless pursuit of wealth can blind us to the needs of the poor and vulnerable, a concern central to Jesus' ministry. He himself declared, "But woe unto you that are rich! for ye have received your consolation" (Luke 6:24). This warning is not an indictment of wealth per se but a prophetic caution against placing wealth above our spiritual and communal duties. It serves as a reminder of the rich young ruler who, despite his adherence to the law, could not follow Christ because he could not part with his great possessions (Mark 10:22).

As stewards of God's resources, church leaders are called to manage finances with integrity, transparency, and fear of the Lord. The mishandling of church funds can lead to scandal and disgrace, tarnishing the church's witness to the world. Therefore, transparency in financial matters should be non-negotiable, ensuring that all dealings are above reproach, as Paul advised in 2 Corinthians 8:21: "Providing for honest things, not only in the sight of the Lord, but also in the sight of men."

Restoring right priorities begins by re-emphasizing the spiritual riches that Christ promised. "Lay not up for yourselves treasures upon earth, where moth and rust doth corrupt, and where thieves break through and steal: But lay up for yourselves treasures in heaven, where neither moth nor rust doth corrupt, and where thieves do not break through nor steal" (Matthew 6:19-20). This directive from Jesus does not merely suggest an alternative investment strategy; it calls for a profound realignment of our values, where eternal outcomes outweigh temporal gains.

How then, can a church re-align itself with the scriptural mandate to prioritize spiritual over material wealth? It begins in the heart of every believer, particularly the leaders. Pastors and church leaders must model contentment and dependence on God, rather than showcasing a lifestyle of luxury that can lead to envy and discontent among the flock. The Apostle Paul sets a profound example in Philippians 4:11-12, stating, "Not that I speak in respect of want: for I have learned, in whatsoever state I am, therewith to be content. I know both how to be abased, and I know how to abound: every where and in all things I am instructed both to be full and to be hungry, both to abound and to suffer need."

Furthermore, churches must actively teach and cultivate a culture of giving and generosity, not as a means to claim God's blessings, but as an act of worship and obedience to God's commands. The widow's mite (Mark 12:41-44) remains a powerful testimony to the heart of giving that God values—sacrificial, cheerful, and from whatever little one may possess.

In the story of the rich young ruler, we see a poignant lesson on the dangers of prioritizing wealth over devotion to God. This man had

CHAPTER 14: SCRIPTURAL GUIDANCE ON MANAGING CHURCH FINANCES

observed the commandments faithfully, yet when Jesus asked him to sell all he had and follow Him, he went away sorrowful. Jesus remarked, "How hardly shall they that have riches enter into the kingdom of God!" (Mark 10:23). The young ruler's attachment to his wealth hindered him from fully committing to Christ, serving as a sobering reminder that our hearts must be free from the love of material possessions to truly follow Him.

A church that emphasizes financial gain over spiritual growth can unwittingly foster a culture of materialism. This mindset can lead to the congregation measuring their worth and success by their financial status rather than their relationship with God. Jesus warned against such misplaced priorities in Luke 12:15, saying, "Take heed, and beware of covetousness: for a man's life consisteth not in the abundance of the things which he possesseth." Our value is found in Christ, not in our wealth.

The pursuit of financial gain can also lead to ethical compromises. When church leaders prioritize fundraising and financial campaigns over discipleship and spiritual growth, it can create an environment where the ends justify the means. This can result in questionable practices and decisions that undermine the church's integrity. James 4:4 warns, "Ye adulterers and adulteresses, know ye not that the friendship of the world is enmity with God? whosoever therefore will be a friend of the world is the enemy of God." The church must maintain its distinctiveness and purity, avoiding the temptation to adopt worldly methods for financial gain.

Transparency in financial matters is essential for maintaining trust and integrity within the church. When Paul collected contributions for the saints in Jerusalem, he ensured accountability by involving multiple trustworthy individuals in the process (2 Corinthians 8:18-21). This practice not only safeguarded the funds but also protected the reputations of those handling them. Similarly, modern churches must implement transparent and accountable financial practices to avoid scandals and maintain credibility.

Churches should also encourage members to view their financial resources as tools for advancing God's kingdom rather than as ends in themselves. This perspective shifts the focus from accumulating wealth to using it for God's purposes. In 1 Timothy 6:17-19, Paul instructs those who are rich to "do good, to be rich in good works, ready to distribute, willing to communicate; Laying up in store for themselves a good foundation against the time to come, that they may lay hold on eternal life." This approach fosters a spirit of generosity and purpose-driven stewardship.

Reevaluating our priorities involves a return to the teachings of Jesus about wealth and possessions. In Matthew 6:24, Jesus makes it clear that we cannot serve both God and mammon. This dichotomy requires us to choose whom we will serve. If our allegiance is to God, then our financial decisions and the way we handle money must reflect His values and purposes. This means prioritizing generosity, humility, and service over accumulation and self-promotion.

Leaders must exemplify these values, living lives of simplicity and contentment. Their example can inspire the congregation to adopt similar attitudes. Hebrews 13:5 advises, "Let your conversation be without covetousness; and be content with such things as ye have: for he hath said, I will never leave thee, nor forsake thee."

CHAPTER 14: SCRIPTURAL GUIDANCE ON MANAGING CHURCH FINANCES

Contentment and trust in God's provision should characterize the lives of believers, contrasting sharply with the relentless pursuit of wealth prevalent in the world.

Moreover, it is crucial for churches to invest in the spiritual development of their members. This involves providing sound biblical teaching that emphasizes the eternal over the temporal. Jesus' parable of the sower in Matthew 13 illustrates the various ways people respond to the word of God. Those who are choked by the cares of this world and the deceitfulness of riches are unfruitful. By focusing on spiritual growth, churches can help their members develop deep roots in their faith, enabling them to withstand the distractions and temptations of wealth.

The church must also remember its mission to care for the poor and marginalized. Jesus' ministry was marked by compassion for the needy, and He calls His followers to do the same. In Matthew 25:40, He says, "Verily I say unto you, Inasmuch as ye have done it unto one of the least of these my brethren, ye have done it unto me." This call to serve those in need should guide the church's use of resources, prioritizing outreach and support for the vulnerable over extravagant expenditures.

Restoring the church's focus on spiritual wealth over material gain is not merely about changing practices but about transforming hearts. This transformation begins with repentance and a renewed commitment to Christ's teachings. Revelation 3:17-18 offers a poignant reminder: "Because thou sayest, I am rich, and increased with goods, and have need of nothing; and knowest not that thou art wretched, and miserable, and poor, and blind, and naked: I counsel thee to buy of me gold tried in the fire, that thou mayest be rich; and white raiment, that thou mayest be clothed, and that the shame of thy nakedness do not appear; and anoint thine eyes with eyesalve, that thou mayest see."

Churches that prioritize spiritual riches will naturally foster a culture of generosity and community. Acts 2:44-45 describes the early believers who "had all things common; And sold their possessions and goods, and parted them to all men, as every man had need." This spirit of sharing and mutual support reflects the heart of Christ and stands in stark contrast to a culture driven by financial gain.

As we navigate the complexities of modern life, the church must continually return to the teachings of Christ and the apostles. By doing so, we ensure that our priorities align with God's will, and our ministries reflect His love and truth. This alignment requires ongoing reflection and willingness to make difficult choices, often countercultural, to remain faithful to the gospel.

In conclusion, as we consider the role of financial management within the church, let us return to the cornerstone of our faith—Christ Jesus, who, though he was rich, for our sakes became poor, that through his poverty we might become rich (2 Corinthians 8:9). This richness is not of the world but is the profound spiritual wealth of knowing Christ and making Him known. The church must, therefore, strive to embody this divine principle, ensuring that its pursuit of financial sustainability never overshadows its spiritual mission.

Chapter 15: Restoring Right Priorities

Restoring right priorities in the church requires a heartfelt return to the foundational principles laid out in Scripture. At the core of this restoration is the understanding that the church's true wealth lies not in its financial reserves, but in the depth of its spiritual vitality. Jesus's encounter with the rich young ruler in Mark 10:21 illustrates this vividly: "One thing thou lackest: go thy way, sell whatsoever thou hast, and give to the poor, and thou shalt have treasure in heaven: and come, take up the cross, and follow me." This passage is not merely about giving away material wealth but about prioritizing spiritual riches above all else. Our journey towards restoring right priorities begins with a willingness to follow Christ wholeheartedly, forsaking all else that might distract or detract from that central commitment.

The early church exemplified this spirit of prioritizing spiritual wealth over material possessions. Acts 2:44-45 tells us, "And all that believed were together, and had all things common; And sold their possessions and goods, and parted them to all men, as every man had need." This radical generosity was a reflection of their deep commitment to Christ and each other. It wasn't about mere redistribution of wealth, but about a community living out the reality of God's kingdom on earth. Today, we must ask ourselves whether our financial strategies and priorities align with this biblical model. Are we focused more on expanding our earthly influence and comfort, or are we committed to fostering a community where spiritual growth and mutual care are paramount?

Churches today face immense pressure to secure financial stability and grow their physical presence. This often leads to a focus on financial gain that can overshadow the mission of spiritual enrichment. However, Ephesians 4:12 reminds us that the purpose of the church is "for the perfecting of the saints, for the work of the ministry, for the edifying of the body of Christ." When financial pursuits become the primary focus, we risk losing sight of these spiritual objectives. Recalibrating our priorities involves a humble return to this mission, ensuring that every budgetary decision reflects our commitment to spiritual growth and community impact.

The allure of financial security is powerful, but it can lead churches astray if not managed with wisdom and integrity. Paul's warning in 1 Timothy 6:10 is especially pertinent: "For the love of money is the root of all evil: which while some coveted after, they have erred from the faith, and pierced themselves through with many sorrows." This passage highlights the spiritual dangers of prioritizing financial gain over faithfulness to God's calling. Church leaders must be vigilant, ensuring that financial goals serve the kingdom's mission rather than becoming an end in themselves.

True restoration of right priorities begins in the heart. A church's collective heart must beat with a rhythm of generosity that mirrors God's own heart. Paul emphasizes this in 2 Corinthians 9:7, saying, "Every man according as he purposeth in his heart, so let him give; not grudgingly, or of necessity: for God loveth a cheerful giver." Generosity should extend beyond financial contributions to include the giving of time, talents, and resources. It reflects a

CHAPTER 15: RESTORING RIGHT PRIORITIES

community committed to living out the Gospel's call to love and serve one another.

Transparency and accountability in financial matters are crucial for maintaining trust and integrity within the church. Luke 16:11 challenges us, "If therefore ye have not been faithful in the unrighteous mammon, who will commit to your trust the true riches?" True riches in the church context are spiritual in nature, encompassing the authority and capacity to impact lives for Christ. Faithful stewardship of earthly resources is a prerequisite for experiencing these true riches. This involves making financial decisions that honor God and reflect our commitment to His mission.

Embracing simplicity and contentment is another essential aspect of restoring right priorities. Paul's words in Philippians 4:11-12 are a powerful reminder: "Not that I speak in respect of want: for I have learned, in whatsoever state I am, therewith to be content. I know both how to be abased, and I know how to abound." Contentment should not be confused with complacency. It is a profound trust in God's provision, challenging us to focus on what truly nourishes the soul. The opulence of a church building or the lavishness of its events should never overshadow the authenticity of its worship and the strength of its community ties.

Church leaders play a pivotal role in modeling these restored priorities. Timothy was instructed in 1 Timothy 4:12 to be "an example of the believers, in word, in conversation, in charity, in spirit, in faith, in purity." Today's church leaders must exemplify financial stewardship that honors God, even when it involves making difficult, unpopular decisions. Such leadership inspires congregations to follow suit, fostering a community committed to spiritual richness over material wealth.

Reflecting on Revelation 3:17-18, where the church in Laodicea is admonished for its lukewarmness and misplaced trust in wealth, we are reminded of the need for constant vigilance in assessing our spiritual health. "Because thou sayest, I am rich, and increased with goods, and have need of nothing; and knowest not that thou art wretched, and miserable, and poor, and blind, and naked: I counsel thee to buy of me gold tried in the fire, that thou mayest be rich." This passage underscores the danger of equating material success with spiritual health. True riches are found in a refined faith, not in earthly abundance.

In restoring right priorities, the church must foster a culture where financial resources are seen as tools for ministry rather than measures of success. Every financial decision should be guided by a commitment to advance God's kingdom, reflecting the principles laid out in Scripture. This includes supporting missions, caring for the needy, and investing in discipleship programs that nurture spiritual growth.

The journey toward financial integrity and spiritual abundance is challenging but essential. As Jesus taught in Matthew 6:19-21, "Lay not up for yourselves treasures upon earth, where moth and rust doth corrupt, and where thieves break through and steal: But lay up for yourselves treasures in heaven, where neither moth nor rust doth corrupt, and where thieves do not break through nor steal: For where your treasure is, there will your heart be also." This teaching calls us to evaluate our priorities and ensure our treasures align with eternal values.

CHAPTER 15: RESTORING RIGHT PRIORITIES

Creating a culture of generosity and transparency involves educating congregations about biblical stewardship. Teaching on passages like Malachi 3:10, "Bring ye all the tithes into the storehouse, that there may be meat in mine house, and prove me now herewith, saith the Lord of hosts, if I will not open you the windows of heaven, and pour you out a blessing, that there shall not be room enough to receive it," helps believers understand the blessings associated with faithful giving. It also instills a sense of responsibility and joy in contributing to God's work.

Restoring right priorities also involves a commitment to prayer and discernment in financial matters. James 1:5 encourages us, "If any of you lack wisdom, let him ask of God, that giveth to all men liberally, and upbraideth not; and it shall be given him." Seeking God's wisdom in financial decisions ensures that our actions are aligned with His will and purpose. It also fosters a dependence on God rather than on human understanding or resources.

As churches embrace these restored priorities, they will experience a shift in focus from financial gain to spiritual growth. This transformation will be evident in the lives of individuals and the community as a whole. The church will become a beacon of hope and light, reflecting the glory of God and drawing others to His kingdom. This aligns with the promise in Proverbs 11:25, "The liberal soul shall be made fat: and he that watereth shall be watered also himself." Generosity and faithfulness lead to spiritual richness and divine blessing.

The road to restoring right priorities is not without its challenges, but it is a journey worth undertaking. It requires intentionality, prayer, and a willingness to align every aspect of church life with biblical principles. As we prioritize spiritual riches over financial gain, we will witness a revival in our churches, marked by genuine worship, deep community ties, and impactful ministry. This revival will not only strengthen the church internally but also extend its influence and reach in the world, fulfilling the Great Commission and glorifying God.

In conclusion, the call to restore right priorities is a call to return to the heart of the Gospel. It is an invitation to forsake the distractions of material wealth and embrace the richness of life in Christ. As we heed this call, we align ourselves with God's eternal purposes, experiencing the fullness of His blessings and becoming effective witnesses of His love and grace. Let us commit to this journey, trusting that God, who began a good work in us, will carry it on to completion until the day of Christ Jesus (Philippians 1:6).

Section 4: Leadership Compromise

Chapter 16: Character over Charisma

In the shifting sands of modern church leadership, the emphasis on charisma over character can often lead to a compromise that undercuts the very foundation of godly governance. Paul's letters to Timothy underscore the non-negotiable need for leaders who are above reproach. As stated in 1 Timothy 3:2, "A bishop then must be blameless, the husband of one wife, vigilant, sober, of good behaviour, given to hospitality, apt to teach." These words are not mere suggestions but prerequisites that set the stage for spiritual integrity and moral clarity. The allure of a charismatic leader can indeed draw crowds, but without a bedrock of solid character, such leadership is as unstable as a house built on sand.

The risk of prioritizing personal charm and dynamic speaking ability above spiritual maturity and ethical steadfastness is a tale as old as time. History is replete with examples where leaders, blessed with the gift of gab and a magnetic personality, led their followers astray due to a lack of moral fiber. Reflecting on Proverbs 27:2, "Let another man praise thee, and not thine own mouth; a stranger, and not thine own lips," we find a powerful admonition against self-promotion. This scripture teaches us that true validation of leadership comes not from one's ability to project an image but from the endorsement of others based on one's inherent godly qualities and deeds.

In our interactions with leaders who focus more on their image than on their duty to shepherd, it becomes evident that such leadership does not endure the trials of time. The scriptures warn us through the wisdom of Solomon in Ecclesiastes 7:1, "A good name is better than precious ointment; and the day of death than the day of one's birth." This vivid comparison underscores the eternal value of a good reputation, which is invariably linked to one's character rather than to one's charisma. Leaders who nurture their character cultivate a legacy that outlives them and continues to bear fruit long after they have gone.

The narrative of King Saul serves as a cautionary tale. Blessed with the physical and charismatic attributes that Israel desired in a king, Saul initially captured the heart of the nation. However, his failure to obey God fully and his propensity to prioritize his public image over divine commands led to his downfall and rejection by God. Samuel's lament in 1 Samuel 15:22, "Hath the LORD as great delight in burnt offerings and sacrifices, as in obeying the voice of the LORD? Behold, to obey is better than sacrifice, and to hearken than the fat of rams," poignantly reminds us that God values obedience over sacrifice. Saul's lack of character, obscured by his charisma, ultimately proved his undoing.

Today's church leaders can draw a lesson from Saul's story. It is imperative that they examine whether their leadership is marked more by a godly character or by the superficiality of charisma. As James 3:1 warns us, "My brethren, be not many masters, knowing that we shall receive the greater condemnation." This scripture speaks directly to those who would lead, emphasizing the serious scrutiny and higher standards to which they are held. It serves as a sober reminder that leadership is a sacred responsibility, not a stage for personal glory.

In nurturing character, leaders must cultivate humility, a trait that is often overshadowed in the race for charisma. Jesus himself demonstrated this in John 13:14 when he washed his disciples' feet, stating, "If I then, your Lord and Master, have washed your feet; ye also ought to wash one another's feet." This act of humility was not just a lesson in service but a profound statement on leadership. The true leader serves, and his actions are driven by a love for others, not by the love of others' admiration.

The emphasis on character extends into how leaders handle criticism and conflict. A leader's true nature is often revealed not in times of peace and popularity but in moments of challenge and controversy. Proverbs 17:27 teaches us, "He that hath knowledge spareth his words: and a man of understanding is of an excellent spirit." A leader rich in character is measured and wise in his responses, seeking resolution and unity rather than division and strife.

Moreover, the development of character in leadership is not a solitary endeavor but a communal responsibility. As the body of Christ, it is incumbent upon us to hold our leaders accountable, to support their growth in grace, and to pray for their spiritual welfare. Galatians 6:1 offers guidance in this regard: "Brethren, if a man be overtaken in a fault, ye which are spiritual, restore such an one in the spirit of meekness; considering thyself, lest thou also be tempted." This mutual accountability safeguards the church and ensures that its leaders can grow in integrity and wisdom.

Character in leadership also involves a commitment to truth, even when it is uncomfortable. Paul exhorts Timothy in 2 Timothy 4:2, "Preach the word; be instant in season, out of season; reprove,

CHAPTER 16: CHARACTER OVER CHARISMA

rebuke, exhort with all longsuffering and doctrine." A leader with godly character will not shy away from proclaiming the whole counsel of God, regardless of the cultural pressures to conform. This unwavering dedication to truth is what distinguishes a leader of character from one who relies solely on charisma.

The foundation of character is built on a leader's personal relationship with God. In Psalm 119:11, the psalmist declares, "Thy word have I hid in mine heart, that I might not sin against thee." Leaders who prioritize their spiritual disciplines—such as prayer, meditation on scripture, and personal holiness—develop a reservoir of character that sustains them through the highs and lows of ministry. This inner spiritual fortitude is what enables them to lead with authenticity and integrity.

Furthermore, character is demonstrated in the consistency of a leader's private and public life. Jesus warns in Matthew 23:27, "Woe unto you, scribes and Pharisees, hypocrites! for ye are like unto whited sepulchres, which indeed appear beautiful outward, but are within full of dead men's bones, and of all uncleanness." This stark warning against hypocrisy highlights the importance of aligning one's private actions with public declarations. Leaders whose lives are marked by such integrity gain the trust and respect of those they lead.

Leadership rooted in character also means prioritizing the well-being of the flock over personal gain. In John 10:11, Jesus proclaims, "I am the good shepherd: the good shepherd giveth his life for the sheep." The ultimate example of sacrificial leadership, Jesus sets the standard for leaders to follow. True leaders lay down their lives, figuratively and literally, for the sake of those they are called to serve. Their primary concern is the spiritual growth and protection of their congregation, not their own advancement.

A leader's character is also evident in their stewardship of resources. Luke 16:10 teaches, "He that is faithful in that which is least is faithful also in much: and he that is unjust in the least is unjust also in much." Leaders who handle church finances and resources with integrity reflect their commitment to accountability and transparency. This faithfulness in small matters translates into greater trust and responsibility in larger ones.

In addition, character in leadership involves a heart for the marginalized and oppressed. Isaiah 1:17 commands, "Learn to do well; seek judgment, relieve the oppressed, judge the fatherless, plead for the widow." Leaders who champion justice and compassion, advocating for those who cannot advocate for themselves, mirror the heart of God. Their actions reflect a deep-seated commitment to living out the gospel in practical, tangible ways.

The testing of character often comes in the form of trials and temptations. James 1:12 encourages, "Blessed is the man that endureth temptation: for when he is tried, he shall receive the crown of life, which the Lord hath promised to them that love him." Leaders who remain steadfast in their faith and principles during difficult times emerge stronger and more resilient. Their perseverance inspires others and strengthens the entire church body.

Ultimately, the fruit of character in leadership is seen in the legacy left behind. Proverbs 22:1 asserts, "A good name is rather to be chosen than great riches, and loving favour rather than silver and gold." Leaders who prioritize character over charisma leave a lasting impact that transcends their tenure. Their influence continues to shape and inspire future generations long after they are gone.

As we reflect on the critical importance of character in leadership, we must also recognize the role of the congregation in fostering and supporting such leaders. Hebrews 13:17 instructs, "Obey them that have the rule over you, and submit yourselves: for they watch for your souls, as they that must give account, that they may do it with joy, and not with grief: for that is unprofitable for you." This mutual respect and support create an environment where leaders can thrive and fulfill their God-given calling.

In conclusion, the call to prioritize character over charisma in church leadership is not just a suggestion but a divine mandate. As we navigate the complexities of modern ministry, let us remember the timeless truths of scripture and strive to raise up leaders who embody the character of Christ. For it is only through such leaders that the church can truly fulfill its mission and stand as a beacon of hope and truth in a world desperate for authentic and godly leadership.

Chapter 17: Accountability Failures

Accountability within church leadership is not just a procedural necessity; it is a spiritual imperative. The Apostle Paul, when he spoke to Timothy, emphasized the need to keep a close watch on both oneself and the doctrine being taught (1 Timothy 4:16). This vigilance ensures that leaders are not only proclaiming the truth but also living it. The absence of such accountability mechanisms has led to a troubling rise in moral and ethical failures within the church, where leaders have succumbed to the very temptations they once preached against. These failures are not just personal missteps; they reverberate through the entire body of Christ, causing disillusionment and spiritual harm to countless believers.

When leaders fall, it often feels like the ground has shifted beneath the feet of their followers. James 3:1 starkly reminds us that those who teach will be judged with greater strictness. This greater judgment is not merely punitive; it reflects the immense influence that leaders hold over their congregations. When a leader stumbles, it can lead to a crisis of faith for those who looked up to them as spiritual guides. This is why the integrity of leadership is so crucial; it forms the bedrock of trust and faith within the church. Without accountability, this trust is easily shattered, leaving a trail of wounded and disillusioned believers in its wake.

A lack of accountability often paves the way for an insidious pride to take root in the hearts of leaders. They begin to see themselves as above reproach, immune to the scrutiny that they once welcomed. Proverbs 16:18 warns us that pride goes before destruction, and a haughty spirit before a fall. This scriptural truth has played out time and again in the annals of church history, where leaders who eschewed accountability found themselves entangled in scandals that could have been avoided with proper oversight. The unchecked power and unchallenged decisions lead to a dangerous isolation, where leaders become insulated from the very feedback and correction that could save them from moral and spiritual peril.

David's grievous sin with Bathsheba serves as a cautionary tale of what happens when leaders operate without accountability. David, a man after God's own heart, found himself in a moral quagmire because he acted without counsel and oversight (2 Samuel 11). His failure to seek accountability led to a series of tragic events that stained his legacy and brought suffering to his house. This biblical account is a powerful reminder that even those with a deep connection to God are vulnerable to the temptations of power when they are not held accountable. It underscores the importance of having trusted voices that can speak truth into our lives, challenging us to stay true to our calling.

True biblical leadership is characterized by humility and a willingness to submit to the counsel of others. Paul's relationship with Barnabas is a testament to this principle. Despite their disagreements, they remained committed to holding each other accountable, ensuring that their ministries were aligned with God's will. This mutual accountability is not a sign of weakness but of strength. It reflects a deep commitment to integrity and a recognition that no one is beyond the need for guidance and correction. When leaders embrace this model, they create a culture where transparency and accountability are valued, fostering an environment of trust and spiritual growth.

The Proverbs declare that iron sharpens iron, so one man sharpens another (Proverbs 27:17). This sharpening process is vital for leaders to maintain their spiritual edge. When accountability is embraced, it becomes a means of refining and strengthening one's ministry. It is not about controlling leaders but about supporting them in their journey of faith. The absence of accountability, on the other hand, dulls the spiritual senses, leading to a gradual drift away from the principles that should guide their actions. This drift is often imperceptible at first but becomes glaringly obvious in the wake of moral failings and ethical breaches.

Restoring accountability in church leadership involves creating systems where feedback is not only given but also received with humility. This might mean establishing oversight boards, conducting regular peer reviews, or inviting external audits of both financial and spiritual governance. The early church practiced this model, as seen in Acts, where the apostles operated in constant consultation with each other, ensuring that their actions were guided by collective wisdom and the Holy Spirit. This communal approach to decision-making prevented any one individual from wielding unchecked power and provided a safeguard against moral and spiritual failures.

When leaders resist accountability, they not only put themselves at risk but also jeopardize the spiritual wellbeing of their congregations. The fall of King Saul is a stark reminder of this truth. Saul's kingdom was torn from him because he valued his own judgment over the commands of God and the counsel of

Samuel (1 Samuel 15:22-23). This narrative warns modern church leaders that God values obedience over sacrifice and expects leaders to model this submission in their administrative and spiritual duties. Saul's downfall was not just a personal tragedy but a national one, illustrating the far-reaching consequences of leadership failures.

Transparency and accountability must be the twin pillars upon which church leadership is built. These principles are not just administrative necessities; they are spiritual disciplines that protect the integrity of the church. Ecclesiastes 4:9-10 highlights the protective and enriching power of accountable relationships: "Two are better than one, because they have a good reward for their toil. For if they fall, one will lift up his fellow." This scripture underscores the importance of having trusted partners in ministry who can offer correction with grace and encouragement in times of challenge. These relationships act as safeguards against the isolating effects of leadership, ensuring that leaders remain grounded in their faith and mission.

In today's church, there is a pressing need to re-establish a culture of accountability that places character and integrity above charisma and oratory skills. This shift requires a concerted effort to train and equip leaders who are not only skilled in their craft but also committed to living out the principles they preach. It means creating an environment where questions are encouraged, and integrity is upheld not out of compulsion but from a genuine desire to honor God. Such a culture fosters trust and spiritual growth, drawing the body of Christ closer to the heart of God.

The path to renewal in church leadership is paved with humility and a willingness to be held accountable. Leaders must recognize that they are not above reproach and that their actions have profound implications for the faith of those they lead. By embracing accountability, they declare their dedication to the truth of the Gospel and their commitment to living it out in every aspect of their ministry. This commitment to integrity and transparency not only protects leaders from moral and spiritual failure but also ensures that the church remains a beacon of hope and truth in a world that desperately needs it.

Scripture provides numerous examples of the benefits of accountable leadership. The story of Moses and Aaron illustrates the strength that comes from shared leadership and mutual accountability. When Moses grew weary, Aaron and Hur held up his hands, ensuring that the Israelites prevailed in battle (Exodus 17:12). This imagery of shared burden and support is a powerful reminder that leaders are not meant to carry their responsibilities alone. They need trusted partners who can help them stay the course and fulfill their God-given mission.

Accountability also involves a willingness to confront and address sin within the church. In 1 Corinthians 5, Paul addresses the issue of immorality within the Corinthian church, urging the leaders to take decisive action to address the sin. This passage highlights the responsibility of church leaders to uphold the moral and spiritual standards of the congregation. Ignoring or downplaying sin within the church not only compromises the integrity of the leadership but also jeopardizes the spiritual health of the entire body. Leaders

CHAPTER 17: ACCOUNTABILITY FAILURES

must be willing to confront difficult issues head-on, guided by love and a commitment to biblical truth.

The journey towards accountability is not an easy one, but it is essential for the health and vitality of the church. Leaders must be willing to open themselves up to scrutiny and correction, recognizing that this is a path to growth and spiritual maturity. Hebrews 12:11 reminds us that "no discipline seems pleasant at the time, but painful. Later on, however, it produces a harvest of righteousness and peace for those who have been trained by it." Embracing accountability may be challenging, but it yields the fruit of righteousness and peace, strengthening the leader and the congregation alike.

As we move forward, let us commit to being leaders who seek not the spotlight, but the strong, steady light of God's truth guiding our paths. Let this be the mark of our leadership, that we loved truth and pursued it, even when it cost us our pride. In doing so, we not only safeguard the integrity of our ministry but also ensure that we are leading our flock towards the everlasting truth of God's word, firmly rooted and built up in Him. This is not just an administrative adjustment but a profound spiritual realignment, echoing the call of scripture to lead with diligence, humility, and a deep-seated fear of the Lord.

The integrity of our leadership is a testimony to the world of the transformative power of the Gospel. When leaders model accountability, they demonstrate that their faith is not just a matter of words but of deep conviction and commitment. This authenticity draws people to Christ, showcasing the beauty of a life lived in alignment with God's principles. It is this witness that the world so desperately needs, a church that stands as a beacon of truth, integrity, and hope in the midst of a culture that often values appearance over substance.

In conclusion, the call to accountability is a call to renewal. It is an invitation to return to the principles that once defined the church, to the humble submission to God's will and the mutual support of the body of Christ. As we heed this call, we can expect to see a church that is not only purified and strengthened but also empowered to fulfill its mission in the world. This is the vision of church leadership that God has set before us, a leadership that is marked by integrity, humility, and a relentless pursuit of His truth. Let us strive to embody this vision, for the glory of God and the sake of His kingdom.

Chapter 18: Biblical Leadership Models

In our pursuit of genuine spiritual leadership, it is paramount that we align ourselves with the models presented in Scripture, where the qualifications and characteristics of leadership are distinctly outlined. The Apostle Paul, understanding the critical role of leadership in shaping the church, offers Timothy comprehensive advice in his pastoral epistles. In 1 Timothy 3:2-7, Paul enumerates the qualities of a church leader, emphasizing virtues such as hospitality, self-control, respectability, and the ability to teach. These traits are not randomly chosen; they are divinely prescribed to ensure that leaders can effectively shepherd the congregation without causing scandal or division. This high standard calls for a deep self-assessment by anyone in or aspiring to a leadership position, prompting a return to humility and service rather than authority and dominance.

Consider the sobering model of Moses, one of the most revered leaders in the Old Testament. His leadership was marked not only by his faithfulness and obedience but also by his humility, which the Bible highlights as exceeding any other man on earth at the time (Numbers 12:3). Moses' reliance on God, his hesitation to step into leadership without God's assurance, and his enduring patience with the people reflect the core attributes that every Christian leader should aspire to embody. His life compels us to ask if our leadership fosters reliance on God's power or on personal charisma. It's a call to evaluate whether our actions guide people towards God or inadvertently towards ourselves.

Furthermore, the example of King David brings an additional layer to our understanding of biblical leadership. Despite his significant failings, David's leadership is consistently celebrated for his heart for God, "a man after God's own heart" (1 Samuel 13:14). His psalms provide a transparent look into his spiritual struggles, showcasing his repentance and fervent pursuit of divine forgiveness. This model teaches us that leadership is not about perfection but about a heartfelt and relentless pursuit of righteousness and reconciliation with God. It underlines the importance of repentance and humility, reminding leaders that they, too, are under the authority of the Almighty.

Jesus Christ himself provided the perfect model of leadership. He washed the feet of His disciples, an act that epitomized servant leadership (John 13:14-15). Through this act, He set a profound example: true leaders are not those who wield power from high positions but those who serve with humility and love. Christ's leadership was devoid of pomp and focused entirely on service, which often meant reaching out to those marginalized by society. This servant leadership model challenges today's leaders to examine whether their leadership style uplifts and serves or whether it seeks to be served.

In the New Testament, we see Paul, a tireless missionary who endured hardships for the sake of the gospel (2 Corinthians 11:24-28). His resilience, focus, and dedication to spreading the message of Christ exemplify a leadership committed to the cause despite personal costs. Paul's life urges leaders today to consider the sacrifices they are making for the spread of the gospel,

CHAPTER 18: BIBLICAL LEADERSHIP MODELS

encouraging a leadership style that prioritizes the eternal impact over temporal gains.

The book of Acts offers insight into the collective leadership of the early church, highlighting the role of the Holy Spirit in guiding decisions (Acts 15:28). This example of communal and spiritual discernment in leadership stands in stark contrast to the isolated decision-making processes often observed in contemporary church leadership. It invites today's leaders to seek divine guidance actively and to value the input of others in the leadership community, fostering a more holistic approach to governance and decision-making.

The prophet Samuel also provides a critical examination of the heart in leadership. When selecting the future king of Israel, God reminds Samuel that while people look at the outward appearance, the Lord looks at the heart (1 Samuel 16:7). This scripture is a poignant reminder for all who lead that God's standards for leadership transcend human criteria; it is the inner character, not the external image, that defines true spiritual leadership.

Nehemiah, tasked with rebuilding the walls of Jerusalem, exemplifies leadership grounded in vision and determination. His ability to rally the people, devise practical strategies, and remain focused despite opposition is a testament to his unwavering commitment to God's call (Nehemiah 4:17-18). Nehemiah's leadership is characterized by a clear purpose and a resilience that did not waver in the face of threats or challenges. His story encourages modern leaders to cultivate a clear, God-given vision and the fortitude to see it through, regardless of the obstacles.

The integrity and wisdom of Joseph, who rose to power in Egypt, offer another compelling leadership model. Despite being sold into slavery and imprisoned, Joseph remained faithful to God. His administrative skills and prophetic insights eventually led to his appointment as second in command to Pharaoh (Genesis 41:39-40). Joseph's story is a powerful reminder that leadership often involves enduring trials and maintaining faithfulness, with the understanding that God's plans and timing are perfect. Leaders today can draw from Joseph's example, learning to trust in God's sovereignty and timing.

Leadership also requires a deep connection with God, as demonstrated by the prophet Elijah. His boldness in confronting the prophets of Baal and his reliance on God's power (1 Kings 18:36-39) underscore the necessity of spiritual intimacy and courage in leadership. Elijah's life shows that true leaders must sometimes stand alone, fortified by their unwavering faith in God. This narrative encourages leaders to cultivate a profound personal relationship with God, enabling them to lead with spiritual authority and confidence.

The wisdom and discernment of Solomon are additional critical attributes for leaders. When God offered him anything he desired, Solomon chose wisdom to govern his people effectively (1 Kings 3:9-12). His choice reflects a profound understanding that leadership requires divine insight and understanding. Solomon's example urges today's leaders to seek God's wisdom above all else, ensuring that their decisions and actions are guided by divine insight rather than human knowledge alone.

CHAPTER 18: BIBLICAL LEADERSHIP MODELS

John the Baptist, the forerunner of Christ, exemplifies humility and the importance of pointing others to Jesus. He famously stated, "He must increase, but I must decrease" (John 3:30). John's life was dedicated to preparing the way for Christ, and his ministry focused on redirecting attention away from himself and towards the Savior. This humility is a crucial lesson for leaders, emphasizing that their primary role is to lead others to Christ rather than seeking personal recognition or glory.

Deborah, a judge and prophetess in Israel, exemplifies leadership marked by wisdom, courage, and faith. Her ability to lead Israel to victory, alongside Barak, and her role as a judge underlines the importance of shared leadership and the inclusion of diverse gifts and perspectives (Judges 4:4-9). Deborah's story encourages leaders to embrace collaboration and to recognize the value of diverse contributions within the body of Christ, fostering a more inclusive and effective leadership model.

Peter, the apostle, provides a model of leadership that embraces transformation and grace. His denial of Christ and subsequent restoration (John 21:15-17) highlight the redemptive power of Christ in a leader's life. Peter's journey from failure to foundational leadership in the early church reminds leaders that their past mistakes do not disqualify them from future service. It's a call to embrace God's grace and to lead from a place of humility and dependence on Him.

Paul's mentorship of Timothy underscores the importance of discipleship in leadership. His letters to Timothy are filled with guidance, encouragement, and doctrinal instruction, demonstrating a model of leadership that invests in the next generation (2 Timothy 2:2). This relational approach to leadership highlights the need for leaders to mentor and develop others, ensuring the continuity of sound doctrine and effective ministry.

Esther's bravery and strategic thinking saved her people from destruction. Her willingness to risk her life to approach the king (Esther 4:16) illustrates the importance of courage and advocacy in leadership. Esther's story challenges leaders to use their influence and position to protect and serve those who are vulnerable, advocating for justice and righteousness.

Barnabas, known as the "Son of Encouragement," played a crucial role in the early church by supporting Paul and others. His willingness to give others a second chance (Acts 9:26-27) and his generosity exemplify a leadership style grounded in encouragement and support. Barnabas's example calls leaders to cultivate an environment of grace and encouragement, fostering growth and unity within the church.

Each of these biblical models provides a facet of what true leadership in the church should look like. They collectively emphasize humility, service, integrity, wisdom, courage, and a deep connection with God. In today's church, where leadership compromise is too often driven by a desire for cultural acceptance and financial gain, returning to these biblical standards is essential. By embracing these models, leaders can guide the church back to its foundational principles, fostering a community that reflects the heart and mission of Christ.

As we navigate the complexities of modern church leadership, these scriptural examples offer a timeless blueprint for integrity and effectiveness. They challenge us to rise above the temptations

CHAPTER 18: BIBLICAL LEADERSHIP MODELS

of contemporary culture, prioritizing God's will and the well-being of the congregation. In doing so, we honor the legacy of biblical leadership and ensure that the church remains a beacon of truth and love in a world desperate for genuine spiritual guidance.

Leadership in the church is a sacred responsibility, one that requires a constant return to the examples set forth in Scripture. These biblical leaders, though flawed and human, achieved great things because they relied on God's strength and guidance. Their lives remind us that our leadership is not about our power or prestige but about our faithfulness to God's call. As we strive to emulate their examples, we commit ourselves to a path of integrity, service, and unwavering devotion to Christ. This commitment is the bedrock upon which true and enduring spiritual leadership is built.

Chapter 19: Scriptural Warning on the Responsibilities of Church Leaders

Leadership within the church carries an extraordinary weight, a divine responsibility that requires vigilance, humility, and unwavering commitment to God's truth. The apostle James offers a profound admonition in James 3:1, "My brethren, be not many masters, knowing that we shall receive the greater condemnation." This verse serves as a stark reminder that those who assume the mantle of leadership are held to a higher standard, subject to greater scrutiny and accountability. The ripple effects of a leader's actions, whether positive or negative, extend far beyond their personal sphere, influencing the entire congregation and shaping the broader perception of the church.

The call to leadership in the church is not a call to personal glory or a platform for showcasing one's charisma. It is, fundamentally, a call to service, rooted in humility and aligned with God's will. The pastoral epistles, particularly Paul's letters to Timothy, underscore the spiritual qualifications required for leadership. These qualifications—sober-mindedness, self-control, respectability, hospitality, and the ability to teach—are not mere suggestions but divine mandates. They serve as essential markers of a leader's capacity to guide their flock away from the pitfalls of worldly temptations and towards spiritual fortitude.

When leaders compromise, the consequences are far-reaching. The biblical narrative offers numerous examples of leaders who faltered and the ensuing repercussions. King David's moral

CHAPTER 19: SCRIPTURAL WARNING ON THE RESPONSIBILITIES OF CHURCH LEADERS

failings, for instance, led to personal grief, national strife, and divine reproof. His profound repentance in Psalm 51 provides a timeless model for leaders today. David's plea, "Create in me a clean heart, O God; and renew a right spirit within me," highlights the necessity of personal holiness and a heart aligned with God's will as the foundation of true leadership. This call to personal integrity is not optional; it is imperative for those who lead God's people.

Jesus' teachings on leadership are revolutionary, challenging the worldly notions of power and authority. In Matthew 20:26-27, He declares, "But it shall not be so among you: but whosoever will be great among you, let him be your minister; And whosoever will be chief among you, let him be your servant." This inversion of worldly leadership paradigms underscores that true greatness in God's kingdom is measured by one's capacity to serve. Leaders are called to a life of service, prioritizing the needs of others over their own ambitions. This scriptural principle demands continuous self-evaluation, urging leaders to examine their motivations and align their hearts with the humility of Christ.

The Bible is replete with examples of leaders who faced divine judgment due to their disobedience and failure to heed God's commands. Saul, Israel's first king, is a poignant example. His rejection by God, as recounted in 1 Samuel 15:22-23, underscores the critical importance of obedience. Samuel's rebuke, "Behold, to obey is better than sacrifice, and to hearken than the fat of rams," serves as a stark reminder that divine appointment carries with it an expectation of absolute obedience and humility. This lesson is as relevant today as it was in ancient Israel, highlighting the uncompromising standards God sets for those who lead His people.

Accountability within church leadership is not merely a safeguard; it is a biblical mandate. The early church practiced a form of mutual accountability that is instructive for contemporary leadership. Acts 4:32-35 describes a community of believers united in heart and mind, sharing everything they had so that no one was in need. This example of communal living underscores the importance of transparency and accountability in leadership, ensuring that decisions are not made in isolation but are weighed against the collective wisdom and spiritual health of the community. This practice fosters an environment where leaders are held accountable to God and to their congregation.

Paul's epistles offer practical advice on maintaining the integrity of church leadership. His instructions to Timothy in 1 Timothy 3:2-7 outline the character and conduct expected of those in leadership. These qualifications emphasize the necessity of a good reputation, even outside the church, reflecting the integrity of the church and its mission. "A bishop then must be blameless, the husband of one wife, vigilant, sober, of good behaviour, given to hospitality, apt to teach," Paul writes. This external testimony is crucial, as it impacts how the church is perceived by the broader community. Leaders must embody these virtues to maintain the church's credibility and witness.

The call to leadership is a divine mandate, not to be taken lightly. Leaders must constantly align themselves with scriptural principles, seeking God's guidance in all aspects of their ministry. The warnings embedded in scripture are not historical relics but

CHAPTER 19: SCRIPTURAL WARNING ON THE RESPONSIBILITIES OF CHURCH LEADERS

urgent messages for today's church. The mission of the church—to bear witness to the grace and truth of Christ—hinges on the credibility and integrity of its leaders. When leaders compromise, the church's witness is compromised. Thus, the call to leadership is a call to a higher standard, requiring constant vigilance, humility, and a heart fixed on serving God and His people.

The prophet Micah encapsulates the essence of divine expectations for leaders in Micah 6:8, "He hath shewed thee, O man, what is good; and what doth the LORD require of thee, but to do justly, and to love mercy, and to walk humbly with thy God?" This scripture highlights the balance of justice, mercy, and humility that should characterize the life and ministry of every leader. These qualities are not mere ideals but essential components of faithful leadership, guiding leaders in their service to God and their congregation.

The story of Moses provides another profound example of the weight of leadership and the consequences of disobedience. Despite his intimate relationship with God and his role in leading Israel out of Egypt, Moses' failure to uphold God's holiness resulted in his exclusion from the Promised Land. Numbers 20:12 records God's rebuke: "Because ye believed me not, to sanctify me in the eyes of the children of Israel, therefore ye shall not bring this congregation into the land which I have given them." Moses' experience serves as a sobering reminder that even the most anointed leaders are not immune to the consequences of disobedience.

Jesus' parable of the talents in Matthew 25:14-30 also provides critical insights into leadership and accountability. The master's expectation of his servants to wisely steward their given resources mirrors God's expectation of church leaders. Those who faithfully multiply what they have been given are rewarded, while those who fail to act with wisdom and diligence face severe consequences. "For unto every one that hath shall be given, and he shall have abundance: but from him that hath not shall be taken away even that which he hath." This parable underscores the principle of responsible stewardship in leadership, emphasizing the need for wisdom and faithfulness.

The apostle Peter, writing to church elders, offers a poignant exhortation in 1 Peter 5:2-3: "Feed the flock of God which is among you, taking the oversight thereof, not by constraint, but willingly; not for filthy lucre, but of a ready mind; Neither as being lords over God's heritage, but being ensamples to the flock." Peter's words highlight the dual responsibility of nurturing and modeling godly behavior. Leaders are called to shepherd their flock willingly and eagerly, setting an example of integrity and godliness. This shepherding is not about exerting power but about serving with a genuine heart.

The responsibility of church leadership extends beyond the pulpit. It involves fostering a community where the spiritual growth of each member is prioritized. Hebrews 13:17 reminds us, "Obey them that have the rule over you, and submit yourselves: for they watch for your souls, as they that must give account, that they may do it with joy, and not with grief: for that is unprofitable for you." This verse emphasizes the weight of responsibility leaders carry, as they are accountable for the spiritual well-being of their

CHAPTER 19: SCRIPTURAL WARNING ON THE RESPONSIBILITIES OF CHURCH LEADERS

congregation. This accountability should inspire leaders to lead with diligence, compassion, and a deep sense of duty.

As we consider the scriptural warnings and the high standards set for leadership, it becomes evident that the church's effectiveness hinges on the faithfulness of its leaders. The call to lead is not merely a call to oversee but to embody the principles of Christ in every aspect of life and ministry. The failures of leaders have profound implications, not just for their personal lives but for the entire body of Christ. Therefore, leaders must approach their roles with a sense of sacred duty, continually seeking God's guidance and striving to live in accordance with His will.

In light of these scriptural imperatives, every leader must engage in regular self-examination and be open to correction. The humility to acknowledge one's flaws and the willingness to seek God's forgiveness and guidance are crucial for maintaining the integrity of one's leadership. The words of 2 Corinthians 13:5, "Examine yourselves, whether ye be in the faith; prove your own selves," serve as a continual reminder for leaders to ensure that their lives and ministries align with God's standards. This self-examination is not a one-time event but a continuous process, essential for spiritual growth and effective leadership.

The role of prayer in leadership cannot be overstated. Leaders must be fervent in prayer, seeking God's wisdom and strength to fulfill their responsibilities. The example of Jesus, who often withdrew to solitary places to pray, as recorded in Luke 5:16, underscores the importance of maintaining a close and personal relationship with God. Through prayer, leaders can gain the clarity and fortitude needed to navigate the complexities of ministry and to lead their congregations faithfully.

Ultimately, the effectiveness of church leadership is measured by its alignment with God's will and its adherence to scriptural principles. Leaders must strive to embody the teachings of Christ, serving as examples of godliness and integrity. The warnings in scripture are not just historical accounts but living messages for today's church, urging leaders to uphold the highest standards of holiness and faithfulness. As Paul exhorts in 1 Corinthians 4:2, "Moreover it is required in stewards, that a man be found faithful." This faithfulness is the cornerstone of effective leadership, ensuring that the church remains a beacon of light in a dark world.

The journey of leadership is fraught with challenges, but it is also filled with the potential for profound impact. Leaders who heed the scriptural warnings and commit to a life of service, integrity, and humility can transform their congregations and communities. The call to lead is a call to embody the love and truth of Christ, guiding others towards a deeper relationship with God. As we navigate the complexities of modern ministry, let us remember the words of Proverbs 3:5-6, "Trust in the LORD with all thine heart; and lean not unto thine own understanding. In all thy ways acknowledge him, and he shall direct thy paths." This trust and acknowledgment of God are the foundation of faithful and effective leadership, ensuring that the church remains steadfast in its mission to glorify God and serve His people.

Chapter 20: Reforming Church Leadership

Reforming church leadership is not merely an administrative task; it is a spiritual mandate that requires both divine wisdom and human diligence. The scripture warns us in James 3:1, "My brethren, be not many masters, knowing that we shall receive the greater condemnation." This solemn admonition serves as a starting point in our conversation about leadership reform. Leaders are held to a higher standard, and rightly so, because their influence permeates the church body. If we aspire to see a true renewal within our churches, it begins with restoring integrity and godly character at the helm.

The challenge we face today in many of our churches is not the absence of charisma or capability among our leaders but rather a profound need for character that aligns with the biblical model of leadership. Titus 1:7-9 outlines the qualifications of a leader, emphasizing that an overseer "must be blameless, not self-willed, not quick-tempered, not given to wine, not violent, not greedy for money." These traits outline not just moral virtues but a character shaped by devotion to Christ and service to others. In pursuing leadership reform, our focus must be on cultivating these enduring qualities, rather than merely seeking out those who can attract large crowds or donations.

As we delve deeper into the necessary steps for reforming church leadership, we must recognize the importance of accountability. Acts 20:28 instructs church leaders to "take heed therefore unto yourselves, and to all the flock, over the which the Holy Ghost hath made you overseers." This scriptural charge reminds us that leadership is not a platform for personal gain but a position of stewardship. It's crucial that leaders are not only accountable to God but also to the congregations they serve. Implementing transparent processes for decision-making and financial management can help restore trust and demonstrate the leaders' commitment to serving rather than being served.

One of the profound ways to encourage reform is through the restoration of prayer in the life of church leaders. Just as Jesus often withdrew to lonely places and prayed (Luke 5:16), leaders too need to cultivate a deep, personal prayer life that anchors them in God's presence and guidance. This spiritual discipline is essential not as a ritual but as a relationship, keeping leaders attuned to the Holy Spirit and safeguarded against the temptations of pride and power.

The scripture offers wisdom about the dangers of isolation in leadership. Proverbs 11:14 tells us, "Where no counsel is, the people fall: but in the multitude of counsellors there is safety." Establishing a council of wise, spiritually mature advisers for leaders can provide them with the counsel and support needed to navigate complex decisions and personal challenges. This network of accountability can act as a bulwark against moral and ethical failures, which have marred the credibility of church leadership in the eyes of both believers and the world.

Training and continuous development must also be a staple in the church leadership diet. Just as Paul mentored Timothy, encouraging him to "study to shew thyself approved unto God, a workman that needeth not to be ashamed, rightly dividing the word of truth" (2 Timothy 2:15), so must our current leaders be

CHAPTER 20: REFORMING CHURCH LEADERSHIP

committed to lifelong learning. This not only includes theological education but also training in ethics, conflict resolution, and pastoral care, ensuring that leaders are well-equipped to shepherd the flock with wisdom and compassion.

The call to reform is also a call to humility. Philippians 2:3 exhorts us, "Let nothing be done through strife or vainglory; but in lowliness of mind let each esteem other better than themselves." In the context of leadership, this means leaders should model servant leadership, exemplified by Jesus when he washed the feet of His disciples. Embracing this mindset requires a radical shift from the celebrity culture that has infiltrated many modern churches, where leaders are often placed on pedestals.

Furthermore, the role of the congregation cannot be understated in the process of leadership reform. As 1 Corinthians 12:26 states, "And whether one member suffer, all the members suffer with it; or one member be honoured, all the members rejoice with it." The body of Christ must be engaged in the selection and affirmation of its leaders, ensuring that these men and women truly represent the values and spiritual maturity the church espouses. This collective involvement can help prevent the rise of autocratic leadership, promoting instead a leadership style that is inclusive and representative of the entire church body.

Praying fervently for our leaders is another critical aspect of reforming church leadership. Hebrews 13:18 urges us, "Pray for us: for we trust we have a good conscience, in all things willing to live honestly." Our leaders need divine strength and wisdom to navigate their roles, and our prayers can be a powerful force in supporting them in their spiritual and practical responsibilities. As we pray, we must ask for God's guidance to help our leaders remain faithful to their calling, free from the lure of worldly temptations.

Reforming church leadership also involves addressing the issue of integrity. Ephesians 4:1-2 calls us to "walk worthy of the vocation wherewith ye are called, with all lowliness and meekness, with longsuffering, forbearing one another in love." Leaders must be models of integrity, walking in the light and demonstrating Christ-like behavior in all aspects of their lives. This integrity must be visible not only in their public roles but also in their private lives, where true character is often revealed.

The necessity of vision cannot be overlooked in the reforming process. Proverbs 29:18 declares, "Where there is no vision, the people perish: but he that keepeth the law, happy is he." A clear, God-given vision provides direction and purpose for both leaders and the congregation. This vision should be rooted in scriptural truths and focused on fulfilling the Great Commission and the Great Commandment. When leaders operate with a clear vision, they can inspire and mobilize the church to accomplish God's purposes.

Addressing the culture within the leadership team is equally important. 1 Peter 5:2-3 advises, "Feed the flock of God which is among you, taking the oversight thereof, not by constraint, but willingly; not for filthy lucre, but of a ready mind; neither as being lords over God's heritage, but being ensamples to the flock." Leaders must foster a culture of mutual respect, collaboration, and servant-heartedness. This culture will be reflected in the way they lead, making them more effective and credible in their ministry.

CHAPTER 20: REFORMING CHURCH LEADERSHIP

It is also vital to address the emotional and mental well-being of church leaders. Galatians 6:2 encourages us to "Bear ye one another's burdens, and so fulfil the law of Christ." Ministry can be incredibly taxing, leading to burnout if leaders are not cared for properly. Providing support systems, counseling, and opportunities for rest and rejuvenation can help leaders maintain their health and effectiveness in ministry.

The reform process must also include confronting and correcting doctrinal errors. 2 Timothy 4:2 commands, "Preach the word; be instant in season, out of season; reprove, rebuke, exhort with all longsuffering and doctrine." Leaders must be vigilant in upholding sound doctrine, correcting errors, and ensuring that the teachings within the church align with the truth of God's Word. This commitment to doctrinal purity will safeguard the church against false teachings and guide the congregation in truth.

Reforming church leadership is about fostering a spirit of servanthood and sacrifice. Mark 10:45 reminds us, "For even the Son of man came not to be ministered unto, but to minister, and to give his life a ransom for many." Leaders should embody the servant leadership model of Christ, prioritizing the needs of others above their own and serving with humility and love. This servant-hearted approach will cultivate a culture of selflessness and generosity within the church.

In reforming church leadership, we must also address the issue of transparency. 1 John 1:7 declares, "But if we walk in the light, as he is in the light, we have fellowship one with another, and the blood of Jesus Christ his Son cleanseth us from all sin." Transparency in decision-making, finances, and ministry activities builds trust and fosters a healthy church environment. Leaders should strive to be open and honest, allowing the light of Christ to shine through their actions and decisions.

Equally important is the development of future leaders. 2 Timothy 2:2 advises, "And the things that thou hast heard of me among many witnesses, the same commit thou to faithful men, who shall be able to teach others also." Investing in the next generation of leaders ensures the sustainability and growth of the church. Mentoring and training programs should be established to equip emerging leaders with the necessary skills and spiritual maturity to carry on the work of the ministry.

Reforming church leadership also involves fostering a spirit of unity and collaboration. Psalm 133:1 proclaims, "Behold, how good and how pleasant it is for brethren to dwell together in unity!" Leaders should work together harmoniously, setting aside personal agendas for the greater good of the church. This unity will create a strong, cohesive leadership team capable of leading the church effectively and fulfilling its mission.

Ultimately, reforming church leadership is about aligning with God's purposes and seeking His glory above all else. Colossians 3:23-24 encourages, "And whatsoever ye do, do it heartily, as to the Lord, and not unto men; Knowing that of the Lord ye shall receive the reward of the inheritance: for ye serve the Lord Christ." Leaders should serve with a heart fully devoted to God, seeking to honor Him in all their endeavors. This God-centered focus will guide the church in fulfilling its divine mandate and experiencing true spiritual renewal.

In conclusion, reforming church leadership is not just about altering structures but transforming hearts. It's about returning to the biblical blueprint where leaders are servants, stewards, and shepherds. By grounding our efforts in scripture and prayer, and by committing to a path of continuous accountability and humility, we can foster a leadership culture that truly reflects Christ's kingdom and prepares the way for a genuine renewal of the church. As we embrace these principles, we will see a transformation that honors God and blesses His people, leading to a vibrant and spiritually healthy church.

Section 5: Doctrine Dilution

Chapter 21: Watered-Down Teachings

In today's church, there is a concerning trend toward watered-down teachings that favor simplicity over depth, often forsaking the robust doctrines that have anchored the Christian faith across centuries. This shift is not merely about making the gospel 'easier' to digest but risks diluting the profound truths that are essential for deep, transformative faith. The Apostle Paul warned Timothy about this very issue, saying, "For the time will come when they will not endure sound doctrine; but after their own lusts shall they heap to themselves teachers, having itching ears" (2 Timothy 4:3). This prophecy seems tailor-made for our times, as we witness a growing number of congregations gathering around messages that scratch popular itches rather than challenge the soul.

The essence of the gospel is not merely to comfort the afflicted but also to afflict the comfortable—to challenge our complacency. When Jesus preached, His words were often tough, piercing the heart with the precision of a surgeon's scalpel. He did not shy away from the difficult truths. In the Sermon on the Mount, He expanded the understanding of the law, deepening not lessening its demands, as He taught, "Ye have heard that it was said by them of old time, Thou shalt not kill; and whosoever shall kill shall be in danger of the judgment: But I say unto you, That whosoever is angry with his brother without a cause shall be in danger of the judgment" (Matthew 5:21-22). His teachings were not just to be heard but to prompt introspection and radical change.

What causes this drift toward doctrinal dilution? Often, it is the pressure to grow numbers and the desire to be seen as 'relevant' or 'inclusive' that leads pastors and teachers to mute the more demanding parts of scripture. Yet, relevance is not about altering the message to fit the times but rather delivering God's unchanging truth in ways that speak powerfully to the here and now. As Hebrews 4:12 reminds us, "For the word of God is quick, and powerful, and sharper than any two-edged sword, piercing even to the dividing asunder of soul and spirit, and of the joints and marrow, and is a discerner of the thoughts and intents of the heart." The Word's cutting ability is vital; it discerns, it judges, it transforms.

This transformation is hindered when we reduce the richness of Biblical teaching to mere platitudes. Consider the depth of theology expressed in Paul's letters, where he delves into the mysteries of Christ's nature, the Church, salvation, and the end times. These are not light topics meant for quick consumption but profound truths meant to be studied, debated, prayed over, and, ultimately, lived out. As believers, if we are to put on the "whole armour of God" (Ephesians 6:11), we must be equipped with more than just the basics. We need the full counsel of God to stand against the wiles of the devil and thrive in our Christian walk.

Moreover, the dilution of doctrine impacts the believer's ability to discern truth from falsehood, a critical need in an age rife with spiritual deception. The early church was continually contending with false teachers, as John points out: "Beloved, believe not every spirit, but try the spirits whether they are of God: because many false prophets are gone out into the world" (1 John 4:1). This

CHAPTER 21: WATERED-DOWN TEACHINGS

discernment comes from a deep engagement with scripture, not a superficial acquaintance with selected, comfortable texts.

How then can we return to a robust doctrinal teaching? It begins with a commitment to preach the whole gospel, to embrace and expound the full narrative of scripture, from Genesis to Revelation. This commitment must be supported by a culture of discipleship that encourages believers to study the Word deeply, engage with it daily, and apply it comprehensively. Pastors and teachers must lead by example, demonstrating a life deeply rooted in scriptural truth and a ministry committed to teaching that truth, regardless of its popularity.

Reviving sound doctrine also means welcoming the Holy Spirit's guidance in our teaching ministries. Jesus promised His disciples, "But the Comforter, which is the Holy Ghost, whom the Father will send in my name, he shall teach you all things, and bring all things to your remembrance, whatsoever I have said unto you" (John 14:26). With the Holy Spirit's help, we can teach with both clarity and depth, ensuring that the church is a pillar and ground of the truth.

Let us, therefore, be bold in our proclamation of the gospel, not shrinking back for fear of offending or losing appeal but trusting that the truth of God's Word will accomplish what He intends. Isaiah 55:11 assures us, "So shall my word be that goeth forth out of my mouth: it shall not return unto me void, but it shall accomplish that which I please, and it shall prosper in the thing whereto I sent it." In an age of compromise, let our message be clear and our teaching deep, that we might see a church not only informed by the truth but transformed by it.

In conclusion, the call to renew our commitment to sound doctrine is not just about preserving theological accuracy but about nurturing a vibrant, life-giving relationship with God. As we align our teachings with the full breadth of scripture, we empower believers to live out their faith with conviction and courage, equipped to face the complexities of modern life with timeless truth. This is not just the path to growth but to genuine spiritual revival.

Our modern culture tends to value instant gratification and convenience, a mindset that has unfortunately infiltrated many church teachings. The deep, sometimes challenging truths of scripture are often glossed over in favor of feel-good messages that attract larger audiences but fail to foster genuine spiritual growth. This is not the example set by Jesus or the early church. Christ's teachings were often challenging, demanding a response that went beyond superficial change. When He said, "If any man will come after me, let him deny himself, and take up his cross daily, and follow me" (Luke 9:23), He was calling for a radical, transformative commitment that is far from easy.

The church's mission is to make disciples, not mere attendees. True discipleship requires a foundation built on solid doctrine. Paul emphasized this when he wrote, "All scripture is given by inspiration of God, and is profitable for doctrine, for reproof, for correction, for instruction in righteousness" (2 Timothy 3:16). Doctrine is not an optional aspect of faith; it is the very bedrock upon which our understanding and practice of Christianity is built. Without it, our faith is shallow and easily shaken.

CHAPTER 21: WATERED-DOWN TEACHINGS

One of the dangers of watered-down teachings is that they often lead to a distorted view of God. When we omit the challenging aspects of His nature and focus solely on His love and mercy, we fail to present a complete picture of who God is. Yes, God is love, but He is also holy and just. The Bible tells us, "It is a fearful thing to fall into the hands of the living God" (Hebrews 10:31). By presenting only a partial view, we create a god in our own image, one who demands little and tolerates much. This is not the God of the Bible.

The health of the church depends on the health of its teaching. If we feed our congregations a steady diet of spiritual junk food, we should not be surprised when they are weak and malnourished in their faith. Jesus Himself emphasized the importance of feeding His sheep with solid food. After His resurrection, He asked Peter three times, "Simon, son of Jonas, lovest thou me?" Each time, Peter affirmed his love, and Jesus responded, "Feed my sheep" (John 21:15-17). This was a charge to nurture the flock with the full counsel of God, not just the palatable parts.

In our quest for relevance, we must remember that the power of the gospel lies not in its ability to conform to cultural trends but in its transformative truth. Paul wrote to the Romans, "For I am not ashamed of the gospel of Christ: for it is the power of God unto salvation to every one that believeth" (Romans 1:16). The gospel's power comes from its truth, a truth that remains constant regardless of the cultural climate. To water it down is to strip it of its power.

Furthermore, the call to sound doctrine is a call to deeper relationship with God. Surface-level teachings produce surface-level relationships. But as we dive deep into the Word, grappling with its complexities and challenges, we come to know God more intimately. The psalmist expressed this longing beautifully: "As the hart panteth after the water brooks, so panteth my soul after thee, O God" (Psalm 42:1). This deep thirst for God can only be quenched by the living water of His Word in its fullness.

Returning to robust doctrinal teaching requires courage and conviction. It means standing firm in the truth of scripture even when it is countercultural. Jesus warned His followers of the cost of discipleship, saying, "And ye shall be hated of all men for my name's sake: but he that endureth to the end shall be saved" (Matthew 10:22). The path of sound doctrine is not always popular, but it is the path to eternal life and true discipleship.

As we seek to restore sound doctrine in our churches, we must also seek the empowerment of the Holy Spirit. Jesus told His disciples, "Howbeit when he, the Spirit of truth, is come, he will guide you into all truth" (John 16:13). The Holy Spirit illuminates the scriptures, helping us understand and apply God's truth in our lives. Without His guidance, our efforts will fall short.

Moreover, we must cultivate a hunger for the Word among our congregations. This means creating environments where deep study and discussion of scripture are encouraged and valued. Small groups, Bible studies, and discipleship programs are vital in fostering this hunger. As leaders, we must model this hunger, demonstrating through our lives the joy and transformation that come from engaging deeply with God's Word.

The call to sound doctrine is ultimately a call to spiritual maturity. Paul lamented to the Corinthians, "I have fed you with milk, and not with meat: for hitherto ye were not able to bear it" (1

CHAPTER 21: WATERED-DOWN TEACHINGS

Corinthians 3:2). His desire was for them to grow beyond the basics and mature in their faith. This is our desire as well, to see believers move from spiritual infancy to maturity, equipped to stand firm in their faith and to share the gospel with boldness.

In this journey, we must be patient and persistent, recognizing that growth takes time. Isaiah reminds us, "But they that wait upon the Lord shall renew their strength; they shall mount up with wings as eagles; they shall run, and not be weary; and they shall walk, and not faint" (Isaiah 40:31). As we commit to sound doctrine, we trust that God will honor our efforts and bring about His purposes in His perfect timing.

Let us not be discouraged by the challenges but inspired by the vision of a church vibrant with truth and love, a beacon of light in a dark world. The stakes are high, but the reward is great. Jesus promised, "He that overcometh shall inherit all things; and I will be his God, and he shall be my son" (Revelation 21:7). This promise is for those who hold fast to His Word, who live out the fullness of the gospel without compromise.

In conclusion, the task before us is not easy, but it is essential. The church must return to sound doctrine, to the rich, full teaching of scripture that transforms lives and communities. As we embrace this call, we will see God's power at work in ways we never imagined. Let us press on with faith and courage, knowing that we serve a God who is faithful to His promises and whose Word never fails.

Chapter 22: Impact on Congregational Depth

In "Church Gone Wild: A Call to Renewal and Restoration," we explore the profound impact that diluted doctrine has had on the spiritual depth of congregations. This chapter delves into how the weakening of doctrinal teachings has led to a shallow, surface-level faith that fails to equip believers for the complexities of life and the spiritual battles they face. As we journey through this examination, it becomes clear that the pursuit of simplicity and cultural relevance has come at a significant cost to the richness and depth of the Gospel message.

One of the most evident consequences of diluted doctrine is the resulting spiritual immaturity within the congregation. Paul's warning to Timothy in 2 Timothy 4:3-4 is particularly pertinent: "For the time will come when they will not endure sound doctrine; but after their own lusts shall they heap to themselves teachers, having itching ears; And they shall turn away their ears from the truth, and shall be turned unto fables." This prophecy is vividly manifested in many modern churches, where teachings are tailored to comfort rather than to challenge. The result is a congregation that lacks the depth needed to withstand trials and temptations, leading to a faith that is easily shaken.

Without robust doctrinal foundations, believers are left vulnerable to the shifting sands of cultural trends and personal whims. Jesus emphasized the importance of a solid foundation in Matthew 7:24-27, where He described the wise man who built his house on the rock. "And the rain descended, and the floods came, and the winds blew, and beat upon that house; and it fell not: for it was founded

CHAPTER 22: IMPACT ON CONGREGATIONAL DEPTH

upon a rock." In contrast, the foolish man built his house on the sand, and it could not withstand the storms. Similarly, when our faith is built on a shallow understanding of scripture, it crumbles under the pressures of life's storms.

Moreover, the dilution of doctrine impacts the church's ability to foster genuine spiritual growth and maturity among its members. Hebrews 5:12-14 highlights this concern, stating, "For when for the time ye ought to be teachers, ye have need that one teach you again which be the first principles of the oracles of God; and are become such as have need of milk, and not of strong meat." The author laments the believers' inability to progress beyond basic teachings to the deeper truths of God's word. This stagnation results in a congregation that remains spiritually infantile, unable to discern good from evil or to apply biblical principles to their lives effectively.

The lack of doctrinal depth also weakens the church's witness to the world. A church that conforms to cultural expectations rather than upholding biblical truth loses its distinctiveness and its power to transform lives. Romans 12:2 exhorts us, "And be not conformed to this world: but be ye transformed by the renewing of your mind, that ye may prove what is that good, and acceptable, and perfect, will of God." When the church mirrors the world instead of reflecting Christ, it fails in its mission to be the light and salt of the earth, as Jesus called us to be in Matthew 5:13-16.

Furthermore, the erosion of doctrinal teaching leads to a superficial sense of community within the church. True fellowship, as described in Acts 2:42, involves "continuing steadfastly in the apostles' doctrine and fellowship, and in breaking of bread, and in prayers." When sound doctrine is neglected, the foundation for meaningful relationships and mutual edification is weakened. The resulting community is one where relationships are shallow, and spiritual support is minimal, making it difficult for believers to bear one another's burdens as instructed in Galatians 6:2.

Another critical impact is on the spiritual discernment of the congregation. Ephesians 4:14 warns, "That we henceforth be no more children, tossed to and fro, and carried about with every wind of doctrine, by the sleight of men, and cunning craftiness, whereby they lie in wait to deceive." Without a deep understanding of biblical truths, believers are easily swayed by false teachings and deceptive philosophies. This lack of discernment not only endangers their spiritual well-being but also leads to the propagation of error within the church.

In addition, the church's capacity to engage in effective spiritual warfare is compromised by doctrinal shallowness. Ephesians 6:10-18 describes the full armor of God, emphasizing the need for truth as the belt that holds everything together. "Stand therefore, having your loins girt about with truth, and having on the breastplate of righteousness." Without a firm grasp of doctrinal truth, believers are ill-equipped to stand against the wiles of the devil and to resist the spiritual forces of darkness.

The pursuit of doctrinal depth is not merely an intellectual exercise but a spiritual discipline that enriches our relationship with God. Psalm 119:105 declares, "Thy word is a lamp unto my feet, and a light unto my path." Engaging deeply with scripture illuminates our path, guiding us through the complexities of life with divine wisdom. This deep engagement fosters a vibrant faith that is rooted

CHAPTER 22: IMPACT ON CONGREGATIONAL DEPTH

in the truth of God's word and alive with the power of the Holy Spirit.

It is essential for church leaders to recognize their responsibility in fostering doctrinal depth. James 3:1 provides a sober reminder, "My brethren, be not many masters, knowing that we shall receive the greater condemnation." Those who teach and lead within the church are held to a higher standard and must be diligent in providing sound, comprehensive biblical teaching. This includes addressing difficult topics and encouraging believers to wrestle with the deeper truths of scripture.

Creating a culture of doctrinal depth within the church involves more than just the pulpit ministry. It requires intentional efforts to develop and nurture an environment where believers are encouraged to study the Word of God diligently. This can be achieved through in-depth Bible studies, small group discussions, and discipleship programs that emphasize the importance of sound doctrine. 2 Timothy 2:15 urges, "Study to shew thyself approved unto God, a workman that needeth not to be ashamed, rightly dividing the word of truth."

As we seek to deepen our doctrinal understanding, it is crucial to remember that this pursuit is inherently relational. John 15:4-5 emphasizes our need to abide in Christ: "Abide in me, and I in you. As the branch cannot bear fruit of itself, except it abide in the vine; no more can ye, except ye abide in me. I am the vine, ye are the branches: He that abideth in me, and I in him, the same bringeth forth much fruit: for without me ye can do nothing." Our growth in doctrinal knowledge must always lead us closer to Jesus, deepening our dependence on Him and enhancing our ability to bear fruit in our lives.

The impact of doctrinal dilution also extends to our worship. True worship, as Jesus described in John 4:24, is worship "in spirit and in truth." When doctrinal truths are compromised, our worship becomes shallow and performative rather than a genuine expression of reverence and adoration for God. Recovering the depth of our doctrinal foundations will naturally enrich our worship, leading us into more profound encounters with the living God.

We must also consider the impact on evangelism. A church grounded in sound doctrine is more effective in sharing the Gospel because its message is clear and unambiguous. 1 Peter 3:15 exhorts us, "But sanctify the Lord God in your hearts: and be ready always to give an answer to every man that asketh you a reason of the hope that is in you with meekness and fear." A deep understanding of our faith enables us to communicate the hope of the Gospel with clarity and conviction, drawing others to the transformative power of Christ.

In reclaiming doctrinal depth, we must also address the issue of biblical literacy. Hosea 4:6 warns, "My people are destroyed for lack of knowledge: because thou hast rejected knowledge, I will also reject thee." This sobering statement underscores the critical need for believers to be well-versed in scripture. Encouraging regular, systematic reading and study of the Bible is vital for fostering a congregation that is knowledgeable and grounded in the truth.

CHAPTER 22: IMPACT ON CONGREGATIONAL DEPTH

As we strive for deeper doctrinal understanding, it is essential to remain humble and teachable. Proverbs 3:5-6 advises, "Trust in the Lord with all thine heart; and lean not unto thine own understanding. In all thy ways acknowledge him, and he shall direct thy paths." Recognizing that our understanding is limited and that we need God's guidance keeps us reliant on Him and open to the leading of the Holy Spirit.

Restoring depth to our doctrinal teachings is not a quick fix but a long-term commitment. It requires perseverance and dedication from both leaders and congregants. Galatians 6:9 encourages us, "And let us not be weary in well doing: for in due season we shall reap, if we faint not." This promise assures us that our efforts to cultivate doctrinal depth will bear fruit in the lives of believers and the church as a whole.

In conclusion, the impact of doctrinal dilution on the depth of congregational life is profound and far-reaching. By recommitting to sound, comprehensive biblical teaching, we can restore the richness and depth that God intends for His church. This restoration will lead to spiritually mature believers who are equipped to navigate life's challenges, engage in effective spiritual warfare, and bear witness to the world with clarity and conviction. Let us heed the call to deepen our understanding of God's word, trusting that as we do, we will see the transformative power of the Gospel at work in our lives and in our congregations. As Colossians 3:16 exhorts, "Let the word of Christ dwell in you richly in all wisdom; teaching and admonishing one another in psalms and hymns and spiritual songs, singing with grace in your hearts to the Lord." Let this be our aim as we seek to restore doctrinal depth within the church.

Chapter 23: Calling for Doctrinal Purity

In the face of an ever-changing world, the need for doctrinal purity within the church stands as a clarion call to all believers. The subtle yet persistent dilution of core Christian doctrines has not only weakened the spiritual fabric of many congregations but also compromised the powerful, transformative message of the Gospel. It is essential to recognize and address this drift with both urgency and care, for our fidelity to the truth of Scripture is not merely an academic exercise but a matter of spiritual life and death. As Paul admonished Timothy, "Take heed unto thyself, and unto the doctrine; continue in them: for in doing this thou shalt both save thyself, and them that hear thee" (1 Timothy 4:16).

The drift away from doctrinal purity often begins with seemingly small compromises, adjustments made in the name of relevance or inclusivity. While the desire to connect with a broader audience is commendable, it must never come at the expense of altering the core truths of our faith. Jesus himself warned against such compromises when He said, "Ye shall know the truth, and the truth shall make you free" (John 8:32). The freedom promised by Christ is anchored in the truth of His Word, and any deviation from that truth enslaves rather than liberates.

One of the most significant areas where doctrinal dilution has taken root is in the nature and character of God. Modern culture often presents a picture of God that is more palatable, more accommodating to human sensibilities. However, Scripture portrays God as both loving and just, merciful and righteous. To understand God fully, we must hold these attributes in tension, not sacrificing one for the sake of emphasizing another. The prophet Isaiah captures this balance beautifully: "For I the Lord love judgment, I hate robbery for burnt offering; and I will direct their work in truth, and I will make an everlasting covenant with them" (Isaiah 61:8).

Equally critical is our understanding of Jesus Christ, His divinity, and His atoning work on the cross. The dilution of the doctrine of Christ's person and work undermines the very foundation of our faith. John emphasizes the importance of this truth, stating, "And every spirit that confesseth not that Jesus Christ is come in the flesh is not of God" (1 John 4:3). Acknowledging Christ's full divinity and humanity is essential for a proper understanding of salvation and the nature of our relationship with God.

The doctrine of salvation itself has not been immune to dilution. In a bid to be more inclusive, some have minimized the necessity of repentance and faith in Christ alone for salvation. Yet, the message of the Gospel is clear: "For by grace are ye saved through faith; and that not of yourselves: it is the gift of God: Not of works, lest any man should boast" (Ephesians 2:8-9). Any teaching that suggests salvation can be earned or achieved through human effort is a direct affront to the grace of God and diminishes the sufficiency of Christ's sacrifice.

The authority of Scripture is another cornerstone of our faith that must be upheld with unwavering commitment. In an age where subjective experiences and personal interpretations often take precedence, it is imperative to reaffirm that the Bible is the inspired, infallible Word of God. Paul's exhortation to Timothy

CHAPTER 23: CALLING FOR DOCTRINAL PURITY

remains as relevant as ever: "All scripture is given by inspiration of God, and is profitable for doctrine, for reproof, for correction, for instruction in righteousness" (2 Timothy 3:16). The Scriptures are our ultimate guide, not merely one source among many, but the definitive revelation of God's will and truth.

To restore doctrinal purity, we must cultivate a rigorous and disciplined approach to teaching and learning within the church. This involves a commitment to deep, exegetical study of the Scriptures, ensuring that our interpretations are rooted in sound hermeneutical principles rather than contemporary trends or personal biases. As Peter exhorts us, "As newborn babes, desire the sincere milk of the word, that ye may grow thereby" (1 Peter 2:2). Spiritual growth is intrinsically linked to our engagement with the Word of God in its purest form.

Leadership within the church carries a profound responsibility in this regard. Those who teach and preach must do so with a deep sense of accountability to God and to their congregations. James' cautionary words should always be at the forefront of our minds: "My brethren, be not many masters, knowing that we shall receive the greater condemnation" (James 3:1). Teaching the Word of God is a solemn task, one that requires both humility and diligence. Leaders must be vigilant, ensuring that their teachings are not swayed by popular opinion or cultural pressures but remain steadfastly anchored in biblical truth.

Involving the congregation in the pursuit of doctrinal purity is also essential. It is not enough for church leaders alone to bear this burden; every believer must be equipped to understand and defend the doctrines of their faith. Paul's charge to the Colossians highlights the importance of collective wisdom and understanding: "Let the word of Christ dwell in you richly in all wisdom; teaching and admonishing one another in psalms and hymns and spiritual songs, singing with grace in your hearts to the Lord" (Colossians 3:16). A church body that is grounded in the Word and actively engaged in mutual teaching and admonition is far less likely to fall prey to doctrinal error.

Furthermore, we must be prepared to confront and correct false teachings whenever they arise. This requires courage and discernment, as well as a deep love for the truth. Paul's instruction to Titus underscores this imperative: "Holding fast the faithful word as he hath been taught, that he may be able by sound doctrine both to exhort and to convince the gainsayers" (Titus 1:9). Correcting false doctrine is not about winning arguments but about preserving the purity of the Gospel and protecting the spiritual well-being of the church.

The role of the Holy Spirit in guiding us into all truth cannot be overstated. Jesus promised, "Howbeit when he, the Spirit of truth, is come, he will guide you into all truth" (John 16:13). As we seek to restore and maintain doctrinal purity, we must rely on the Spirit's guidance, praying for wisdom, insight, and discernment. The Spirit works through the Word, illuminating our understanding and helping us to apply it rightly.

Cultural pressures to conform are ever-present, and the church must stand firm against these forces. Paul's admonition to the Romans is particularly relevant: "And be not conformed to this world: but be ye transformed by the renewing of your mind, that ye may prove what is that good, and acceptable, and perfect, will

CHAPTER 23: CALLING FOR DOCTRINAL PURITY

of God" (Romans 12:2). This transformation is ongoing, requiring continual immersion in the Word and a steadfast commitment to living out its truths, regardless of societal trends.

We must also consider the impact of doctrinal purity on our witness to the world. When the church compromises on core doctrines, it sends a confusing message to both believers and non-believers alike. Jesus prayed for His disciples, "Sanctify them through thy truth: thy word is truth" (John 17:17). Our sanctification and our witness are intrinsically linked to the truth of God's Word. A church that stands firm on doctrinal purity is a powerful testimony to the world of God's unchanging truth and His transformative power.

Addressing doctrinal dilution involves a return to spiritual disciplines that foster a deep and abiding relationship with God. Prayer, fasting, and meditation on the Word are essential practices that keep us aligned with God's truth. As we engage in these disciplines, we invite the Holy Spirit to work in us, transforming our hearts and minds and strengthening our commitment to doctrinal purity. David's prayer in Psalm 51:10 is a model for us: "Create in me a clean heart, O God; and renew a right spirit within me."

The journey to doctrinal purity is not without its challenges. It requires perseverance, humility, and a willingness to be corrected and to grow. Yet, the rewards are immeasurable. A church that is committed to doctrinal purity is a church that experiences the fullness of God's blessing and power. As Paul wrote to the Ephesians, "That he might sanctify and cleanse it with the washing of water by the word, That he might present it to himself a glorious church, not having spot, or wrinkle, or any such thing; but that it should be holy and without blemish" (Ephesians 5:26-27).

In our pursuit of doctrinal purity, we must also remember the importance of unity within the body of Christ. While we stand firm on essential doctrines, we must approach secondary issues with grace and charity. Paul's appeal to the Philippians is instructive: "Let this mind be in you, which was also in Christ Jesus" (Philippians 2:5). Humility and a servant's heart are crucial as we navigate doctrinal differences, always seeking to maintain the unity of the Spirit in the bond of peace (Ephesians 4:3).

As we draw this discussion to a close, let us be encouraged by the promise of God's faithfulness. He who began a good work in us will carry it on to completion until the day of Christ Jesus (Philippians 1:6). Our commitment to doctrinal purity is not borne out of fear or legalism but out of a deep love for God and a desire to honor Him in all that we do. Let us press on, confident that as we seek first His kingdom and His righteousness, all these things will be added unto us (Matthew 6:33).

In conclusion, the call to doctrinal purity is a call to faithfulness. It is a call to return to the ancient paths, to stand firm on the truths of God's Word, and to live out those truths in our daily lives. May we, as the church, rise to this challenge with courage and conviction, holding fast to the faithful word as we have been taught, and proclaiming the unchanging gospel of Jesus Christ to a world in desperate need of His saving grace. As we do so, we can trust that God will honor our efforts, and His truth will indeed set us free.

Chapter 24: Scriptural Insight on the Dangers of Diluted Doctrine

In today's ever-changing spiritual landscape, where messages are often adapted to fit modern sensibilities, it's crucial we hold fast to the bedrock of our faith—the inerrant Word of God. Paul, understanding the risks of the times, admonished Timothy in 2 Timothy 4:3-4, warning that a time would come when people would not endure sound doctrine, but according to their own desires, they would heap up for themselves teachers and turn their ears away from the truth. This foresight into human nature underlines the inherent danger of diluting divine truths for comfort rather than conviction.

As anointed leaders and members of Christ's body, it is imperative that we remain vigilant, ensuring that the doctrines we uphold are not merely reflections of societal preferences but are deeply rooted in scriptural truth. The allure of modifying our teachings to increase appeal or to align with popular opinion is a profound temptation that must be resisted with every fiber of our spiritual being. Remember, our calling is not to conform but to transform, as Paul so eloquently states in Romans 12:2, urging us not to be conformed to this world, but to be transformed by the renewal of our mind, that by testing we may discern what is the will of God, what is good and acceptable and perfect.

Why, then, do we find ourselves at this junction where the purity of our teachings is at risk? It may stem from a desire to make the gospel more accessible or perhaps more palatable to those we wish to reach. However, in making the Word more 'accessible,' we must guard against the loss of its potency. The gospel of Christ is inherently powerful and needs no embellishment. It is sharper than any two-edged sword, as described in Hebrews 4:12, piercing to the division of soul and spirit, of joints and marrow, and discerning the thoughts and intentions of the heart.

It is our responsibility, therefore, to preach this unadulterated gospel, to teach it in its fullness as it was entrusted to us. The church must act as the pillar and ground of the truth, as stated in 1 Timothy 3:15. Our role is not only to uphold this truth but to propagate it through teaching that echoes the teachings of Christ and the apostles without dilution. This requires courage, for often, the truth is countercultural, it convicts, and it challenges.

In reflecting on the words of Christ in Matthew 5:13, where He calls us the "salt of the earth," we are reminded of our duty to preserve the flavor of divine truth in the world. Salt, by its very nature, prevents decay and adds flavor, but if it loses its saltiness, it becomes ineffective. Similarly, if our teachings lose their grounding in scripture, they lose their ability to effect true spiritual change and preservation in our world.

Let us also consider the nurturing aspect of our role. Just as Peter was instructed by Jesus in John 21:17 to feed His sheep, we are called to nourish the flock with wholesome, substantial spiritual food. This nourishment comes from the whole counsel of God—every book, chapter, and verse holds value and is beneficial for teaching, rebuking, correcting, and training in righteousness, as 2 Timothy 3:16-17 declares. Our teaching should leave no room for

CHAPTER 24: SCRIPTURAL INSIGHT ON THE DANGERS OF DILUTED DOCTRINE

spiritual malnutrition but should aim to fully equip the saints for every good work.

Therefore, the question we must continually ask ourselves is not whether our teachings are popular or acceptable to the masses but whether they are true to the Word of God. The benchmarks for our teachings are not modern-day analytics or attendance figures; they are the timeless scriptures. As we craft our sermons, lead our Bible studies, or write our spiritual literature, our constant reference should be the Bible, asking like the Bereans did in Acts 17:11, who examined the Scriptures daily to see if what Paul said was true.

In this journey of faith, let us be inspired by the courage of the prophets and the apostles who, despite opposition and persecution, proclaimed the Word of God with boldness and without compromise. They did not shy away from declaring the whole will of God, aware of the cost yet driven by the eternal impact of their mission.

We must also remember that God's Word is not just a collection of ancient texts but the living, breathing revelation of His will. Hebrews 4:12 reminds us that the Word of God is alive and active. It is this living Word that has the power to transform lives, convict hearts, and guide us into all truth. When we dilute this Word, we rob it of its transformative power and fail to fulfill our calling as messengers of the gospel.

Consider the example of the early church, as described in Acts 2:42, where the believers devoted themselves to the apostles' teaching and to fellowship, to the breaking of bread and to prayer. This commitment to sound doctrine and communal living was the foundation of their faith and their effectiveness in spreading the gospel. It was not a message tailored to please, but one that demanded repentance, change, and a radical shift in lifestyle.

Today, many churches face the challenge of balancing relevance with reverence. There is a fine line between making the gospel accessible and watering it down to the point where it loses its essence. Jesus, in His earthly ministry, never compromised on the truth. He spoke with authority, often delivering messages that were hard to hear, yet they were the words of eternal life. John 6:68 recounts Peter's declaration, "Lord, to whom shall we go? You have the words of eternal life." This is the message we are entrusted with—the words of eternal life that should not be altered to suit human preferences.

As shepherds of God's flock, we must also be vigilant against false teachings that creep into the church. Paul warned the elders of Ephesus in Acts 20:29-30 that savage wolves would come in among them, not sparing the flock. These false teachers would distort the truth to draw away disciples after them. Our vigilance must include a steadfast commitment to teaching and defending sound doctrine, ensuring that what we teach aligns with the truth of Scripture.

The impact of diluted doctrine is not just theoretical; it has real consequences for the spiritual health of believers. When the church shifts its focus from the gospel to feel-good messages, it fails to prepare its members for the trials and challenges of the Christian walk. Jesus warned us in Matthew 7:15 to beware of false prophets who come in sheep's clothing but inwardly are ravenous wolves. Their messages may be comforting, but they lead away from the narrow path that leads to life.

CHAPTER 24: SCRIPTURAL INSIGHT ON THE DANGERS OF DILUTED DOCTRINE

Moreover, diluted doctrine can lead to a weakened witness. The church is called to be a light in the world, a city set on a hill that cannot be hidden (Matthew 5:14). When our teachings lose their distinctiveness, we blend into the world rather than standing out as beacons of truth and hope. Our mission is to make disciples of all nations, baptizing them and teaching them to obey everything Jesus has commanded (Matthew 28:19-20). This great commission requires a commitment to the full, unaltered gospel.

In our pursuit of doctrinal purity, we must also cultivate humility and a teachable spirit. James 1:21 urges us to receive with meekness the implanted word, which is able to save our souls. Recognizing that we do not have all the answers and that our understanding is continually being shaped by the Holy Spirit is crucial. This humility allows us to remain open to correction and growth, aligning our teachings ever closer to the truth of Scripture.

Let us not forget the role of the Holy Spirit in guiding us into all truth. Jesus promised in John 16:13 that the Spirit of truth would guide us into all truth. As we seek to teach and uphold sound doctrine, we must rely on the Spirit's guidance, trusting that He will illuminate our minds and hearts to understand and convey God's Word accurately.

As we reflect on these truths, let us commit to being guardians of the gospel, unwavering in our dedication to sound doctrine. The words of Paul in 1 Corinthians 2:2 resonate deeply: "For I resolved to know nothing while I was with you except Jesus Christ and him crucified." This singular focus on Christ and His redemptive work should underpin all our teachings, ensuring that we do not stray into areas that detract from the central message of the gospel.

Our teaching must also be practical, addressing the real-life challenges and questions that believers face. Paul's letters are rich with doctrine but also with practical advice on living out the Christian faith. Colossians 3:16 exhorts us to let the word of Christ dwell in us richly, teaching and admonishing one another in all wisdom. This balance of doctrine and practical application helps believers to not only understand their faith but to live it out effectively.

In closing, let us embrace the responsibility bestowed upon us with a renewed sense of purpose and reverence. The stakes are high, and the spiritual well-being of many rests on the integrity of our teachings. By committing to scriptural insight and rejecting the dilution of doctrine, we can ensure that we are faithful stewards of the mysteries of God, as Paul described in 1 Corinthians 4:1.

May we be found diligent in our study of the Word, uncompromising in our teaching, and unwavering in our commitment to the truth. Let us be inspired by the words of Jude 1:3, urging us to contend earnestly for the faith that was once for all delivered to the saints. This is our calling and our privilege, to stand firm in the truth and to lead others in the same path of righteousness.

Chapter 25: Reviving Sound Doctrine

In the heart of every believer lies a profound yearning for truth, an intrinsic call to anchor our lives in the immutable Word of God. This desire, though often clouded by the distractions of modern life, remains a beacon, guiding us back to the foundational doctrines of our faith. As we stand on the precipice of a new era in the church, the urgency to revive sound doctrine is more pressing than ever. The Apostle Paul's admonition to Timothy resonates deeply: "Hold fast the form of sound words, which thou hast heard of me, in faith and love which is in Christ Jesus" (2 Timothy 1:13). This isn't a mere suggestion; it's a divine imperative to cling tenaciously to the truth handed down through the scriptures.

The erosion of sound doctrine is often a gradual process, like the slow wearing away of rock by water. It begins subtly, with the adoption of appealing yet unscriptural ideas that prioritize comfort over conviction and acceptance over the fear of God. Over time, these ideas permeate the church, diluting the rich, robust truths of the gospel. We see this in how difficult, yet essential, biblical topics are frequently glossed over, leaving congregations ill-equipped to navigate the complexities of faith. The prophet Hosea's lament echoes through the ages: "My people are destroyed for lack of knowledge" (Hosea 4:6). This ignorance is not due to a dearth of information but a departure from the divine wisdom that once guided the early church.

Reviving sound doctrine requires a deliberate return to the sacred texts, approaching them not as ancient relics but as the living, breathing Word of God. Paul's words to Timothy underscore this necessity: "All scripture is given by inspiration of God, and is profitable for doctrine, for reproof, for correction, for instruction in righteousness" (2 Timothy 3:16). The scriptures are designed to equip us fully, building up the body of Christ so we may stand mature and fully convinced in all the will of God. It is through diligent study and application of these truths that the church can begin to repair its doctrinal foundations.

One might ask, how can we foster a culture that embraces such rigorous scriptural engagement? It begins with leadership. Those who teach and preach must themselves be deeply rooted in the Word, embodying the life they proclaim. As Paul instructed Titus, leaders must "hold fast the faithful word as he hath been taught, that he may be able by sound doctrine both to exhort and to convince the gainsayers" (Titus 1:9). The authenticity of a leader's walk with Christ, their commitment to truth, and their courage to proclaim it set a powerful example for the congregation to follow.

Moreover, reviving sound doctrine necessitates a community committed to accountability. When believers gather, it should be with the intention of sharpening one another, as "iron sharpeneth iron" (Proverbs 27:17). In such a community, correction is not feared but welcomed as a means of grace, guiding us back to the path of righteousness. This community must be marked by a relentless pursuit of truth, a place where questions are encouraged, and answers are sought together in the light of scripture. James 5:16 exhorts us to confess our faults one to another and pray for one another, fostering a spirit of mutual edification and growth.

Such a pursuit is not for the faint-hearted. It calls for humility and patience, recognizing that growth in understanding is a gradual

CHAPTER 25: REVIVING SOUND DOCTRINE

process. As we delve deeper into the mysteries of God's Word, we must also dwell in prayer, seeking the guidance of the Holy Spirit who Jesus promised would lead us into all truth (John 16:13). It is the Spirit who breathes life into the written word, transforming it from ink on paper to a transformative force in our lives. Without the Spirit's illumination, our study remains purely academic, devoid of the power to change hearts.

In practical terms, reviving sound doctrine means reintroducing the disciplines of Biblical exposition and theological education at every level of church life. From Sunday sermons to small group studies, the content must consistently drive us deeper into the truths of our faith, challenging our presuppositions and inspiring our devotion. As we commit to this path, we must also embrace the diverse heritage of the church's theological reflections, engaging with the thoughts and struggles of believers across the ages. This engagement not only broadens our understanding but also roots us in a rich tradition of faithful interpretation.

This revival of sound doctrine will not only fortify the church internally but will enhance its witness to the world. A church solid in its theological convictions is clear in its mission and bold in its outreach. It stands as a beacon of truth in a society often tossed by the waves of relativism and skepticism. Peter reminds us, we must always be ready to give an answer to every man that asketh us a reason for the hope that is in us, doing so with meekness and fear (1 Peter 3:15). Our ability to respond hinges on our depth of understanding and the integrity of our doctrine.

Furthermore, reviving sound doctrine demands that we address the uncomfortable truths head-on. It involves preaching and teaching on sin, repentance, holiness, and the cost of discipleship. Jesus' call to take up our cross and follow Him (Matthew 16:24) is not a call to a comfortable life but to a life of radical obedience and self-denial. These are not popular messages, but they are essential to a faith that is grounded in the reality of God's holiness and our need for redemption.

Another critical aspect of reviving sound doctrine is the commitment to a holistic gospel. This means proclaiming not only the saving grace of Christ but also His lordship over every aspect of life. The gospel transforms our personal lives, our families, our communities, and our world. It speaks to issues of justice, mercy, and faithfulness, calling us to live out our faith in tangible ways. Micah 6:8 encapsulates this beautifully: "He hath shewed thee, O man, what is good; and what doth the Lord require of thee, but to do justly, and to love mercy, and to walk humbly with thy God?"

Incorporating sound doctrine also means being vigilant against false teachings. The New Testament is replete with warnings against false prophets and teachers who would lead the flock astray. Jude urges us to "contend for the faith which was once delivered unto the saints" (Jude 1:3). This contending is an active, ongoing process of defending the truth against all forms of error. It requires discernment, wisdom, and a deep commitment to the purity of the gospel message.

Reviving sound doctrine involves a return to exegetical preaching, where scripture is expounded systematically and contextually. This approach ensures that the full counsel of God is proclaimed, not just the parts that are easy or convenient. As Paul charged Timothy, we must "preach the word; be instant in season, out of season;

CHAPTER 25: REVIVING SOUND DOCTRINE

reprove, rebuke, exhort with all longsuffering and doctrine" (2 Timothy 4:2). This method of preaching not only informs but transforms, as the Holy Spirit works through the faithful proclamation of His Word.

The role of discipleship in reviving sound doctrine cannot be overstated. Discipleship is the process of teaching and training believers to follow Jesus closely, to understand His teachings deeply, and to live them out daily. It is a relational process, where mature believers invest in the growth of others, modeling what it means to live according to the Word. Jesus' Great Commission to make disciples of all nations (Matthew 28:19-20) includes teaching them to observe all that He has commanded, highlighting the importance of doctrinal soundness in the discipleship process.

As we undertake the task of reviving sound doctrine, we must also embrace the role of suffering in the Christian life. The New Testament is clear that suffering is an integral part of following Christ. Paul wrote, "Yea, and all that will live godly in Christ Jesus shall suffer persecution" (2 Timothy 3:12). This is not to be feared but embraced as part of our identification with Christ. Sound doctrine prepares us to endure suffering with grace and faith, knowing that it produces perseverance and maturity (James 1:2-4).

The revival of sound doctrine will also lead to a renewed emphasis on holy living. The call to be holy, as God is holy (1 Peter 1:16), is a call to live set apart, reflecting God's character in every area of our lives. This involves a conscious rejection of worldliness and a passionate pursuit of godliness. Holiness is not about legalism but about a heart transformed by the grace of God, desiring to please Him in all things.

Ultimately, reviving sound doctrine is about returning to the heart of worship. True worship is grounded in truth, as Jesus declared that true worshipers will worship the Father in spirit and truth (John 4:24). This truth is found in the scriptures, and as we immerse ourselves in them, our worship becomes a response to the revelation of God's character and works. Sound doctrine fuels our worship, giving it depth and authenticity.

As we embark on this journey, let us be encouraged by the promise of God's faithfulness. He has pledged to build His church, and the gates of hell shall not prevail against it (Matthew 16:18). Our role is to remain faithful stewards of the truth, proclaiming it boldly, living it authentically, and teaching it diligently. In doing so, we align ourselves with God's purposes and participate in the glorious work of His kingdom.

In conclusion, the revival of sound doctrine is not merely an academic exercise but a spiritual imperative. It calls us to return to the scriptures with renewed passion, to commit ourselves to the truth, and to live out that truth with integrity and courage. As we do so, we will see the church strengthened, believers equipped, and the gospel proclaimed with power. Let us heed the call to revive sound doctrine, knowing that in doing so, we honor God and fulfill our calling as His people.

Section 6: Social Justice vs. Scriptural Justice

Chapter 26: Modern Social Movements and the Gospel

In today's rapidly evolving society, the church finds itself at a crossroads, grappling with the challenges and opportunities presented by modern social movements. As followers of Christ, it is crucial to discern the lines where cultural shifts align with scriptural truths and where they diverge. The apostle Paul reminds us in Romans 12:2, "And be not conformed to this world: but be ye transformed by the renewing of your mind, that ye may prove what is that good, and acceptable, and perfect, will of God." This scripture serves as a guiding light, urging us to transform and not merely conform to societal pressures that may stray from God's will.

Social movements today often champion values such as justice, equality, and the dignity of all human beings—values that deeply resonate with the Gospel's teachings. However, as these movements grow and evolve, they sometimes adopt ideologies that can conflict with biblical doctrines. For instance, movements that advocate for behaviors contrary to biblical teachings present a complex scenario for believers. We must ask ourselves how Jesus would navigate these waters. He engaged with all members of society in love, yet He never compromised His divine principles.

The challenge lies in engaging with these movements constructively. The book of Titus offers wisdom in chapter 3, verses 1-2, advising believers "to speak evil of no man, to be no brawlers, but gentle, showing all meekness unto all men." Thus,

CHAPTER 26: MODERN SOCIAL MOVEMENTS AND THE GOSPEL

our engagement should not be contentious or combative but characterized by gentleness and respect, aiming to build bridges rather than walls. By demonstrating Christ's love, we can be beacons of light in discussions that often become polarized and fraught with anger.

Yet, in our pursuit of justice, we must also maintain a clear focus on the Gospel's core message. Social justice initiatives must be rooted in the transformative power of the Gospel, which provides not only temporal relief but eternal hope. Galatians 3:28 declares, "There is neither Jew nor Greek, there is neither bond nor free, there is neither male nor female: for ye are all one in Christ Jesus." This powerful statement reminds us that in Jesus, all human barriers fall away; our primary identity is in Him, and our primary mission is to bring others into this eternal fellowship.

As we align our efforts with God's kingdom, we encounter the profound truth that the Gospel itself is the ultimate answer to the world's cries for justice. In the ministry of Jesus, we see a perfect balance of truth and grace—meeting physical needs while pointing people to the deeper spiritual realities. James 1:27 encapsulates this dual mandate, "Pure religion and undefiled before God and the Father is this, To visit the fatherless and widows in their affliction, and to keep himself unspotted from the world." This scripture not only calls us to address the physical and social needs but also to live lives of holiness that testify to the transforming power of Christ.

The engagement of the church with social movements should also be prophetic, not just echoing societal trends but calling society to a higher standard. As in the days of the prophets, today's church is called to be a voice in the wilderness, challenging both the world and our congregations to repentance and deeper commitment to Christ's ways. Micah 6:8 teaches us, "He hath shewed thee, O man, what is good; and what doth the LORD require of thee, but to do justly, and to love mercy, and to walk humbly with thy God?" This scripture does not merely suggest, but requires us to pursue justice and mercy, grounded in a humble walk with God.

Moreover, as we consider the role of the church in modern social movements, we must also reflect on our motivations. Are our social justice efforts driven by a desire to be seen as relevant and progressive by the world, or are they motivated by a genuine compassion and love that flows from a deep, abiding connection with Christ? The Sermon on the Mount, as recorded in Matthew 5, calls us to be the salt and light of the earth, influencing the world by our distinct flavor of divine love and truth, not by blending indistinguishably into the cultural milieu.

In navigating these complex waters, wisdom and discernment are indispensable. The wisdom of Proverbs 2:6, "For the LORD giveth wisdom: out of his mouth cometh knowledge and understanding," should be continually sought in prayer. Engaging with social movements requires more than human understanding; it requires divine insight that comes from a relationship with God and a commitment to studying His Word.

The heart of the Gospel is transformative. It changes individuals, families, communities, and nations. When the church engages with social movements, it should do so with the intent to bring about this transformation, aligning with God's redemptive plan. Second Corinthians 5:17 proclaims, "Therefore if any man be in Christ, he

CHAPTER 26: MODERN SOCIAL MOVEMENTS AND THE GOSPEL

is a new creature: old things are passed away; behold, all things are become new." This renewal must be the goal of our social justice endeavors, reflecting the hope and change that come through Christ.

As we participate in these movements, we must always point back to Jesus. Our actions and advocacy should clearly demonstrate His love and His call to repentance. John 8:12 reminds us, "Then spake Jesus again unto them, saying, I am the light of the world: he that followeth me shall not walk in darkness, but shall have the light of life." We must ensure that our involvement illuminates the path to Christ, not leading others into the darkness of confusion or compromise.

Furthermore, it is essential to recognize that not all social movements align with biblical values. Some may begin with noble intentions but can become vehicles for ideologies that oppose Christian teachings. In such cases, believers must exercise discernment, standing firm in the truth of the Gospel. Ephesians 6:13-14 encourages us, "Wherefore take unto you the whole armour of God, that ye may be able to withstand in the evil day, and having done all, to stand. Stand therefore, having your loins girt about with truth, and having on the breastplate of righteousness." This spiritual armor equips us to engage with the world without compromising our faith.

The church's response to social movements must also be marked by humility and repentance. We must acknowledge where we have failed to address injustices and where we have allowed worldly values to infiltrate our mission. Second Chronicles 7:14 provides a timeless directive, "If my people, which are called by my name, shall humble themselves, and pray, and seek my face, and turn from their wicked ways; then will I hear from heaven, and will forgive their sin, and will heal their land." Healing begins with humility and a turning back to God.

Our engagement should be rooted in the understanding that true justice flows from the heart of God. Isaiah 61:8 declares, "For I the LORD love judgment, I hate robbery for burnt offering; and I will direct their work in truth, and I will make an everlasting covenant with them." This covenant of truth and justice calls us to align our efforts with God's righteous standards, ensuring that our pursuit of justice does not deviate from His commands.

As we strive for social justice, we must remember that it is ultimately about people—souls in need of God's love and salvation. Mark 8:36 challenges us, "For what shall it profit a man, if he shall gain the whole world, and lose his own soul?" Our advocacy must never lose sight of the eternal destiny of those we seek to help. The church's mission is to bring the message of salvation to all, ensuring that social justice efforts are intertwined with evangelism and discipleship.

Additionally, the church must be a place of refuge and healing for those affected by injustice. Jesus, in Matthew 11:28, invites, "Come unto me, all ye that labour and are heavy laden, and I will give you rest." Our communities should embody this invitation, offering support, comfort, and hope to those burdened by societal injustices. This holistic approach addresses both physical and spiritual needs, reflecting the comprehensive nature of Christ's ministry.

CHAPTER 26: MODERN SOCIAL MOVEMENTS AND THE GOSPEL

The pursuit of social justice also requires the church to challenge and inspire its members to live out their faith in practical ways. James 2:17 emphasizes, "Even so faith, if it hath not works, is dead, being alone." Faith must be active and visible, demonstrated through actions that reflect Christ's love and compassion. This active faith serves as a powerful testimony to the world, showcasing the transformative power of the Gospel.

In engaging with social movements, we must also be mindful of the power of unity within the body of Christ. Jesus prayed for this unity in John 17:21, "That they all may be one; as thou, Father, art in me, and I in thee, that they also may be one in us: that the world may believe that thou hast sent me." Our collective efforts, rooted in unity and love, can have a profound impact, demonstrating to the world the cohesive and redemptive power of the church.

Furthermore, the church must advocate for justice with the understanding that it is a part of God's redemptive plan for humanity. Colossians 1:20 reveals, "And, having made peace through the blood of his cross, by him to reconcile all things unto himself; by him, I say, whether they be things in earth, or things in heaven." This reconciliation extends to all areas of life, including social justice, where the peace of Christ can heal and restore broken systems and relationships.

It is also imperative that the church teaches its members to engage critically and thoughtfully with social movements. Hosea 4:6 warns, "My people are destroyed for lack of knowledge." Education and awareness are crucial in helping believers navigate complex social issues without being swayed by every wind of doctrine. A well-informed church can engage more effectively and righteously in social justice initiatives.

Our engagement with social justice should also inspire hope. Romans 15:13 offers a powerful blessing, "Now the God of hope fill you with all joy and peace in believing, that ye may abound in hope, through the power of the Holy Ghost." This hope is not just for the future but for the present, providing the assurance that God is actively working through His church to bring about justice and restoration.

In conclusion, the church's engagement with modern social movements is a delicate balance of upholding biblical truths while addressing the pressing needs of our world. It requires wisdom, humility, and a deep reliance on the Holy Spirit. As we navigate these challenging waters, let us remain steadfast in our commitment to Christ and His Gospel, ensuring that our actions reflect His love, justice, and transformative power. May our efforts be a testament to the world of God's unchanging truth and boundless grace, drawing many to the light and hope found only in Jesus Christ.

Chapter 27: The Role of the Church in Society

The role of the church in society is not a mere peripheral aspect of our faith; it lies at the very heart of our calling as followers of Christ. As believers, we are commissioned to be a transformative presence in the world, reflecting the light and love of Jesus in all that we do. This calling is not only about personal piety but also about how we engage with and impact the broader community around us. In Matthew 5:13-16, Jesus tells us that we are the salt of the earth and the light of the world. These metaphors underscore our responsibility to preserve what is good, to bring out the God-flavors in this world, and to shine brightly in the darkness.

Engaging with society means addressing the myriad of social issues that confront us daily. It is not enough for the church to remain cloistered within the safety of its walls, detached from the struggles and injustices that plague our communities. The prophet Isaiah admonishes us in Isaiah 1:17 to "Learn to do well; seek judgment, relieve the oppressed, judge the fatherless, plead for the widow." This scriptural mandate compels us to take action, to be actively involved in seeking justice and righteousness on behalf of those who are marginalized and vulnerable.

Our engagement must be rooted in love, the very essence of God's nature. Jesus summarized the law and the prophets with two commandments: to love God with all our heart, soul, and mind, and to love our neighbor as ourselves (Matthew 22:37-40). This dual commandment encapsulates our mission. Loving our neighbor means advocating for their well-being, standing up against injustices, and working towards a society that reflects God's justice and mercy. It is this love that must drive our involvement in social issues, ensuring that our actions are not about gaining recognition but about genuinely caring for others.

The early church provides a profound example of how this love was manifested in communal life. In Acts 2:44-45, we read that "all that believed were together, and had all things common; and sold their possessions and goods, and parted them to all men, as every man had need." This radical expression of community and generosity was a powerful testament to the transformative power of the Gospel. It showed that the church was not only a spiritual family but also a social institution that addressed the practical needs of its members.

Today, the church must reclaim this vision of community. We must be places where people can find support, encouragement, and practical help. Our congregations should be exemplars of the kingdom values of justice, mercy, and humility, providing a counter-narrative to the individualism and materialism that pervade society. In doing so, we become living testimonies to the reality of God's kingdom, drawing others to Christ through our witness.

However, our engagement with society must be discerning. While we are called to be in the world, we are not to be of the world (John 17:16). This distinction is crucial. It means that while we engage with social issues, we must do so from a place of biblical conviction, not merely adopting the trends and ideologies of the day. The Apostle Paul warns us in Romans 12:2, "And be not conformed to this world: but be ye transformed by the renewing of

CHAPTER 27: THE ROLE OF THE CHURCH IN SOCIETY

your mind, that ye may prove what is that good, and acceptable, and perfect, will of God." Our minds must be continually renewed by Scripture, guiding our actions and ensuring that our engagement is both prophetic and transformative.

One of the most significant social issues the church faces today is the question of justice. In a world rife with inequality and oppression, the church's voice must be clear and unwavering. Micah 6:8 lays out God's requirements for us: "to do justly, and to love mercy, and to walk humbly with thy God." This tripartite calling—justice, mercy, and humility—should shape our social engagement. It calls us to stand against injustice wherever we see it, to act with compassion and kindness, and to remain humble, recognizing that we are but instruments of God's grace.

In addressing social justice, the church must also confront its own shortcomings. We must be willing to acknowledge and repent of the ways in which we have failed to live up to our calling. This involves not only personal repentance but also corporate repentance for the ways in which the church has been complicit in systems of oppression and injustice. 2 Chronicles 7:14 provides a powerful promise: "If my people, which are called by my name, shall humble themselves, and pray, and seek my face, and turn from their wicked ways; then will I hear from heaven, and will forgive their sin, and will heal their land." This verse underscores the importance of repentance and prayer in our efforts to bring about societal change.

Moreover, the church's role in society includes advocating for the marginalized and oppressed. Proverbs 31:8-9 instructs us to "Open thy mouth for the dumb in the cause of all such as are appointed to destruction. Open thy mouth, judge righteously, and plead the cause of the poor and needy." Advocacy is a vital part of our mission. It involves speaking out against injustice, supporting those who are voiceless, and working to change systems and structures that perpetuate inequality.

The church must also be a place of reconciliation. In a world marked by division and conflict, we are called to be peacemakers. Jesus said in Matthew 5:9, "Blessed are the peacemakers: for they shall be called the children of God." Our role is to foster reconciliation, both within our communities and in the broader society. This involves building bridges across divides, promoting understanding and forgiveness, and working towards unity.

As we engage with society, we must also remember that our ultimate goal is not merely social reform but the transformation of hearts and lives through the Gospel. Social action and evangelism are not mutually exclusive; they are two sides of the same coin. The Great Commission in Matthew 28:19-20 calls us to make disciples of all nations, teaching them to observe all that Christ has commanded. This includes addressing social injustices as part of our discipleship, demonstrating how the Gospel transforms not only individual lives but also societal structures.

In doing so, the church must maintain its prophetic voice. We are called to speak truth to power, to challenge the status quo, and to call people back to God's ways. This prophetic role is not always comfortable or popular, but it is essential. The prophets of the Old Testament, like Amos and Isaiah, were often unpopular because they spoke out against the injustices and idolatries of their time. Yet their messages were crucial for calling God's people back to

CHAPTER 27: THE ROLE OF THE CHURCH IN SOCIETY

faithfulness. In the same way, the church today must be willing to take a stand, even when it is costly.

In our engagement with society, we must also ensure that we are embodying the values we espouse. James 1:27 reminds us that "Pure religion and undefiled before God and the Father is this, To visit the fatherless and widows in their affliction, and to keep himself unspotted from the world." Our actions must reflect our faith, showing the world what it means to follow Jesus. This means caring for the vulnerable, living with integrity, and maintaining our distinctiveness as God's people.

Finally, the church's role in society is to offer hope. In a world that is often dark and despairing, we are bearers of the hope of the Gospel. This hope is not a naive optimism but a confident expectation based on God's promises. Romans 15:13 declares, "Now the God of hope fill you with all joy and peace in believing, that ye may abound in hope, through the power of the Holy Ghost." Our hope is rooted in the resurrection of Jesus and the promise of His return, and it is this hope that we are called to share with the world.

In conclusion, the church's role in society is multifaceted and deeply significant. We are called to be salt and light, to engage with social issues from a place of biblical conviction, to advocate for justice, to foster reconciliation, to maintain our prophetic voice, to embody our faith, and to offer hope. As we do so, we must remain grounded in Scripture, guided by the Holy Spirit, and motivated by love. It is a daunting task, but one that we undertake with the assurance that we do not go alone. Jesus promised in Matthew 28:20, "And lo, I am with you always, even unto the end of the world." With His presence and power, we can fulfill our calling and make a lasting impact on the world around us.

Chapter 28: Scriptural Examples of Justice

In our pursuit of understanding and applying justice, it is essential to ground our perspectives in the timeless truths of Scripture. The Bible, replete with narratives, commandments, and prophetic declarations, offers a rich tapestry of what true justice looks like in the eyes of God. This exploration into scriptural examples of justice will not only enlighten our minds but also stir our hearts towards embodying this divine principle in our daily lives.

Consider the laws given in Leviticus, where God commands, "Ye shall do no unrighteousness in judgment: thou shalt not respect the person of the poor, nor honor the person of the mighty: but in righteousness shalt thou judge thy neighbour" (Leviticus 19:15). This directive encapsulates the essence of impartial justice, reminding us that true justice must transcend social and economic boundaries. Whether dealing with the poor or the rich, our judgments must be fair and rooted in righteousness. This principle is a stark contrast to many modern practices where favoritism and bias often distort justice.

Reflecting on Jesus' interactions during His earthly ministry, we see a profound commitment to justice, particularly in His treatment of the marginalized. One striking example is His encounter with Zacchaeus, the tax collector. Despite Zacchaeus' notorious reputation, Jesus' decision to dine with him was an act of restoring dignity and offering redemption (Luke 19:1-10). Jesus' approach here teaches us that justice often involves recognizing and uplifting the inherent worth of every individual, regardless of their past or societal status. This act of inclusion transformed Zacchaeus, leading him to make restitution and commit to a life of integrity.

The parable of the Good Samaritan further expands our understanding of justice. In this parable, Jesus subverts societal prejudices by presenting a Samaritan—a group despised by the Jews—as the hero who shows mercy and compassion to an injured man, unlike the priest and the Levite who pass by on the other side (Luke 10:25-37). This story challenges us to redefine our notions of neighborliness and justice, urging us to act with compassion and love towards those in need, irrespective of their background or ethnicity. True justice, as illustrated here, is active, inclusive, and bound by love.

Paul's letter to Philemon about Onesimus is another compelling scriptural narrative on justice. Onesimus, a runaway slave, becomes a believer and Paul appeals to Philemon to receive him back not as a slave but as a beloved brother in Christ (Philemon 1:16). This appeal underscores the transformative power of the gospel, which redefines social relationships and calls for a justice that is restorative rather than punitive. Paul's approach models how we should advocate for those under our influence, promoting reconciliation and dignity.

King Solomon's wisdom in resolving the dispute between the two women claiming to be the mother of a baby exemplifies the divine insight needed for just judgments. Solomon's proposal to divide the living child revealed the true mother, highlighting that true justice often involves discernment and wisdom that goes beyond surface-level facts (1 Kings 3:16-28). This account serves as a

CHAPTER 28: SCRIPTURAL EXAMPLES OF JUSTICE

reminder that our quest for justice must be undergirded by a prayerful dependence on divine wisdom, ensuring our decisions bring about genuine restoration and peace.

The Old Testament prophets, such as Amos and Micah, were ardent advocates for justice. Amos' passionate declaration, "But let judgment run down as waters, and righteousness as a mighty stream" (Amos 5:24), calls us to a relentless pursuit of justice that is as powerful and cleansing as a rushing stream. Amos condemned the exploitation and corruption prevalent among the leaders of Israel, urging them to return to God's standards of justice. His message is a timeless reminder that our social structures and personal lives must be continually aligned with God's righteous standards.

Micah's call to "do justly, and to love mercy, and to walk humbly with thy God" (Micah 6:8) distills the essence of biblical justice into actionable mandates. Justice, in Micah's vision, is intertwined with mercy and humility, creating a holistic approach to living out God's commands. This prophetic call challenges us to integrate these qualities into our lives, ensuring that our actions towards others are not just fair but also merciful and humble. It is a call to reflect God's character in our daily interactions and societal structures.

The psalms also resonate with a profound sense of justice, particularly in their call to defend the vulnerable. "Defend the poor and fatherless: do justice to the afflicted and needy. Deliver the poor and needy: rid them out of the hand of the wicked" (Psalm 82:3-4). This plea highlights the divine mandate to protect and uplift those who are most susceptible to injustice. It reminds us that true justice involves proactive efforts to rescue and support the marginalized, ensuring they receive fair treatment and opportunities for a dignified life.

In the New Testament, James exhorts believers to live out their faith through actions that reflect God's justice. "Pure religion and undefiled before God and the Father is this, To visit the fatherless and widows in their affliction, and to keep himself unspotted from the world" (James 1:27). This definition of true religion ties together personal piety with social justice, emphasizing that our faith must manifest in caring for those in distress and maintaining personal integrity. It challenges us to examine whether our religious practices truly align with God's heart for justice.

The story of Ruth and Boaz offers a beautiful illustration of justice intertwined with kindness and mercy. Boaz, recognizing Ruth's vulnerability as a foreign widow, extends protection and provision to her, going beyond the requirements of the law (Ruth 2:8-16). His actions reflect a justice that is compassionate and generous, providing a model for how we can support and uplift those in precarious situations. This narrative encourages us to consider how we can extend God's justice through acts of kindness and generosity in our communities.

Jesus' confrontation with the Pharisees about their hypocritical practices further elucidates His commitment to true justice. He rebukes them for neglecting the weightier matters of the law—judgment, mercy, and faith—while being meticulous about minor rituals (Matthew 23:23). This highlights the importance of prioritizing the core principles of justice and mercy over mere religious formalities. Jesus' critique calls us to ensure that our

CHAPTER 28: SCRIPTURAL EXAMPLES OF JUSTICE

pursuit of justice is rooted in genuine care for others, rather than superficial adherence to rules.

The Acts of the Apostles provides early church examples of communal justice. Believers shared their possessions so that there was no needy person among them (Acts 4:32-35). This radical sharing was a practical expression of justice within the community, ensuring that everyone's needs were met. It presents a powerful model of economic justice that challenges contemporary practices of individualism and materialism, urging us towards a more communal and caring approach to resources.

The parable of the sheep and the goats in Matthew 25:31-46 is perhaps one of the most vivid depictions of divine justice. In this parable, Jesus identifies with the hungry, thirsty, stranger, naked, sick, and imprisoned, declaring that whatever is done for them is done for Him. This teaching makes it clear that justice in God's kingdom is measured by how we treat the least among us. It underscores the critical importance of compassion and action towards those who are suffering, presenting a sobering call to align our lives with this standard of divine justice.

The letter of James also addresses economic injustice, warning the rich of the misery that awaits them for exploiting the laborers and living in luxury while others suffer (James 5:1-6). This prophetic warning serves as a stark reminder of the consequences of economic oppression and the necessity for fair wages and just treatment of workers. It urges us to examine our economic systems and personal practices to ensure they reflect God's justice and righteousness.

The narrative of Joseph, who forgives and provides for his brothers despite their betrayal, is a powerful example of restorative justice (Genesis 50:15-21). Joseph's response to his brothers, "But as for you, ye thought evil against me; but God meant it unto good," reflects a heart that seeks restoration and reconciliation over retribution. This story encourages us to pursue justice that heals and restores relationships, promoting peace and unity rather than perpetuating cycles of harm and vengeance.

Throughout His ministry, Jesus exemplified justice through His miracles and teachings, consistently addressing the needs of the marginalized. Whether healing the sick, feeding the hungry, or forgiving the sinner, His actions were always aligned with the principles of God's kingdom. The healing of the man at the pool of Bethesda (John 5:1-15) is one such example, where Jesus' compassion led to both physical healing and a deeper call to righteousness. These acts challenge us to consider how our efforts in justice can also lead to holistic transformation.

The early church's practice of appointing deacons to ensure fair distribution of food highlights the importance of organizational justice (Acts 6:1-7). This decision was made to address the complaints of the Hellenistic Jews who felt their widows were being neglected. It shows the church's commitment to addressing inequalities and ensuring that everyone, regardless of background, received fair treatment. This practice calls us to implement structures that promote equity and justice within our organizations and communities.

Finally, the vision of the New Jerusalem in Revelation offers a future hope of perfect justice. John describes a city where God

Himself will dwell with His people, wiping away every tear, and where there will be no more death, mourning, crying, or pain (Revelation 21:1-4). This vision provides us with the ultimate goal of justice—a restored creation where peace and righteousness reign. It inspires us to work towards this vision in our present context, embodying the principles of God's kingdom as we await its full realization.

As we reflect on these scriptural examples, it becomes evident that God's justice is comprehensive, encompassing legal fairness, social equity, economic integrity, and relational restoration. It challenges us to examine our lives and communities, aligning them with these divine principles. By embracing the scriptural mandate for justice, we participate in God's redemptive work, bringing His kingdom of righteousness, peace, and joy closer to fruition in our world. Let us commit to this high calling, ensuring that our pursuit of justice reflects the heart of our just and merciful God.

Chapter 29: Dangers of Political Entanglement

The pursuit of justice is a timeless mandate embedded in the fabric of Scripture. As we navigate the complexities of modern society, it's imperative to ground our understanding of justice in the examples provided in the Bible. These scriptural narratives offer a profound insight into God's heart for justice and serve as a guiding light for the church today. As we delve into these examples, let us remember Micah 6:8, which succinctly encapsulates God's requirement: "He hath shewed thee, O man, what is good; and what doth the Lord require of thee, but to do justly, and to love mercy, and to walk humbly with thy God?"

One of the earliest examples of justice in Scripture is found in the story of Cain and Abel. When Cain killed his brother Abel, God confronted him with a piercing question in Genesis 4:9, "Where is Abel thy brother?" This question, followed by the declaration in Genesis 4:10, "The voice of thy brother's blood crieth unto me from the ground," highlights God's awareness of injustice and His commitment to addressing it. The ensuing judgment on Cain underscores the principle that God does not ignore wrongdoing; He calls it out and acts upon it.

Moving forward in biblical history, the story of Joseph provides a powerful narrative of justice, forgiveness, and reconciliation. Sold into slavery by his brothers and unjustly imprisoned, Joseph's rise to power in Egypt is nothing short of divine orchestration. In Genesis 50:20, Joseph addresses his brothers with remarkable

CHAPTER 29: DANGERS OF POLITICAL ENTANGLEMENT

grace, saying, "But as for you, ye thought evil against me; but God meant it unto good, to bring to pass, as it is this day, to save much people alive." This statement not only reflects Joseph's understanding of God's sovereignty but also illustrates how God's justice often includes redemption and restoration.

The Exodus narrative offers another profound example of God's justice. The oppression of the Israelites in Egypt and their subsequent deliverance is a testament to God's active involvement in liberating the oppressed. Exodus 3:7-8 reveals God's heart for justice: "And the Lord said, I have surely seen the affliction of my people which are in Egypt, and have heard their cry by reason of their taskmasters; for I know their sorrows; And I am come down to deliver them out of the hand of the Egyptians." This passage reminds us that God is deeply moved by the suffering of His people and is committed to their deliverance.

In the period of the Judges, we see repeated cycles of Israel's disobedience, oppression by enemies, and God's deliverance through appointed leaders. One such leader, Deborah, stands out as a remarkable figure of justice. Her story in Judges 4-5 highlights not only her role as a prophetess and judge but also her courage and leadership in delivering Israel from Canaanite oppression. Judges 4:14 captures a pivotal moment: "And Deborah said unto Barak, Up; for this is the day in which the Lord hath delivered Sisera into thine hand: is not the Lord gone out before thee?" Deborah's faith and decisiveness exemplify how God can use individuals to bring about justice in times of need.

The prophetic books of the Old Testament are replete with calls for justice. The prophet Amos is particularly vocal about God's demand for justice and righteousness. In Amos 5:24, he declares, "But let judgment run down as waters, and righteousness as a mighty stream." This imagery conveys the overwhelming and pervasive nature of true justice as envisioned by God. Amos's ministry underscores the idea that justice is not merely a legal or social concept but a divine imperative that should flow freely and abundantly in the lives of God's people.

Isaiah, another major prophet, frequently addresses issues of justice. Isaiah 1:17 issues a direct call to action: "Learn to do well; seek judgment, relieve the oppressed, judge the fatherless, plead for the widow." This verse encapsulates the practical outworking of justice, emphasizing the need to protect and uplift the vulnerable in society. Isaiah's prophetic ministry highlights that true worship of God is intrinsically linked to the pursuit of justice and righteousness.

The life and ministry of Jesus Christ provide the ultimate example of divine justice. Jesus' inaugural sermon in Luke 4:18-19 sets the tone for His mission: "The Spirit of the Lord is upon me, because he hath anointed me to preach the gospel to the poor; he hath sent me to heal the brokenhearted, to preach deliverance to the captives, and recovering of sight to the blind, to set at liberty them that are bruised, To preach the acceptable year of the Lord." Jesus' ministry was characterized by acts of compassion, healing, and liberation, embodying the very essence of God's justice on earth.

Jesus' encounter with the woman caught in adultery in John 8:1-11 further illustrates His approach to justice. When the Pharisees brought the woman before Him, seeking to trap Him into condoning her stoning, Jesus responded with both wisdom and

CHAPTER 29: DANGERS OF POLITICAL ENTANGLEMENT

mercy. In John 8:7, He said, "He that is without sin among you, let him first cast a stone at her." This response not only diffused the situation but also highlighted the importance of self-examination and mercy in the administration of justice. Jesus' final words to the woman, "Neither do I condemn thee: go, and sin no more" (John 8:11), underscore the balance of justice and grace.

The parable of the Good Samaritan in Luke 10:25-37 offers a poignant lesson on social justice. When asked, "Who is my neighbor?" Jesus tells the story of a Samaritan who, unlike the religious leaders, stops to help a man beaten and left for dead. In Luke 10:37, Jesus concludes, "Go, and do thou likewise." This parable challenges us to extend justice and mercy beyond social, ethnic, and religious boundaries, embodying God's inclusive love and compassion.

The early church in the Book of Acts provides practical examples of justice within a community of believers. Acts 4:34-35 describes the radical generosity of the early Christians: "Neither was there any among them that lacked: for as many as were possessors of lands or houses sold them, and brought the prices of the things that were sold, And laid them down at the apostles' feet: and distribution was made unto every man according as he had need." This communal approach ensured that the needs of all members were met, reflecting a profound commitment to justice and equity.

Paul's letters also contain numerous exhortations to uphold justice. In Romans 12:17-18, he advises, "Recompense to no man evil for evil. Provide things honest in the sight of all men. If it be possible, as much as lieth in you, live peaceably with all men." These verses emphasize personal integrity and the pursuit of peace, foundational elements of a just society. Paul's teachings consistently urge believers to embody the principles of justice in their interactions with others.

James, known for his practical wisdom, addresses the issue of partiality in the church. In James 2:1, he admonishes, "My brethren, have not the faith of our Lord Jesus Christ, the Lord of glory, with respect of persons." He further illustrates this with a scenario in James 2:2-4, criticizing favoritism towards the wealthy and neglect of the poor. This teaching calls the church to embody impartial justice, treating all individuals with equal dignity and respect.

The book of Revelation provides a vision of ultimate justice. Revelation 21:4 offers a glimpse of God's final act of justice: "And God shall wipe away all tears from their eyes; and there shall be no more death, neither sorrow, nor crying, neither shall there be any more pain: for the former things are passed away." This promise assures us that God's justice will prevail, bringing an end to all forms of suffering and injustice.

As we reflect on these scriptural examples, it becomes clear that justice is not merely a human endeavor but a divine mandate that flows from the very character of God. Psalm 89:14 declares, "Justice and judgment are the habitation of thy throne: mercy and truth shall go before thy face." This verse beautifully captures the essence of God's reign, where justice and mercy coexist in perfect harmony.

The call to justice is also a call to reflect God's character in our lives and communities. Proverbs 31:8-9 instructs us to "Open thy mouth for the dumb in the cause of all such as are appointed to

CHAPTER 29: DANGERS OF POLITICAL ENTANGLEMENT

destruction. Open thy mouth, judge righteously, and plead the cause of the poor and needy." This charge challenges us to advocate for those who cannot speak for themselves, ensuring that justice is accessible to all.

In conclusion, the scriptural examples of justice provide a robust framework for the church to engage in social justice today. By grounding our actions in biblical principles, we can ensure that our pursuit of justice aligns with God's will. As we navigate the challenges of modern society, let us remain steadfast in our commitment to justice, guided by the timeless truths of Scripture. Isaiah 58:6-7 reminds us of the true fast God desires: "Is not this the fast that I have chosen? to loose the bands of wickedness, to undo the heavy burdens, and to let the oppressed go free, and that ye break every yoke? Is it not to deal thy bread to the hungry, and that thou bring the poor that are cast out to thy house? when thou seest the naked, that thou cover him; and that thou hide not thyself from thine own flesh?" This passage encapsulates the heart of biblical justice—actions that liberate, uplift, and restore dignity to those in need.

As we embrace this divine mandate, let us be inspired by the examples set before us in Scripture, ensuring that our pursuit of justice is always in harmony with the righteousness and mercy of our Creator.

Chapter 30: Emphasizing Biblical Justice

In today's world, the call for social justice echoes through the corridors of our society, urging institutions, including the church, to respond. As the body of Christ, we are summoned not merely to react according to the prevailing winds of societal change but to act firmly rooted in the principles laid out in Scripture. The Bible speaks clearly on issues of justice, reminding us in Micah 6:8 that the Lord requires us to "do justly, and to love mercy, and to walk humbly with thy God." This divine mandate sets a standard that transcends time and culture, calling the church to embody justice that is not shaped by the trends of the day but by the timeless commands of our Lord.

As followers of Christ, we are instructed to defend the oppressed and care for the poor, a directive deeply embedded in the fabric of Scripture. Psalm 82:3 commands us to "Defend the poor and fatherless: do justice to the afflicted and needy." This is not a passive suggestion but a command to engage actively in the alleviation of suffering and the correction of wrongs. The challenge for the church today is to discern how these commands are best applied in a modern context without losing the essence of what it means to follow Christ. It is a call to action that demands integrity, compassion, and a steadfast commitment to the truth of God's Word.

The risk of aligning too closely with political movements or social trends in the pursuit of justice is that we may drift away from our biblical foundations. Romans 12:2 warns us not to be conformed to this world, but to be transformed by the renewing of our minds,

CHAPTER 30: EMPHASIZING BIBLICAL JUSTICE

that we may prove what is that good, and acceptable, and perfect, will of God. It is essential, therefore, that our actions as a church are not mere reflections of the current social climate but are informed by and infused with biblical truth. Our commitment to justice must be a reflection of God's unchanging character, not the shifting sands of cultural focus. This steadfastness in truth allows us to act justly while maintaining our distinct identity as the people of God.

Moreover, the Bible does not merely call us to act justly but to love mercy. How we pursue justice is as important as the pursuit itself. In the zeal to rectify wrongs, the church must guard against the temptation to adopt the world's often harsh and retributive approaches to justice. Instead, we are to mirror God's mercy, as highlighted in Ephesians 4:32: "And be ye kind one to another, tenderhearted, forgiving one another, even as God for Christ's sake hath forgiven you." Our approach to justice must therefore be tempered with compassion and forgiveness, hallmarks of Christ's dealings with us. This compassionate approach ensures that our pursuit of justice does not become another form of oppression.

In addressing the injustices of the world, the church must also ensure that it does not neglect the gospel's call to spiritual justice. The message of salvation—the ultimate deliverance from injustice through Christ—must remain central to our mission. As we advocate for societal changes, we must not lose sight of the transformative power of the gospel, which changes hearts and, consequently, societies. Galatians 3:28 reminds us that in Christ, there is neither Jew nor Greek, there is neither bond nor free, there is neither male nor female: for ye are all one in Christ Jesus. Our pursuit of justice must always be a testament to this profound spiritual truth, promoting unity and equality through the lens of the gospel. This holistic approach ensures that our efforts are rooted in the ultimate source of justice and redemption.

The practical outworking of biblical justice in the church involves active listening and humble learning. We must be willing to hear the voices of those who have been marginalized and understand their experiences. James 1:19 advises us to be "swift to hear, slow to speak, slow to wrath," which is vital in our approach to justice. By listening, we validate the experiences and pains of others and align our responses to the empathy and love that Christ shows us. This active listening creates a foundation of trust and respect, which is essential for meaningful engagement and effective ministry.

Furthermore, biblical justice involves advocacy and action. It's not enough to listen and empathize; we must also be the hands and feet of Jesus in a broken world. Isaiah 1:17 exhorts us to "Learn to do well; seek judgment, relieve the oppressed, judge the fatherless, plead for the widow." The church is called to be an active participant in society, working to bring about the justice that reflects the kingdom of heaven. This active participation requires courage and a willingness to confront injustice wherever it is found, regardless of the cost.

In this pursuit, it is crucial for the church to maintain its prophetic voice. The prophets in the Bible did not shy away from calling out injustice, nor did they mince words about the necessity of returning to God's ways. Like them, the church today must be bold in proclaiming truth and justice, rooted in biblical teachings and led

CHAPTER 30: EMPHASIZING BIBLICAL JUSTICE

by the Holy Spirit. As we align ourselves with the divine call to justice, we must remember the words of Amos 5:24, "But let judgment run down as waters, and righteousness as a mighty stream." This imagery is powerful, depicting justice as a forceful, unending torrent that cleanses and renews. Our prophetic voice must echo this call for righteousness, demanding that justice flow unhindered in our communities and beyond.

The journey towards emphasizing biblical justice in the church is ongoing. It requires continuous reflection, constant prayer, and an unwavering commitment to aligning our actions with God's word. The process is not about reaching a destination but about striving to live out God's commandments every day. As we do so, we must cling to the promise found in 2 Chronicles 7:14, that if we humble ourselves, pray, seek His face, and turn from our wicked ways, then God will hear from heaven, will forgive our sin, and will heal our land. Through our commitment to biblical justice, the church not only obeys God but also becomes a beacon of hope and a testament to His unfailing love and righteousness in a world that desperately needs it.

As we pursue justice, we must recognize that it is ultimately God's justice we seek to manifest. Human systems of justice are inherently flawed and limited, but God's justice is perfect and complete. Psalm 9:7-8 declares, "But the Lord shall endure for ever: he hath prepared his throne for judgment. And he shall judge the world in righteousness, he shall minister judgment to the people in uprightness." Our role is to be instruments of His justice, guided by His Spirit and grounded in His Word. This divine perspective ensures that our efforts are not merely human endeavors but part of God's redemptive plan for humanity.

The pursuit of justice also demands personal integrity and accountability. As individuals and as a church, we must reflect the justice we preach. Matthew 7:3-5 warns us to first remove the plank from our own eye before addressing the speck in our brother's eye. This self-examination is crucial in maintaining credibility and authenticity in our advocacy for justice. By living justly in our personal lives, we model the principles we seek to promote in the wider society, creating a ripple effect that can lead to broader cultural transformation.

In a world rife with injustice, it is easy to become overwhelmed and discouraged. However, Scripture offers us hope and assurance. Psalm 37:27-29 encourages us, "Depart from evil, and do good; and dwell for evermore. For the Lord loveth judgment, and forsaketh not his saints; they are preserved for ever: but the seed of the wicked shall be cut off. The righteous shall inherit the land, and dwell therein for ever." This promise reminds us that our efforts are not in vain and that God's justice will ultimately prevail. This assurance strengthens our resolve to continue striving for justice, even in the face of significant challenges.

In our pursuit of justice, we must also cultivate a spirit of humility. Micah 6:8 calls us to walk humbly with our God. This humility recognizes that we do not have all the answers and that our understanding is limited. It opens us to continual learning and growth, allowing God to refine our perspectives and approaches. By walking humbly, we create space for God's wisdom and

CHAPTER 30: EMPHASIZING BIBLICAL JUSTICE

guidance to direct our paths, ensuring that our pursuit of justice remains aligned with His will.

The church's role in promoting biblical justice extends beyond addressing societal issues; it includes fostering environments where justice, mercy, and humility are practiced daily. This involves nurturing communities where the marginalized are welcomed, the voiceless are heard, and the oppressed are uplifted. Luke 4:18-19 recounts Jesus' mission, "The Spirit of the Lord is upon me, because he hath anointed me to preach the gospel to the poor; he hath sent me to heal the brokenhearted, to preach deliverance to the captives, and recovering of sight to the blind, to set at liberty them that are bruised, To preach the acceptable year of the Lord." As His followers, we are called to continue this mission, embodying His compassion and justice in our daily interactions and communal life.

The commitment to biblical justice requires perseverance. Galatians 6:9 encourages us, "And let us not be weary in well doing: for in due season we shall reap, if we faint not." This perseverance is fueled by faith, knowing that God is at work even when we cannot see immediate results. It is a long-term commitment to seeing God's kingdom come on earth as it is in heaven, trusting in His timing and sovereignty.

As we engage in the work of justice, it is vital to remain rooted in prayer. Philippians 4:6-7 instructs us, "Be careful for nothing; but in every thing by prayer and supplication with thanksgiving let your requests be made known unto God. And the peace of God, which passeth all understanding, shall keep your hearts and minds through Christ Jesus." Prayer keeps us connected to God's heart, aligns our desires with His, and empowers us to act with divine wisdom and strength. It is through prayer that we find the guidance, encouragement, and sustenance needed to persist in the often challenging work of justice.

Finally, the ultimate goal of our pursuit of justice is to glorify God and advance His kingdom. Matthew 5:16 exhorts us, "Let your light so shine before men, that they may see your good works, and glorify your Father which is in heaven." Our actions are meant to reflect God's character and draw others to Him. By emphasizing biblical justice, we demonstrate the transformative power of the gospel and offer a compelling witness to the world of God's love, righteousness, and redemption.

In conclusion, emphasizing biblical justice is not just a response to the world's call for fairness; it is a fulfillment of God's mandate for His people. It is a commitment to living out the principles of justice, mercy, and humility as revealed in Scripture. As we align ourselves with this divine mandate, we become agents of change in a world desperate for true justice. Let us, therefore, strive to embody the justice of God in all we do, continually seeking His guidance and strength, and trusting that His justice will ultimately prevail. Through our efforts, may the church shine brightly as a beacon of hope, reflecting the justice, mercy, and love of our Lord and Savior, Jesus Christ.

Section 7: Worship Trends and True Worship

Chapter 31: Entertainment over Worship

In today's church, a subtle yet profound shift has occurred, transforming sacred assemblies into stages of performance where the essence of worship is often overshadowed by a desire to entertain. This trend reflects a deeper cultural influence where entertainment is prized above introspection and spiritual connection. Worship, as intended in Scripture, is a profound, personal engagement with God, driven by a spirit of reverence and awe. The Apostle Paul underscores this in Ephesians 5:19, urging us to speak to one another with psalms, hymns, and songs from the Spirit, singing and making music from the heart to the Lord. It's a heart-to-heart interaction with our Creator, not merely a performance for the congregation.

The move towards entertainment-focused worship often begins with an innocent desire to make church services more accessible and engaging. While the intention might be noble, the execution can stray far from the biblical purpose of worship—to honor and glorify God. When King David brought the Ark of the Covenant to Jerusalem, his dance was one of genuine spiritual exuberance, not choreographed for spectator approval (2 Samuel 6:14). David's display was a personal expression of his relationship with God, a stark contrast to the polished, rehearsed productions that sometimes characterize modern worship.

This performance-oriented approach can lead to a congregation that values the quality of the music or the charisma of the leader more than the spiritual message and connection the worship is supposed to facilitate. Jesus addressed this when He spoke to the

CHAPTER 31: ENTERTAINMENT OVER WORSHIP

Samaritan woman at the well in John 4:24, saying, "God is spirit, and his worshipers must worship in the Spirit and in truth." This is a call to transcend the superficial layers of worship, urging us to reach into the depth of genuine, spirit-led worship that seeks truth over comfort or entertainment.

Moreover, the trend of entertainment over worship has a numbing effect on the congregation's spiritual sensitivity. When services are designed primarily to entertain, they often shy away from the convicting power of the Holy Spirit, which is essential for spiritual growth and transformation. The Book of Acts (2:43) speaks of a reverent awe that came upon every soul in the early church, leading to profound miracles and deep community bonding. Such awe is often absent in a church that prioritizes spectacle over substance.

It's important to remember that worship is not about attracting the masses with dazzling performances but about gathering the faithful to experience the divine presence. The Psalms offer numerous insights into the nature of true worship, with Psalm 95:6 inviting us to bow down in worship and kneel before our Maker. This posture of humility and reverence seems far removed from the high-energy displays that can dominate today's church services, yet it is fundamental to a meaningful worship experience.

In addressing this issue, church leaders need to evaluate the long-term spiritual health of their congregation. Are we fostering a community that delights in the presence of God, or are we simply entertaining an audience that might be momentarily inspired but is ultimately unchanged? As Paul warns in 2 Timothy 4:3-4, a time will come when people will not endure sound teaching, but having itching ears, they will accumulate for themselves teachers to suit their own passions. This prophecy is poignant, reminding us of the responsibility we have to anchor our worship in scriptural truth rather than popular appeal.

Restoring true worship requires courage to resist the current cultural currents within and outside the church. It means reorienting our focus from the applause of men to the approval of God. As Matthew 6:1 advises, we should take care not to practice our righteousness in front of others to be seen by them. Instead, our acts of worship must stem from a deep, internal conviction, aimed solely at glorifying God, not impressing others.

This recalibration towards true worship might involve reeducating our congregations about the purpose and power of worship. It might mean simplifying our services to emphasize prayer, scripture reading, and congregational singing, where every voice is valued over the few on stage. Such changes will undoubtedly challenge the status quo, but they are essential if we are to lead our congregations into a deeper, more authentic relationship with God.

Let us strive to be like the believers described in Acts 4:31, who, after praying, were filled with the Holy Spirit and spoke the word of God boldly. They were not performers on a stage but faithful servants witnessing the power of God moving in their midst. Their focus was not on the reaction of their audience but on the response of God to their sincere worship.

Consider the biblical account of Paul and Silas in prison. Stripped of any comfort or audience, they prayed and sang hymns to God. Their worship was so powerful that it caused an earthquake and opened the prison doors (Acts 16:25-26). This raw, unfiltered worship was not about presentation but about a heart posture

CHAPTER 31: ENTERTAINMENT OVER WORSHIP

before God. It's a potent reminder that worship's true power lies not in how it is presented but in the sincerity and depth of our connection with the Divine.

The drive for entertainment has also created an environment where worship teams feel pressured to perform rather than lead. The result can be a focus on technical excellence over spiritual authenticity. Psalm 33:3 encourages us to play skillfully and with a shout of joy, but this skillfulness is meant to enhance, not overshadow, the heartfelt expression of worship. The balance is delicate but crucial, ensuring that excellence in music and performance supports rather than supplants the spiritual experience.

It's essential to foster a culture where the congregation participates actively in worship rather than passively consuming a religious product. True worship is a communal act, where each member contributes to a collective expression of faith. Colossians 3:16 emphasizes teaching and admonishing one another with all wisdom through psalms, hymns, and songs from the Spirit, singing to God with gratitude in our hearts. This mutual edification through worship strengthens the church body, uniting them in purpose and spirit.

Addressing entertainment-focused worship also involves examining the content of our worship songs. Lyrics that focus more on personal feelings and less on the majesty and holiness of God can shift the emphasis from God's glory to our emotions. Isaiah 6:1-5 describes Isaiah's vision of the Lord, high and exalted, with the train of His robe filling the temple. The seraphim called out, "Holy, holy, holy is the Lord Almighty; the whole earth is full of his glory." This vision of God's holiness should inspire our worship, leading us to focus on His attributes and character.

In contrast, the Psalms are filled with examples of worship that extol God's attributes, recount His deeds, and call the worshiper to a posture of awe and reverence. Psalm 145:3 declares, "Great is the Lord and most worthy of praise; his greatness no one can fathom." Such declarations remind us of the object of our worship, guiding our hearts and minds to honor God for who He is and what He has done.

Leaders must also model true worship. When leaders prioritize authenticity over performance, it sets a powerful example for the congregation. King Jehoshaphat's leadership during a time of national crisis exemplifies this. He led the people in fasting and prayer, seeking God's guidance and protection (2 Chronicles 20:3-4). His leadership in worship was not about show but about sincere dependence on God. This authenticity in leadership encourages the congregation to seek God earnestly.

Furthermore, true worship involves surrender and sacrifice. Romans 12:1 urges us to offer our bodies as living sacrifices, holy and pleasing to God—this is our true and proper worship. Such worship transcends mere singing or performance; it encompasses our entire lives, dedicated to God's service. It's a call to live out our faith daily, allowing our actions to reflect our worship.

The story of Mary anointing Jesus' feet with expensive perfume (John 12:3) is a powerful example of worship that involves costly sacrifice. Her act was not about public approval but about deep, personal devotion to Jesus. This kind of worship challenges us to evaluate what we are willing to sacrifice for our Lord. It calls us to

CHAPTER 31: ENTERTAINMENT OVER WORSHIP

give our best to God, not out of obligation but out of profound love and reverence.

As we seek to restore true worship, it's crucial to remember that worship is ultimately about encountering God. Moses' encounter with God at the burning bush (Exodus 3:1-6) was marked by reverence and awe. God's presence was so holy that Moses had to remove his sandals. This encounter reminds us that worship brings us into God's holy presence, requiring a response of humility and reverence.

In this journey towards restoring true worship, let us be mindful of Jesus' rebuke to the Pharisees in Matthew 15:8-9: "These people honor me with their lips, but their hearts are far from me. They worship me in vain; their teachings are merely human rules." This sobering reminder calls us to examine our hearts, ensuring that our worship is not just outward expression but a true reflection of our devotion to God.

As we navigate these challenges, let us draw inspiration from the early church, whose worship was characterized by simplicity, sincerity, and spiritual depth. Acts 2:46-47 describes the believers breaking bread in their homes and eating together with glad and sincere hearts, praising God and enjoying the favor of all the people. This vibrant, heartfelt worship attracted many to the faith, demonstrating the power of genuine worship.

May we strive to create worship environments where God's presence is tangibly felt, where hearts are drawn to repentance, and where lives are transformed. Let us prioritize God's glory over human applause, seeking to honor Him in spirit and in truth. In doing so, we align ourselves with the true purpose of worship, fulfilling our calling to be a people set apart for God's praise and glory.

In conclusion, as we reflect on the nature and direction of our worship services, may we always prioritize the heart over the spectacle. Let us return to the roots of biblical worship, where every song, every prayer, and every sermon draws us closer to the heart of God, fostering a community truly reflective of His love and grace. After all, as we are reminded in Revelation 4:11, our Lord and God deserves to receive glory, honor, and power, for He created all things, and by His will, they were created and have their being. In our worship, may this profound truth resonate above all else.

Chapter 32: The Purpose of Worship

In exploring the essence of worship within the modern church, we find ourselves at a crossroads between tradition and transformation. Worship, as delineated in Scripture, is far more than the songs we sing or the rituals we perform. It is a profound expression of our reverence and love for God, deeply rooted in our spirits. Jesus Himself taught, "God is a Spirit: and they that worship him must worship him in spirit and in truth" (John 4:24). This divine instruction compels us to look beyond the surface, urging us to cultivate a worship experience that transcends mere formality and engages the depth of our souls.

Yet, how often do our worship services mirror a concert or a performance, prioritizing entertainment over true spiritual connection? In these settings, it's easy to lose sight of the primary purpose of worship: to honor and glorify God. Worship should never be reduced to a passive activity where congregants merely observe. Instead, it should be an active, communal experience that lifts the hearts of the people towards God. In doing so, worship unites us, drawing us closer to the Lord and to one another in the shared pursuit of His presence.

The transformation of worship into a performance can subtly shift our focus from God to man. When the metrics of good worship become tied to production values or emotional highs, we risk departing from the biblical model. The Psalmist declares, "O come, let us worship and bow down: let us kneel before the LORD our maker" (Psalm 95:6). Here, worship is an act of humility, a physical and spiritual posture of bowing before our Creator, acknowledging His supremacy and our utter dependence on Him.

In reviving the true purpose of worship, we must also confront the consumer mentality that pervades many congregations today. Worship is not about what we can receive, but what we give to God out of our love and reverence for Him. Each melody sung, each word spoken, each silent prayer offered should be an outpouring of our gratitude and adoration toward the One who "inhabiteth the praises of Israel" (Psalm 22:3). Our gatherings should be less about pleasing ourselves and more about pleasing God, shifting from self-centeredness to God-centeredness.

Authentic worship involves the whole being. It is a response to God's revelation of Himself, reflecting our awe and reverence. Paul's exhortation to the Romans resonates deeply here, as he calls believers to present their bodies as a living sacrifice, holy and acceptable unto God, which is their reasonable service (Romans 12:1). Worship, then, is not just a momentary act but a lifestyle, extending beyond the walls of the church into every aspect of our lives, expressing our ongoing commitment to God's lordship over us.

We must also consider the communal aspect of worship, which fosters unity and reflects the unity of the Body of Christ. As we come together in worship, our individual praises and prayers merge into a single chorus of adoration, echoing the unity Christ prayed for in John 17:21, "That they all may be one; as thou, Father, art in me, and I in thee, that they also may be one in us: that the world may believe that thou hast sent me." This unity in

CHAPTER 32: THE PURPOSE OF WORSHIP

worship is a powerful testimony to the world of the love and presence of God among His people.

True worship also acts as a conduit of God's healing and restoration. As we lift our voices and hearts in genuine adoration, we open ourselves to the transformative power of God's Spirit. The Scriptures remind us in 2 Chronicles 7:14 that if God's people, who are called by His name, will humble themselves, pray, seek His face, and turn from their wicked ways, then He will hear from heaven, will forgive their sin, and will heal their land. Worship, therefore, is integral to the spiritual and communal health of the church.

The heart of worship is not confined to music or praise alone; it encompasses every act of our lives that glorifies God. Colossians 3:17 instructs us, "And whatsoever ye do in word or deed, do all in the name of the Lord Jesus, giving thanks to God and the Father by him." This scripture expands the definition of worship to include our everyday actions, demonstrating that worship is a lifestyle dedicated to honoring God in all we do.

In examining the life of King David, we see a model of what it means to be a true worshiper. David was known as a man after God's own heart, and his psalms are filled with expressions of worship that range from joyous praise to deep lament. His life was marked by an unrelenting pursuit of God's presence, often saying, "One thing have I desired of the LORD, that will I seek after; that I may dwell in the house of the LORD all the days of my life, to behold the beauty of the LORD, and to inquire in his temple" (Psalm 27:4). David's example teaches us that worship is about longing for God, seeking His presence continually, and finding our deepest satisfaction in Him alone.

The purity of worship is often tested by our circumstances. It is easy to worship God when life is going well, but true worship is tested and proven in the trials. Job's story is a powerful testament to this truth. Despite losing everything, Job's response was one of worship: "Then Job arose, and rent his mantle, and shaved his head, and fell down upon the ground, and worshipped, and said, Naked came I out of my mother's womb, and naked shall I return thither: the LORD gave, and the LORD hath taken away; blessed be the name of the LORD" (Job 1:20-21). Job's unwavering devotion in the face of immense suffering reveals that authentic worship comes from a heart that trusts and honors God, regardless of the circumstances.

The modern church faces the challenge of balancing cultural relevance with scriptural fidelity. In our efforts to attract and engage, we must be vigilant not to compromise the sacredness of worship. Jesus warned in Matthew 15:8-9, "This people draweth nigh unto me with their mouth, and honoureth me with their lips; but their heart is far from me. But in vain they do worship me, teaching for doctrines the commandments of men." These words serve as a sober reminder that true worship must come from the heart and align with God's truth, rather than conforming to human traditions or societal trends.

As worship leaders and participants, we have a responsibility to foster an atmosphere that encourages genuine encounters with God. This begins with a commitment to prayer and preparation, seeking God's guidance in crafting worship experiences that are

CHAPTER 32: THE PURPOSE OF WORSHIP

Spirit-led and biblically grounded. The story of the woman with the alabaster jar in Luke 7:37-38 illustrates the beauty of sacrificial worship. She poured out her most valuable possession at Jesus' feet, anointing Him with costly perfume as an act of deep love and reverence. Jesus acknowledged her act of worship, saying, "Her sins, which are many, are forgiven; for she loved much" (Luke 7:47). This powerful moment teaches us that worship involves giving our best to God, holding nothing back, and expressing our love for Him with all that we are.

In our quest to return to the heart of worship, we must also address the issue of idolatry. Idolatry in worship occurs when we place anything above God, whether it be traditions, preferences, or even the act of worship itself. Exodus 20:3-4 commands, "Thou shalt have no other gods before me. Thou shalt not make unto thee any graven image." Worship must be directed solely toward God, free from distractions and competing affections. This requires a continual examination of our hearts and motives, ensuring that God remains the central focus of our worship.

The story of the Samaritan woman at the well provides profound insights into the nature of true worship. In John 4, Jesus engaged in a transformative conversation with her, revealing that worship is not about location or tradition but about spirit and truth. Jesus declared, "But the hour cometh, and now is, when the true worshippers shall worship the Father in spirit and in truth: for the Father seeketh such to worship him" (John 4:23). This conversation underscores that genuine worship is rooted in a personal relationship with God, transcending external forms and rituals.

Moreover, worship has a missional aspect that often goes overlooked. When we worship God in spirit and truth, we bear witness to His greatness and draw others into His presence. Psalm 96:3 calls us to "Declare his glory among the heathen, his wonders among all people." Our worship should not only edify the church but also serve as a powerful testimony to the world, inviting others to experience the transformative love of God.

In the corporate setting, worship plays a vital role in building and sustaining the community of believers. Acts 2:46-47 describes the early church's practice of worship: "And they, continuing daily with one accord in the temple, and breaking bread from house to house, did eat their meat with gladness and singleness of heart, praising God, and having favour with all the people." This passage highlights the joy and unity that comes from communal worship, as well as its impact on the wider community. When the church gathers in genuine worship, it strengthens the bonds of fellowship and creates a space where the Holy Spirit can move powerfully.

Finally, worship is a foretaste of the eternal praise we will offer in heaven. Revelation 7:9-10 paints a vivid picture of a great multitude from every nation, tribe, people, and language, standing before the throne and before the Lamb, crying out, "Salvation to our God which sitteth upon the throne, and unto the Lamb." This heavenly vision reminds us that our worship here on earth is part of a larger, cosmic chorus that will continue for all eternity. It calls us to worship with reverence and anticipation, looking forward to the day when we will join the heavenly hosts in perfect praise.

Let us then strive to reclaim the sanctity of worship in our churches. May our worship be a reflection of our deep reverence

CHAPTER 32: THE PURPOSE OF WORSHIP

for God, stripped of pretense and performance. As we return to the heart of worship, let us remember that it is all about Jesus, and nothing else. Let our worship be as the Psalmist says in Psalm 29:2, "Give unto the LORD the glory due unto his name; worship the LORD in the beauty of holiness." It is in this spirit of holiness and awe that we can truly touch the heart of God.

As leaders and participants in worship, we carry the responsibility to foster an environment where true worship can flourish—an environment where the Spirit of God moves freely and powerfully among His people. By focusing on these biblical truths, we can guide our congregations back to the essence of worship that pleases God and fulfills the deepest longings of our hearts.

In conclusion, let us be vigilant and intentional in our approach to worship. Let it always be spirit-filled, truth-laden, and God-centered. As we do so, we will witness a renewal in our personal lives and in the life of the church, fulfilling our call to worship in spirit and truth, thereby attracting the very presence of God into our midst. This is the heart and soul of worship, and this is what we are called to rediscover and restore in our congregations across the globe.

Chapter 33: Scriptural Foundations for Worship

The modern church finds itself at a crossroads where the true essence of worship is being challenged by the allure of entertainment and cultural acceptance. This shift has resulted in a form of worship that often prioritizes emotional engagement and aesthetic appeal over genuine spiritual connection. As we navigate this landscape, it becomes imperative to return to the scriptural foundations of worship, which call us to engage with God in spirit and in truth. Jesus emphasized this in John 4:24, saying, "God is a Spirit: and they that worship him must worship him in spirit and in truth." This directive from our Savior is not merely a suggestion but a divine mandate that shapes the core of our worship practices.

True worship, as depicted in the Bible, is a profound act of the heart, transcending the superficial elements that often dominate modern services. It requires a posture of humility and reverence, recognizing the sovereignty and holiness of God. Psalm 95:6 invites us to "O come, let us worship and bow down: let us kneel before the LORD our maker." This invitation is not just a call to a physical act but a summons to a spiritual posture of submission and adoration. In an age where self-promotion and personal gratification are celebrated, bowing down before God requires a countercultural shift that places His glory above our own desires.

The early church provides a compelling example of what it means to live a life of worship. Acts 2:46-47 describes believers who,

CHAPTER 33: SCRIPTURAL FOUNDATIONS FOR WORSHIP

"continuing daily with one accord in the temple, and breaking bread from house to house, did eat their meat with gladness and singleness of heart, praising God, and having favour with all the people." Their worship was not confined to a specific time or place but was a continuous expression of their faith, woven into the fabric of their daily lives. This holistic approach to worship created a vibrant, Spirit-filled community that drew others to the gospel through their genuine expressions of faith and love.

Moreover, worship according to Scripture is inherently transformative. It is designed to realign our hearts with God's will, reshape our desires, and influence our interactions with the world. Romans 12:1 exhorts us, "I beseech you therefore, brethren, by the mercies of God, that ye present your bodies a living sacrifice, holy, acceptable unto God, which is your reasonable service." This verse encapsulates the sacrificial nature of true worship. It calls us to offer our entire being to God, not just in moments of corporate worship but as a daily act of devotion. This type of worship transforms us from the inside out, enabling us to reflect God's holiness in our lives.

However, the shift towards performance-based worship in many modern churches has led to a consumer mentality, where congregants evaluate worship services based on their personal enjoyment rather than their spiritual edification. This trend can create an environment where emotional highs and charismatic leadership overshadow the true purpose of worship, which is to encounter and honor God. Hebrews 13:15 reminds us, "By him therefore let us offer the sacrifice of praise to God continually, that is, the fruit of our lips giving thanks to his name." Worship, therefore, should be a continual offering of praise and gratitude, flowing from a heart transformed by God's grace.

To restore the scriptural foundations of worship, churches must refocus on fostering deep, personal connections with God that transcend the confines of a service. Matthew 15:8 warns, "This people draweth nigh unto me with their mouth, and honoureth me with their lips; but their heart is far from me." True worship must engage our hearts, not just our lips. It must be an authentic expression of our devotion to God, driven by a desire to honor Him above all else. Leaders play a crucial role in guiding congregations back to this authentic worship by living out these principles themselves and teaching them with clarity and conviction.

The call to return to the essence of worship is not about rejecting all modern innovations but about ensuring that these elements serve to enhance, rather than replace, our genuine encounter with God. 2 Chronicles 29:30 provides a powerful example of this balance as King Hezekiah and the people worshipped with songs of praise written by David and Asaph the seer, rejoicing in the restoration of proper worship. This passage reminds us that the heart of worship is not found in the new or the old but in the sincerity and purity of our devotion to God.

True worship is also deeply rooted in community. It is not an isolated act but a collective expression of faith that builds up the body of Christ. Ephesians 5:19-20 encourages us to speak to one another "in psalms and hymns and spiritual songs, singing and making melody in your heart to the Lord; giving thanks always for all things unto God and the Father in the name of our Lord Jesus Christ." Worship in the early church was a communal experience

CHAPTER 33: SCRIPTURAL FOUNDATIONS FOR WORSHIP

that fostered unity, encouragement, and spiritual growth. Restoring this sense of community in our worship practices can help us move beyond individualism and create environments where the Spirit of God can move freely among His people.

Furthermore, worship is an act of obedience. It is not merely about singing or praying but about living in a way that honors God in every aspect of our lives. 1 Samuel 15:22 emphasizes this point: "Hath the LORD as great delight in burnt offerings and sacrifices, as in obeying the voice of the LORD? Behold, to obey is better than sacrifice, and to hearken than the fat of rams." Our acts of worship must be accompanied by a lifestyle of obedience to God's commands. This obedience is the true measure of our worship, reflecting our commitment to live according to His will.

Worship is also a declaration of God's worthiness. Revelation 4:11 proclaims, "Thou art worthy, O Lord, to receive glory and honour and power: for thou hast created all things, and for thy pleasure they are and were created." When we worship, we acknowledge God's supreme worth and declare His glory. This declaration is not limited to our words but is expressed through our actions, attitudes, and the way we live our lives. It is a recognition that God alone is worthy of our highest praise and deepest devotion.

As we seek to restore true worship, we must also address the distractions that can hinder our focus on God. Luke 10:41-42 recounts Jesus' words to Martha: "Martha, Martha, thou art careful and troubled about many things: But one thing is needful: and Mary hath chosen that good part, which shall not be taken away from her." In our worship, we must strive to be like Mary, choosing to focus on the one thing that is truly needed—our relationship with Jesus. This means setting aside distractions and making time to sit at His feet, listening to His words and experiencing His presence.

Additionally, worship is a response to God's revelation. When we encounter the majesty and holiness of God, our natural response should be one of awe and reverence. Isaiah 6:1-5 illustrates this beautifully as Isaiah sees the Lord high and lifted up, and his immediate response is to acknowledge his own unworthiness and the holiness of God. This encounter leads to a profound transformation in Isaiah's life and ministry. Similarly, our worship should be a response to who God is and what He has done, leading to transformation and a deeper commitment to His purposes.

Worship is also a weapon in spiritual warfare. 2 Chronicles 20:21-22 recounts how King Jehoshaphat appointed singers to praise the Lord as they went out before the army, and as they began to sing and praise, the Lord set ambushes against their enemies. This passage reminds us that worship has the power to break strongholds and bring victory in our lives. When we lift up our voices in praise, we are declaring God's sovereignty and inviting His power to work on our behalf. This aspect of worship is often overlooked but is a critical part of our spiritual arsenal.

Moreover, worship is a foretaste of heaven. Revelation 7:9-10 gives us a glimpse of the heavenly worship, where a great multitude from every nation, tribe, people, and language stands before the throne and before the Lamb, crying out, "Salvation to our God which sitteth upon the throne, and unto the Lamb." This heavenly scene reminds us that our worship here on earth is a preparation for the eternal worship we will experience in heaven.

It connects us with the greater reality of God's kingdom and aligns our hearts with His eternal purposes.

In restoring true worship, we must also cultivate a heart of gratitude. Colossians 3:16-17 encourages us to let the word of Christ dwell in us richly, teaching and admonishing one another in all wisdom, singing psalms and hymns and spiritual songs, with thankfulness in our hearts to God. Gratitude is a vital component of worship, reminding us of God's goodness and faithfulness. It shifts our focus from our circumstances to His character, filling our hearts with joy and our mouths with praise.

As we journey towards a deeper understanding of worship, let us remember the promise of James 4:8, "Draw nigh to God, and he will draw nigh to you." This assurance that God responds to our sincere efforts to seek Him is both comforting and motivating. It underscores the reciprocal nature of worship—when we draw near to God in spirit and truth, He meets us with His presence, grace, and power. This divine encounter is the heart of worship, transforming us and drawing us closer to His heart.

In conclusion, true worship is not about the style or the setting but about the posture of our hearts before God. It is a lifestyle of reverence, obedience, and love, rooted in the truth of Scripture and expressed in every aspect of our lives. As we return to the scriptural foundations of worship, let us commit to honoring God in spirit and in truth, creating environments where His presence is welcomed and His glory is revealed. By doing so, we not only fulfill our highest calling but also pave the way for others to encounter the living God and be transformed by His grace.

Chapter 34: Correcting Course

In "Church Gone Wild: A Call to Renewal and Restoration," the chapter "Correcting Course" addresses the urgent need for the church to return to authentic, biblically grounded worship. As we look around today, it's clear that many churches have allowed the pursuit of entertainment to overshadow the true purpose of worship. This shift has transformed what should be a sacred encounter with the divine into a mere spectacle designed to please the masses. Yet, worship must be rooted in the essence of spirit and truth, as Jesus emphasized in John 4:24, "God is a Spirit: and they that worship him must worship him in spirit and in truth."

The transformation begins with a heartfelt realignment of our priorities. Worship should be about engaging with God, not just putting on a show. Psalm 100:2 reminds us, "Serve the LORD with gladness: come before his presence with singing." The essence of worship is service and joyful submission to God's presence, not merely performing for an audience. This distinction is crucial, as it redirects our focus from human approval to divine encounter, ensuring that every element of our worship—whether music, prayer, or preaching—serves to glorify God rather than entertain people.

In many congregations, the tendency to turn worship into a performance has created an environment where the congregation becomes passive spectators. This passive stance is contrary to the biblical model of worship, which calls for active participation. Colossians 3:16 exhorts us, "Let the word of Christ dwell in you richly in all wisdom; teaching and admonishing one another in

CHAPTER 34: CORRECTING COURSE

psalms and hymns and spiritual songs, singing with grace in your hearts to the Lord." True worship involves the entire body of believers, teaching, admonishing, and singing together, thereby creating a dynamic and participatory worship experience.

Church leaders play a pivotal role in this transformation. They must guide their teams with a clear vision that prioritizes God's glory above all. 1 Peter 4:10-11 instructs, "As every man hath received the gift, even so minister the same one to another, as good stewards of the manifold grace of God. If any man speak, let him speak as the oracles of God; if any man minister, let him do it as of the ability which God giveth: that God in all things may be glorified through Jesus Christ." This scripture underscores the responsibility of leaders to steward their gifts for God's glory, ensuring that their ministry reflects His grace and truth.

To correct our course, we must also embrace silence and reflection within our worship services. In today's fast-paced world, moments of quiet can seem counterintuitive, yet they are profoundly biblical. 1 Kings 19:12 recounts how God spoke to Elijah not through wind, earthquake, or fire, but in a "still small voice." Silence in worship allows us to listen attentively to God's voice, fostering a deeper, more intimate connection with Him. These moments of quiet contemplation can transform our worship, making space for the Holy Spirit to move in ways that loud music and busy schedules cannot.

Teaching the congregation about the true purpose and power of worship is another crucial step. Worship is not just a prelude to the sermon; it is an act of surrender and adoration that stands on its own. Romans 12:1-2 teaches us, "I beseech you therefore, brethren, by the mercies of God, that ye present your bodies a living sacrifice, holy, acceptable unto God, which is your reasonable service. And be not conformed to this world: but be ye transformed by the renewing of your mind, that ye may prove what is that good, and acceptable, and perfect, will of God." Worship is our reasonable service, a transformative act of presenting ourselves to God.

Incorporating diverse expressions of worship is also vital. The early church exemplified a vibrant and diverse worship life, as seen in Acts 2:46-47, where they broke bread from house to house, praising God together. This model shows that worship can be both communal and personal, formal and informal. By embracing various forms of worship—whether through traditional hymns, contemporary songs, or spontaneous praise—we can create a richer, more inclusive worship experience that resonates with all members of the congregation.

Openness to the Holy Spirit's guidance is essential for correcting our course. Romans 8:26 reminds us, "Likewise the Spirit also helpeth our infirmities: for we know not what we should pray for as we ought: but the Spirit itself maketh intercession for us with groanings which cannot be uttered." Being sensitive to the Spirit's leading ensures that our worship services are not just well-planned events but dynamic encounters with God. This sensitivity can lead to spontaneous moments of prayer, prophecy, or repentance, making our worship services truly Spirit-led.

Correcting our course also involves understanding the power of worship to transform lives. When worship is done in spirit and truth, it has the power to change hearts, break chains, and bring

CHAPTER 34: CORRECTING COURSE

healing. Isaiah 61:3 speaks of giving "beauty for ashes, the oil of joy for mourning, the garment of praise for the spirit of heaviness." Worship can lift us from our burdens and usher us into God's presence, where we find joy, peace, and restoration.

Restoring the focus of worship on God's glory also means reevaluating the content of our worship songs. Songs should be rich in theology and scripture, not merely catchy or emotionally appealing. Ephesians 5:19 encourages us to speak "to yourselves in psalms and hymns and spiritual songs, singing and making melody in your heart to the Lord." Our songs should reflect the depth and beauty of God's word, teaching and admonishing us as we sing.

Encouraging personal worship practices outside of the corporate setting is another way to correct our course. Worship should not be confined to Sunday mornings; it should be a daily practice. Psalm 34:1 declares, "I will bless the LORD at all times: his praise shall continually be in my mouth." Teaching congregants to develop personal worship habits—through prayer, song, and scripture reading—can deepen their relationship with God and make corporate worship even more meaningful.

As we strive to correct our course, we must remember the communal aspect of worship. Hebrews 10:24-25 exhorts us to "consider one another to provoke unto love and to good works: not forsaking the assembling of ourselves together, as the manner of some is; but exhorting one another: and so much the more, as ye see the day approaching." Worshiping together strengthens the body of Christ, fostering unity and mutual encouragement.

The role of creativity in worship cannot be overlooked. God is a creator, and He has endowed us with creativity. Psalm 96:1 says, "O sing unto the LORD a new song: sing unto the LORD, all the earth." Encouraging creativity in worship—whether through new songs, artistic expressions, or innovative service formats—can breathe new life into our worship experiences, making them fresh and engaging while still rooted in biblical truth.

Transparency and authenticity in worship are also crucial. God desires worship that is genuine and heartfelt, not just ritualistic. Psalm 51:17 reminds us, "The sacrifices of God are a broken spirit: a broken and a contrite heart, O God, thou wilt not despise." Encouraging congregants to come as they are, with all their struggles and burdens, fosters an environment where true, transformative worship can occur.

Leaders must model the worship they seek to cultivate. Their authenticity and passion for God set the tone for the congregation. 1 Corinthians 11:1 exhorts us, "Be ye followers of me, even as I also am of Christ." When leaders demonstrate a deep, authentic worship life, it inspires the congregation to follow suit, creating a ripple effect throughout the church.

Balancing tradition with innovation is another key aspect. While new forms of worship can be refreshing, it is important to honor and preserve the traditions that have sustained the church through the ages. Matthew 13:52 says, "Then said he unto them, Therefore every scribe which is instructed unto the kingdom of heaven is like unto a man that is an householder, which bringeth forth out of his treasure things new and old." Blending the old with the new can create a worship experience that is both grounded and dynamic.

CHAPTER 34: CORRECTING COURSE

Worship is also a powerful witness to the world. John 13:35 declares, "By this shall all men know that ye are my disciples, if ye have love one to another." When the church worships in unity and truth, it becomes a beacon of God's love and grace, drawing others to Him. Our worship should therefore be a reflection of the gospel, proclaiming the good news of Jesus Christ to all who see and hear.

In our pursuit of correcting course, we must remain humble and teachable. 2 Chronicles 7:14 gives a powerful promise, "If my people, which are called by my name, shall humble themselves, and pray, and seek my face, and turn from their wicked ways; then will I hear from heaven, and will forgive their sin, and will heal their land." Humility and repentance are key to experiencing God's healing and renewal in our worship practices.

As we journey towards restoring true worship, let us be encouraged by the promise of God's presence. James 4:8 assures us, "Draw nigh to God, and he will draw nigh to you." As we draw near to Him with sincere hearts and pure worship, He will meet us, transform us, and use us for His glory. Let us commit to this journey, knowing that as we correct our course, we align ourselves with God's divine purpose for His church.

Chapter 35: Case Studies of Authentic Worship

In the realm of modern worship, it's easy to become entangled in the spectacle and miss the heart of true worship. As we explore case studies of authentic worship, let us remember the wisdom of Scripture, where Jesus declares in John 4:24, "God is a Spirit: and they that worship him must worship him in spirit and in truth." This foundational truth guides our examination of congregations that exemplify worship that transcends mere performance and deeply connects with the divine.

One inspiring example is a small community church in rural Georgia. Despite lacking the technological advancements and polished bands prevalent in urban megachurches, this congregation demonstrates a profound depth of worship. Their services, filled with heartfelt hymns and spontaneous prayer, embody Paul's instruction in Ephesians 5:19, "Speaking to yourselves in psalms and hymns and spiritual songs, singing and making melody in your heart to the Lord." This scene is a powerful testament to the beauty of simplicity in worship, reminding us that genuine connection with God doesn't require grandiosity.

Contrastingly, consider a church in Chicago, where despite the presence of cutting-edge audio-visual systems and an award-winning Christian recording artist serving as pastor, the leaders consciously strive to keep the focus on Christ. They regularly incorporate moments of silent reflection and congregational prayer, aligning with Colossians 3:16, where we are urged to "let

CHAPTER 35: CASE STUDIES OF AUTHENTIC WORSHIP

the word of Christ dwell in you richly in all wisdom; teaching and admonishing one another in psalms and hymns and spiritual songs, with grace in your hearts to the Lord." This balance of modernity and reverence offers a blueprint for larger churches seeking to maintain the core of worship amid external allure.

In the heart of South Africa, another vibrant church community gathers under a tent, their voices united in powerful acapella worship. Their commitment to worshipping in spirit and truth, regardless of their modest surroundings, brings to life the essence of 2 Chronicles 29:30, which highlights King Hezekiah's encouragement for the Levites to praise the Lord with the words of David and Asaph the seer. This example serves as a poignant reminder that worship is ultimately about communal expression of faith and adoration towards God, not the venue in which it occurs.

Another profound instance of authentic worship can be found in a recovery group meeting in a small church hall in New Mexico. Here, individuals broken by life's trials find solace in worship as a form of healing and connection with a Higher Power. They cling to Psalms 147:3, "He healeth the broken in heart, and bindeth up their wounds." The raw, unpolished worship conducted here may not look like what many consider traditional church service, yet it's deeply spiritual and transformative for its participants.

Across the ocean in a historic cathedral in England, worshippers engage in liturgical worship that has been practiced for centuries. The structured format, including choral renditions of ancient psalms, reflects a deep respect for tradition and the continuity of faith as depicted in Lamentations 3:22-23, "It is of the Lord's mercies that we are not consumed, because his compassions fail not. They are new every morning: great is thy faithfulness." This form of worship emphasizes a connection to the past and a reverence for the patterns that have brought countless generations closer to God.

In a bustling city in Brazil, a contemporary church has integrated dance and visual arts into their worship, celebrating the creativity bestowed by the Creator. This expression is aligned with Exodus 35:35, where the artisans are endowed by God with skill to perform all manner of work. This church's approach showcases the diversity in worship methods that can effectively bring different cultures and personalities closer to God through their unique expressions.

A quiet, contemplative service in a monastery in the Swiss Alps focuses on meditation and the quiet chanting of scriptures. This practice mirrors the biblical encouragement found in Joshua 1:8, "This book of the law shall not depart out of thy mouth; but thou shalt meditate therein day and night, that thou mayest observe to do according to all that is written therein." The monks' worship through meditation underscores the personal and introspective relationship one can have with God, highlighting the peace and wisdom that comes from such deep spiritual engagement.

In the southern United States, a church organizes community gospel sing-alongs that bring together diverse groups to celebrate through soul-stirring music. This gathering not only provides spiritual uplift but also community bonding, resonating with Acts 2:46-47, "And they, continuing daily with one accord in the temple, and breaking bread from house to house, did eat their meat with gladness and singleness of heart, Praising God, and having

CHAPTER 35: CASE STUDIES OF AUTHENTIC WORSHIP

favour with all the people." The unity and joy evident in these sessions exemplify the communal aspect of worship that reinforces bonds among believers.

Another striking example can be found in an urban church in Seoul, South Korea, where early morning prayer meetings are a cornerstone of their worship practice. Congregants gather before dawn, seeking God with fervor and dedication, reminiscent of Jesus' own practice as noted in Mark 1:35, "And in the morning, rising up a great while before day, he went out, and departed into a solitary place, and there prayed." These gatherings emphasize the importance of prioritizing communion with God, even at the sacrifice of comfort and convenience.

In a remote village in Kenya, worship takes on a communal form where the entire village participates. The worship here is deeply connected to their daily lives, reflecting the holistic approach described in Romans 12:1, "I beseech you therefore, brethren, by the mercies of God, that ye present your bodies a living sacrifice, holy, acceptable unto God, which is your reasonable service." This integration of worship and daily living highlights how true worship is not confined to a particular time or place but is a continuous act of devotion.

In a small, hidden church in a persecuted region, believers gather in secret, their worship marked by a profound sense of reverence and urgency. Here, every song and prayer is offered with the awareness of the potential cost, echoing the courage and dedication found in Hebrews 10:24-25, "And let us consider one another to provoke unto love and to good works: Not forsaking the assembling of ourselves together, as the manner of some is; but exhorting one another: and so much the more, as ye see the day approaching." This environment of worship is a powerful reminder of the privilege and freedom many take for granted.

A church in the heart of New York City embraces a diverse congregation, and their worship services are a tapestry of various cultures and traditions. This melting pot of worship styles reflects Revelation 7:9, "After this I beheld, and, lo, a great multitude, which no man could number, of all nations, and kindreds, and people, and tongues, stood before the throne, and before the Lamb, clothed with white robes, and palms in their hands." This congregation's approach exemplifies the beauty and richness that diversity brings to the worship experience.

In an impoverished area of India, a small church meets under a tree, their worship marked by a simplicity and sincerity that cuts through any pretense. They sing with heartfelt passion, their voices lifted in faith despite their material lack, embodying the truth of James 2:5, "Hearken, my beloved brethren, Hath not God chosen the poor of this world rich in faith, and heirs of the kingdom which he hath promised to them that love him?" This community's worship serves as a poignant reminder of the power of faith and the presence of God among the humble and lowly.

In a modern suburban church in Australia, worship is marked by a focus on social justice and community service. The worshippers here are deeply involved in outreach programs, reflecting the teaching of Isaiah 58:6-7, "Is not this the fast that I have chosen? to loose the bands of wickedness, to undo the heavy burdens, and to let the oppressed go free, and that ye break every yoke? Is it not to deal thy bread to the hungry, and that thou bring the poor that

CHAPTER 35: CASE STUDIES OF AUTHENTIC WORSHIP

are cast out to thy house? when thou seest the naked, that thou cover him; and that thou hide not thyself from thine own flesh?" This form of worship through action underscores the importance of living out one's faith through tangible acts of love and compassion.

In a vibrant church in Lagos, Nigeria, the worship experience is filled with dance, vibrant music, and expressive praise. This exuberant worship style reflects Psalm 150:4, "Praise him with the timbrel and dance: praise him with stringed instruments and organs." The joy and energy in their worship not only uplift the congregation but also serve as a powerful witness to the life-transforming power of the Gospel.

In a quiet, reflective service in a Quaker meeting house, worship is characterized by silence and waiting upon the Lord. This practice aligns with Psalm 46:10, "Be still, and know that I am God." The silence allows for deep introspection and a heightened awareness of God's presence, offering a stark contrast to more expressive forms of worship and reminding us of the value of quietness and contemplation in our spiritual lives.

In an intergenerational church in Canada, worship services are intentionally designed to include both the young and the old, fostering a sense of unity and mutual edification. This practice brings to mind Psalm 145:4, "One generation shall praise thy works to another, and shall declare thy mighty acts." The interweaving of different generations in worship enriches the community, providing a platform for the transmission of faith and wisdom from one generation to the next.

These diverse examples of worship, from rural simplicity to urban complexity, from joyful exuberance to silent reflection, each illustrate different facets of what it means to worship in spirit and truth. They challenge us to look beyond the surface and rediscover the heart of worship as a profound encounter with the living God. As we reflect on these case studies, let us be inspired to reevaluate our own practices of worship, ensuring they align with the divine mandate to worship in spirit and truth, thus restoring the heart of worship in our communities and in our own hearts.

Section 8: Church Community vs. Individualism

Chapter 36: The Rise of Individualistic Christianity

In today's church, a troubling shift has emerged—a rise of individualistic Christianity that starkly contrasts with the communal faith depicted in the New Testament. As followers of Christ, we are called to live out our faith in a community, yet many believers now approach their spiritual journey with a "me first" mentality. This drift from collective spirituality to individualism mirrors broader societal changes but carries significant spiritual consequences. Acts 2:42-47 paints a picture of the early church where believers were devoted to the apostles' teaching and to fellowship, to the breaking of bread and to prayer. This community shared everything, living in a unity that today's church often lacks.

Our contemporary culture emphasizes personal independence and self-sufficiency, values that have insidiously influenced the church. This influence has led to a version of Christianity where personal spiritual fulfillment takes precedence over collective growth and accountability. Galatians 6:2 exhorts us to "bear one another's burdens, and so fulfill the law of Christ." However, in a culture that celebrates individual achievement, the notion of carrying each other's burdens becomes foreign, leading to isolation rather than the interconnectedness God intended.

The digital age has further fueled this individualistic approach. With the advent of online church services and virtual worship, many believers now choose convenience over community. While

CHAPTER 36: THE RISE OF INDIVIDUALISTIC CHRISTIANITY

these technological advances provide accessibility, they also risk creating a detached faith experience. Hebrews 10:25 warns us not to forsake assembling together, emphasizing the importance of physical presence in fostering a strong, supportive Christian community. When worship becomes a solitary act consumed through a screen, we lose the richness of fellowship and the collective encouragement that comes from being physically present with one another.

Personalization of faith via digital platforms often leads to a selective consumption of doctrine. Believers can choose sermons, teachings, and even entire churches that align with their personal preferences, avoiding challenging or convicting messages. This behavior is reminiscent of 2 Timothy 4:3, where Paul cautions that people will seek out teachers who say what their itching ears want to hear. The danger here is a fragmented faith, tailored to individual desires rather than grounded in the holistic truth of the gospel.

Worship, once a corporate expression of devotion to God, is now often treated as a personalized experience designed to meet individual tastes. The essence of worship in spirit and truth, as described in John 4:24, is lost when the focus shifts to what makes us feel good rather than what honors God. This shift not only diminishes the communal aspect of worship but also fosters a consumer mentality, where believers attend church for personal gain rather than to offer collective praise and service to God.

The trend towards individualism also manifests in how we perceive our spiritual responsibilities. Many believers now view their faith as a personal matter, something to be nurtured privately without the need for accountability or communal involvement. Yet, the Bible is clear that we are members of one body, each part indispensable to the whole. Romans 12:4-5 reminds us that just as each of us has one body with many members, so in Christ, we who are many form one body, and each member belongs to all the others. Our spiritual health and growth are intertwined with that of our fellow believers.

This individualistic mindset can lead to a lack of accountability, where personal interpretations and practices go unchecked. Without the guidance and correction that come from being part of a community, believers are more susceptible to doctrinal errors and spiritual pitfalls. Proverbs 27:17 states, "Iron sharpeneth iron; so a man sharpeneth the countenance of his friend." The sharpening process implies friction and challenge, something that is often missing when we isolate ourselves from the community.

The rise of individualism in the church can also be seen in our approach to discipleship and service. The Great Commission in Matthew 28:19-20 calls us to make disciples of all nations, teaching them to observe all that Jesus commanded. This mission is inherently communal, requiring the collective effort of the church body. However, when discipleship becomes a personal project rather than a shared endeavor, its impact is diminished. The communal support, shared wisdom, and mutual encouragement that come from discipling within a community are lost.

Moreover, individualism affects how we engage with the world. The church, as the body of Christ, is called to be a light to the nations, a collective witness to the transformative power of the gospel. Isaiah 60:1-3 calls us to arise and shine, for our light has come. This call to shine is not to individuals alone but to the church

CHAPTER 36: THE RISE OF INDIVIDUALISTIC CHRISTIANITY

as a unified body. When our witness becomes fragmented by individualism, the strength and clarity of our collective testimony are weakened.

The emphasis on personal spirituality can also lead to a neglect of communal prayer and worship. Acts 1:14 describes how the early believers were constantly in prayer, united in their devotion. This unity in prayer is powerful, fostering a sense of collective dependence on God and solidarity among believers. In contrast, when prayer becomes an individualistic activity, we miss out on the profound experience of shared spiritual battles and victories.

Another consequence of this shift is the erosion of the church's role in providing support and care. James 1:27 defines pure and undefiled religion as caring for orphans and widows in their distress and keeping oneself from being polluted by the world. This mandate is best fulfilled through a community that collectively meets the needs of its members. When believers prioritize personal spiritual journeys over communal responsibilities, the church's ability to provide comprehensive care and support is compromised.

The rise of individualistic Christianity also impacts how we interpret and apply scripture. Bible study, once a communal activity where believers learned and grew together, is now often a solitary pursuit. While personal study is important, it should complement, not replace, communal study. Colossians 3:16 urges us to let the word of Christ dwell in us richly as we teach and admonish one another with all wisdom. This communal interaction with scripture ensures a balanced and holistic understanding of God's word.

The consequences of this shift extend to our understanding of spiritual gifts. 1 Corinthians 12:7-11 teaches that the manifestation of the Spirit is given for the common good. Spiritual gifts are intended to build up the body of Christ, not just the individual. When believers focus solely on their personal spiritual experiences, they miss the opportunity to contribute to the growth and edification of the church.

Our approach to fellowship has also been affected by individualism. Genuine fellowship, as described in 1 John 1:7, involves walking in the light as He is in the light, resulting in fellowship with one another. This depth of relationship requires vulnerability, accountability, and a commitment to communal living that is often lacking in an individualistic culture. True fellowship cannot thrive in isolation; it requires a collective commitment to live out our faith together.

In light of these reflections, it is imperative that we reevaluate and realign our faith practices with the biblical model of community. The early church thrived not because of individual efforts but because of their collective devotion to one another and to God. Acts 4:32 highlights that all the believers were one in heart and mind, sharing everything they had. This unity and selflessness stand in stark contrast to the individualistic tendencies we see today.

As we seek to address this issue, we must start by fostering a culture that values community. This involves creating spaces for genuine fellowship, encouraging communal worship, and prioritizing collective prayer and service. By doing so, we honor the biblical mandate to live out our faith in community,

CHAPTER 36: THE RISE OF INDIVIDUALISTIC CHRISTIANITY

strengthening the body of Christ and enhancing our collective witness.

Furthermore, church leaders play a crucial role in guiding their congregations away from individualism. By emphasizing the importance of community, modeling communal practices, and holding believers accountable, leaders can help cultivate a church culture that reflects the interconnectedness described in scripture. Ephesians 4:11-13 underscores the role of church leaders in equipping the saints for the work of ministry, for building up the body of Christ, until we all attain unity in the faith.

Finally, as individual believers, we must be intentional about engaging with our church communities. This means prioritizing communal activities, seeking accountability, and being willing to share our lives with others. Philippians 2:3-4 encourages us to do nothing out of selfish ambition or vain conceit but in humility consider others better than ourselves, looking not only to our own interests but also to the interests of others. This attitude of humility and selflessness is essential for fostering a thriving church community.

In conclusion, the rise of individualistic Christianity poses a significant challenge to the church today. However, by returning to the biblical model of community, we can overcome this challenge and strengthen the body of Christ. As we do so, we fulfill Jesus' prayer in John 17:21 that all of us may be one, just as He and the Father are one, so that the world may believe that the Father sent Him. Let us commit to this vision, striving for unity and communal living that reflects the heart of our faith and the teachings of scripture.

Chapter 37: Biblical Community Life

In "Church Gone Wild: A Call to Renewal and Restoration," we address a critical shift that has subtly infiltrated many of our modern churches: the drift towards individualism. The essence of biblical community life, deeply rooted in scripture, stands in stark contrast to this trend. From the very inception of the church, believers were called to live in a profound fellowship, a koinonia, that is far more than mere social interaction. Acts 2:44 states, "And all that believed were together, and had all things common." This depiction of early Christians sharing their lives and resources reflects a divine blueprint for how the body of Christ is meant to function.

The erosion of this biblical model is not always glaringly obvious. Often, it manifests in subtle shifts, where personal preferences and individual desires begin to overshadow the collective calling of the church. This self-centered focus can infiltrate our spiritual lives without notice, but its impact is deeply corrosive. Reflecting on Hebrews 10:24-25, we see an urgent call to not neglect meeting together but to encourage one another. This scripture highlights the New Testament church's emphasis on mutual edification and collective spiritual growth, which are not just beneficial but essential for maturing in faith.

The Bible does not merely suggest community; it commands it, portraying it as a life-giving network where each member plays a crucial role. Paul writes in 1 Corinthians 12:12, "For as the body is one, and hath many members, and all the members of that one body, being many, are one body: so also is Christ." This passage

CHAPTER 37: BIBLICAL COMMUNITY LIFE

challenges the modern celebration of individualism by asserting that our individual roles in the church are not for personal fulfillment alone but for the edification of the whole body. Each believer's contribution is indispensable, reflecting the intricate design of the body of Christ.

In today's churches, the push towards individualism often manifests in how services are conducted, how messages are preached, and how church activities are organized. It's as though the service has turned into a spiritual buffet, where members pick what suits their taste, neglecting the communal dining table where the early church once sat together. Such a model starkly contrasts with the practice of the early believers who "continued steadfastly in the apostles' doctrine and fellowship, and in breaking of bread, and in prayers" (Acts 2:42). Their commitment was to a shared life, a unified pursuit of spiritual growth that naturally fostered a strong community.

To restore this biblical model of community, we must begin by realigning our church's focus from catering to individual preferences to fostering environments where spiritual relationships can thrive. True community life begins not when we gather to receive but when we gather to give, to support, and to build up one another. Galatians 6:2 instructs us, "Bear ye one another's burdens, and so fulfil the law of Christ." This mutual bearing of burdens is not just about offering emotional support; it's about creating a culture where every believer feels responsible for the spiritual welfare of their brothers and sisters.

One profound aspect often overlooked in the scriptural portrayal of community is the concept of accountability. In the Epistle of

James, we are encouraged to confess our faults to one another and to pray for each other so that we may be healed (James 5:16). This level of transparency and interdependence can seem daunting in a society that prizes privacy and independence, but it is a critical element of the life-changing community that scripture advocates. Accountability in the church fosters spiritual growth and prevents the isolation that can lead to spiritual decline.

Furthermore, the restoration of biblical community life also involves embracing the diversity within the body of Christ. Just as Paul celebrated the different gifts within the church, we too must learn to appreciate and integrate the varied contributions of all members. "But now hath God set the members every one of them in the body, as it hath pleased him" (1 Corinthians 12:18). Each person's unique abilities and spiritual gifts are not just for personal development but are intended to complement and strengthen the community. This diversity, when embraced, leads to a richer, more dynamic church life.

The call to community is also a call to radical love. Love is the ultimate mark of a disciple and the binding agent of community. Jesus said in John 13:35, "By this shall all men know that ye are my disciples, if ye have love one to another." Love motivates us to lay down our preferences, our time, and our resources for the benefit of others. It calls us out of isolation and into the beautiful, messy, and holy experience of shared life. In this love, the church finds its true expression, not as a collection of individuals pursuing personal spirituality but as a united body reflecting Christ's love to a broken world.

CHAPTER 37: BIBLICAL COMMUNITY LIFE

The modern shift towards individualism also affects how we view our participation in church life. Many treat church as a place to receive spiritual goods and services rather than a community where we invest ourselves. This consumer mentality stands in stark contrast to the sacrificial commitment seen in the early church. In Acts 4:32, we read, "And the multitude of them that believed were of one heart and of one soul: neither said any of them that ought of the things which he possessed was his own; but they had all things common." This passage exemplifies the depth of unity and selflessness that characterized the early believers.

Rebuilding this sense of community requires intentional effort. It starts with teaching and preaching that emphasize the biblical call to communal life. Leaders must model this commitment by being transparent, accessible, and deeply involved in the lives of their congregation. Church programs should facilitate not just attendance but meaningful connections. Small groups, mentorship programs, and service projects can all contribute to creating an environment where relationships flourish and spiritual growth is a collective journey.

The strength of a church community is often tested in times of crisis. When members face trials, the support of the church can be a powerful testament to the love of Christ. Romans 12:15 encourages us to "Rejoice with them that do rejoice, and weep with them that weep." This empathy and shared experience deepen bonds and demonstrate the practical outworking of our faith. A community that can stand together in joy and sorrow is a true reflection of the kingdom of God on earth.

Prayer is another foundational element of biblical community life. The early church was devoted to prayer, not just individually but corporately. Acts 1:14 tells us, "These all continued with one accord in prayer and supplication." Corporate prayer binds the community together, aligns their hearts with God's will, and invites the Holy Spirit's power into their midst. It is in these collective moments of seeking God that a church finds strength, direction, and unity.

Another crucial aspect of biblical community life is shared mission. The early church was united in their purpose to spread the gospel and serve others. This common mission gave them a sense of purpose and direction. Matthew 28:19-20, the Great Commission, is a call not just to individuals but to the church collectively. When a church embraces this shared mission, it transcends personal agendas and becomes a powerful force for the kingdom of God.

Forgiveness and reconciliation are also essential components of a healthy church community. Inevitably, conflicts and misunderstandings arise, but how we handle them can either strengthen or weaken our fellowship. Colossians 3:13 instructs us, "Forbearing one another, and forgiving one another, if any man have a quarrel against any: even as Christ forgave you, so also do ye." This practice of forgiveness fosters a culture of grace and humility, essential for maintaining unity.

Discipleship within the context of community is another vital practice. The Great Commission calls us to make disciples, and this process is deeply relational. 2 Timothy 2:2 describes this model: "And the things that thou hast heard of me among many

CHAPTER 37: BIBLICAL COMMUNITY LIFE

witnesses, the same commit thou to faithful men, who shall be able to teach others also." Discipleship in community allows for teaching, modeling, and mutual growth, ensuring that the faith is passed on robustly and effectively.

Generosity is a hallmark of biblical community life. The early church was known for its radical generosity, ensuring that no member was in need. Acts 4:34-35 recounts, "Neither was there any among them that lacked: for as many as were possessors of lands or houses sold them, and brought the prices of the things that were sold, and laid them down at the apostles' feet: and distribution was made unto every man according as he had need." This selfless sharing is a powerful witness to the world and a tangible expression of God's love.

The church is also called to be a place of healing and restoration. James 5:14-16 speaks to this, urging believers to pray for the sick and confess sins to one another for healing. This communal care reflects the heart of Jesus' ministry and creates an environment where people can experience God's grace and power. A community committed to healing and restoration becomes a beacon of hope and a safe haven for the broken.

Biblical community life is ultimately about embodying the kingdom of God on earth. It is a foretaste of the heavenly community we will one day fully experience. Revelation 7:9 paints a picture of this future reality: "After this I beheld, and, lo, a great multitude, which no man could number, of all nations, and kindreds, and people, and tongues, stood before the throne, and before the Lamb, clothed with white robes, and palms in their hands." Our church communities should reflect this diverse, unified worship and fellowship, giving the world a glimpse of God's eternal kingdom.

As we confront the trends of individualism in our churches, let us recall the profound interconnectedness that scripture lays out for us. Let us work towards restoring the biblical community life where every believer is actively engaged in the welfare, growth, and spiritual journey of one another. This is not merely an idealistic return to the past but a prophetic call to the future—a future where the church stands as a vibrant testament to the power of collective faith lived out in love and unity. This call to community is a call to live out our faith in the fullest expression of Christ's love, demonstrating to the world that we are His disciples.

Chapter 38: Restoring Community

Restoring community within the church is not just a lofty ideal; it is an essential return to the very heart of Christian faith. The apostle Paul vividly describes the church as the body of Christ in 1 Corinthians 12:12-27, emphasizing that every member is indispensable. When we understand this divine blueprint, we see that community is not optional. Each of us, regardless of our role or status, is a crucial part of this living, breathing body. The church flourishes when we embrace this interconnectedness, realizing that we are stronger together, supporting each other through the highs and lows of life.

Imagine a church where everyone truly feels like they belong, where every individual is valued and every contribution is recognized. This vision is not far-fetched. It mirrors the early church described in Acts 2:42-47, where believers devoted themselves to the apostles' teaching, to fellowship, to the breaking of bread, and to prayer. Their community life was marked by genuine care and mutual support, and the Lord added to their number daily those who were being saved. This model is not a relic of the past but a blueprint for the present. Our challenge is to recreate this vibrant, loving community in today's context, resisting the pull of individualism that isolates and divides.

One of the most profound aspects of community is the practice of bearing one another's burdens, as instructed in Galatians 6:2. This is not merely about solving each other's problems but about sharing the weight of life's challenges. When we come alongside each other in times of need, we fulfill the law of Christ, demonstrating

His love in tangible ways. It's in these moments of shared vulnerability and support that the true essence of community shines. We are not just fellow churchgoers; we are family, bound together by the love of Christ.

However, building such a community requires intentional effort. It demands that we move beyond superficial interactions and engage in meaningful relationships. In Romans 12:10, Paul urges us to be devoted to one another in love and to honor one another above ourselves. This devotion is more than a feeling; it is a commitment to prioritize others, to listen, to empathize, and to act in ways that demonstrate our love. True community is forged in the fires of everyday life, in the small acts of kindness and the sacrificial giving of our time and resources.

We must also be willing to create spaces where authentic relationships can flourish. Small groups or home fellowships are crucial in this regard. They provide a setting where people can share their lives more deeply, study Scripture together, and pray for one another. In these intimate gatherings, we experience the truth of Matthew 18:20, where Jesus promises that where two or three gather in His name, He is there with them. These small communities within the larger church body become the lifeblood of our fellowship, places where trust is built and faith is strengthened.

Restoring community also means embracing diversity within the body of Christ. Ephesians 2:14-16 reminds us that Christ has broken down the dividing wall of hostility, creating in Himself one new humanity. The church should reflect this divine unity in diversity, welcoming people from all backgrounds and walks of

CHAPTER 38: RESTORING COMMUNITY

life. This inclusivity is not merely a social nicety; it is a gospel imperative. By embracing our differences and valuing each person, we paint a vivid picture of the kingdom of God, where every tribe, tongue, and nation finds its place.

Discipleship plays a key role in fostering community. Older, more mature believers are called to mentor and guide younger ones, as outlined in Titus 2:3-5. This pattern of passing down wisdom and experience ensures that the faith is transmitted effectively across generations. It also creates a sense of belonging and purpose, as each member finds their place in the continuum of the church's life. Mentorship is not just about imparting knowledge; it is about walking alongside someone, sharing in their journey, and helping them grow into the fullness of Christ.

Moreover, the restoration of community involves a commitment to transparency and accountability. James 5:16 exhorts us to confess our sins to one another and pray for each other so that we may be healed. This level of openness fosters a culture of trust and support, where people feel safe to be honest about their struggles and failures. It's in this environment of grace and truth that genuine transformation happens. We are not perfect people pretending to have it all together; we are a community of broken individuals being healed and restored by the grace of God.

Celebration is another vital aspect of community life. Throughout the Psalms, we see calls to worship and rejoice together, as in Psalm 95:1-2, which invites us to come before the Lord with thanksgiving and extol Him with music and song. Celebrations within the church are not just social events; they are spiritual gatherings that remind us of God's goodness and faithfulness. They strengthen our bonds as we share in the joy of milestones, baptisms, and answered prayers. These moments of collective joy are essential for a vibrant and healthy community.

Service to others is a natural outflow of a restored community. In Matthew 25:40, Jesus teaches that whatever we do for the least of these, we do for Him. Our love for one another should extend beyond the walls of the church, reaching into our neighborhoods and beyond. Acts of service and compassion not only meet practical needs but also testify to the love of Christ in action. When we serve together, we strengthen our unity and fulfill our mission as the body of Christ, bringing His light to a world in need.

The journey to restoring community is not without its challenges. It requires perseverance and a willingness to confront the barriers that individualism has erected. But we are not alone in this endeavor. The Holy Spirit empowers us, guiding and equipping us to build the kind of community that reflects the heart of God. In John 17:21, Jesus prayed for His followers to be one, just as He and the Father are one. This unity is not a human achievement but a divine gift that we must steward and nurture.

Prayer is foundational to this process. In Colossians 4:2, we are instructed to devote ourselves to prayer, being watchful and thankful. Prayer unites us with God and with each other, aligning our hearts with His purposes and interceding for one another's needs. A praying community is a powerful community, rooted in the presence and guidance of the Holy Spirit. As we seek God's face together, we find the strength and wisdom needed to navigate the complexities of communal life.

Forgiveness is also essential for community restoration. In Ephesians 4:32, Paul urges us to be kind and compassionate to one another, forgiving each other just as in Christ God forgave us. Forgiveness breaks the chains of bitterness and resentment, allowing us to move forward in unity. It acknowledges the reality of hurt and betrayal but chooses to extend grace and seek reconciliation. A community that practices forgiveness reflects the redemptive love of Christ and paves the way for deeper, more meaningful relationships.

As we work towards restoring community, let us not forget the ultimate goal: to glorify God and make His name known. In John 13:35, Jesus said that by this everyone will know that we are His disciples if we love one another. Our love and unity are powerful testimonies to the world of the transforming power of the gospel. When the church lives out this calling, it becomes a beacon of hope and a place of refuge for those seeking truth and belonging.

In our pursuit of community, let us also embrace the simplicity and beauty of shared meals and fellowship, as depicted in Acts 2:46. Breaking bread together is a sacred act that fosters intimacy and connection. It allows us to slow down, share our stories, and build relationships in a relaxed and personal setting. These communal meals are more than just eating; they are opportunities to nurture our souls and deepen our bonds as brothers and sisters in Christ.

Let us also be mindful of the importance of encouragement. Hebrews 3:13 advises us to encourage one another daily, so that none of us may be hardened by sin's deceitfulness. Encouragement is the lifeblood of a thriving community. It lifts us up in times of doubt, strengthens us in times of trial, and propels us forward in our walk with God. A community that actively encourages one another creates an environment where faith can flourish and hope can be renewed.

The restoration of community is not a task for a select few; it is the responsibility of every member of the church. In 1 Peter 4:10, we are reminded that each of us should use whatever gift we have received to serve others, as faithful stewards of God's grace in its various forms. Every believer has a role to play in building up the body of Christ. When we each contribute our unique gifts and talents, we create a mosaic of grace that reflects the fullness of God's love and wisdom.

As we move forward, let us be inspired by the promise in Matthew 18:20, where Jesus assures us that where two or three gather in His name, He is there with them. This promise is a cornerstone of our community life. It reminds us that our efforts to restore community are not in vain. Christ Himself is present with us, empowering us, and blessing our endeavors. With His presence, we can overcome the challenges and build a community that truly honors Him.

In conclusion, the call to restore community within the church is a call to return to our roots, to the simple yet profound principles that define the body of Christ. It is a journey that requires dedication, humility, and a reliance on the Holy Spirit. But it is also a journey that brings immense joy and fulfillment as we see the church become a vibrant, loving, and united family. Let us embrace this call with passion and commitment, knowing that as we do, we fulfill the prayer of Jesus in John 17:21 and bring glory to our Heavenly Father.

Chapter 39: Scriptural Encouragement to Build a Strong Church Community

In today's fragmented world, where the pursuit of individualism often overshadows collective well-being, the church faces a profound challenge. This challenge extends beyond maintaining relevance; it is about cultivating a biblical community that mirrors the values and principles taught by Christ. Hebrews 10:24-25 urges us, "And let us consider one another to provoke unto love and to good works: Not forsaking the assembling of ourselves together, as the manner of some is; but exhorting one another: and so much the more, as ye see the day approaching." This passage serves as a powerful reminder of the necessity of gathering together—not just in physical spaces but in heart and purpose—to foster a community bound by love and committed to mutual encouragement.

Reflecting on this scripture, we see that the early church thrived on a model of mutual edification. Acts 2:46-47 describes the first Christians continuing daily with one accord in the temple, breaking bread from house to house, and eating their meat with gladness and singleness of heart, praising God and having favor with all the people. Here, the sense of community is palpable. It wasn't merely about being together; it was about being one in spirit, which propelled the church's influence and growth. This unity and communal approach is something modern churches can sometimes lose sight of amidst the drive towards personal spiritual achievements and self-focused faith journeys.

In our current context, the concept of individualism within the church has often led to isolated faith experiences where believers feel disconnected from one another. This isolation can diminish our collective strength in Christ. Galatians 6:2 teaches us to "Bear ye one another's burdens, and so fulfil the law of Christ." The law of Christ is fulfilled not in isolation but in community, through the love we show and the burdens we share. The church, therefore, must be a place where individuals feel intrinsically linked and responsible for each other's spiritual and emotional well-being.

The implications of embracing a true biblical community are vast. In a world where loneliness and individual struggles are rampant, the church offers a beacon of hope and connection. Romans 15:7, "Wherefore receive ye one another, as Christ also received us to the glory of God," underscores the call to acceptance and mutual support. By receiving each other—flaws and all—we mirror Christ's unconditional acceptance, fostering an environment where every member can grow and thrive.

Building a strong community means more than just encouraging attendance at services. It involves creating meaningful relationships that go beyond superficial interactions. Just as 1 Thessalonians 5:11 advises, "Wherefore comfort yourselves together, and edify one another, even as also ye do," our interactions should be nurturing, offering comfort and edification. This doesn't happen by accident but through intentional, thoughtful engagement with each other's lives. We are called to invest time, energy, and genuine care into the lives of our fellow believers, ensuring that no one walks their faith journey alone.

CHAPTER 39: SCRIPTURAL ENCOURAGEMENT TO BUILD A STRONG CHURCH COMMUNITY

Moreover, the challenge of fostering community over individualism is not merely about increasing numbers or filling pews; it's about deepening the spiritual connections that bind us as a body of believers. Ephesians 4:16 teaches us, "From whom the whole body fitly joined together and compacted by that which every joint supplieth, according to the effectual working in the measure of every part, maketh increase of the body unto the edifying of itself in love." This scripture paints a vivid picture of a church where each member contributes to the strength and growth of the whole. Each person's unique gifts and talents are essential, and their contributions are valued.

Confronting the spirit of individualism with the strength of community also involves recognizing the diverse gifts within a congregation. As 1 Corinthians 12:25-26 instructs, "That there should be no schism in the body; but that the members should have the same care one for another. And whether one member suffer, all the members suffer with it; or one member be honoured, all the members rejoice with it." In a truly integrated community, everyone's successes and struggles are shared, reflecting the interconnectedness that God intends for His church. This sense of shared experience fosters a deeper bond and a stronger, more resilient community.

The path to restoring a vibrant church community also means revisiting our worship practices to ensure they are not merely performances but times of genuine spiritual communion. John 4:24 says, "God is a Spirit: and they that worship him must worship him in spirit and in truth." This directive calls us to seek authenticity in our worship as a community, where every voice is valued, and every heart is engaged, not just those leading from the front. True worship involves the collective hearts of the congregation lifted together in praise and adoration of God, creating a powerful spiritual experience that unites us in His presence.

Furthermore, the concept of fellowship in the Bible goes beyond social gatherings. It speaks to a profound spiritual kinship. Acts 2:42 states, "And they continued stedfastly in the apostles' doctrine and fellowship, and in breaking of bread, and in prayers." This verse encapsulates the essence of Christian community—teaching, fellowship, breaking of bread, and prayer. Each element is crucial in building a strong and united church. Fellowship, in particular, is about sharing life together, supporting each other, and growing in faith collectively. It is about creating a space where believers can be vulnerable, share their struggles, and receive support and encouragement.

James 5:16 adds another layer to this community dynamic: "Confess your faults one to another, and pray one for another, that ye may be healed. The effectual fervent prayer of a righteous man availeth much." Confession and prayer are powerful tools in building a transparent and supportive community. By confessing our faults to one another, we build trust and openness, fostering a culture of accountability and mutual growth. Praying for one another strengthens these bonds and brings collective healing and spiritual fortitude.

The apostle Paul, in his letters, often highlighted the importance of unity and harmony within the church. Philippians 2:2-3 exhorts, "Fulfil ye my joy, that ye be likeminded, having the same love, being of one accord, of one mind. Let nothing be done through

CHAPTER 39: SCRIPTURAL ENCOURAGEMENT TO BUILD A STRONG CHURCH COMMUNITY

strife or vainglory; but in lowliness of mind let each esteem other better than themselves." This call to unity is a reminder that our actions within the church should always be driven by love and humility. Esteeming others above ourselves creates a selfless community focused on serving each other and glorifying God.

Another vital aspect of fostering a strong church community is mentorship and discipleship. Titus 2:3-4 instructs, "The aged women likewise, that they be in behaviour as becometh holiness, not false accusers, not given to much wine, teachers of good things; That they may teach the young women to be sober, to love their husbands, to love their children." Mentorship bridges generational gaps and ensures that wisdom and faith are passed down, nurturing the next generation in their walk with Christ. This relational dynamic strengthens the church as a whole, creating a continuous cycle of learning and growth.

Hospitality is another cornerstone of biblical community. Romans 12:13 encourages us to be "Distributing to the necessity of saints; given to hospitality." Opening our homes and hearts to one another builds trust and deepens relationships. It allows us to share our lives more intimately, breaking down barriers and fostering a sense of belonging. Hospitality is not just about entertaining; it's about creating a welcoming environment where people feel loved, valued, and part of a family.

In Galatians 3:28, Paul emphasizes the inclusivity of the church: "There is neither Jew nor Greek, there is neither bond nor free, there is neither male nor female: for ye are all one in Christ Jesus." This radical inclusivity must be reflected in our church communities today. Every believer, regardless of their background, status, or gender, should feel equally valued and included. This unity in diversity is a powerful testimony to the world of the transformative power of the gospel.

Moreover, the unity of the church is a testament to the world of God's love. John 13:35 states, "By this shall all men know that ye are my disciples, if ye have love one to another." The love we exhibit within our church community is a witness to others. It is through our love and unity that the world will see the reality of Christ's message. A divided church cannot effectively witness to a divided world; only through unity can we demonstrate the transformative power of God's love.

The strength of a church community is also seen in how it supports its members during times of need. 1 John 3:17 challenges us, "But whoso hath this world's good, and seeth his brother have need, and shutteth up his bowels of compassion from him, how dwelleth the love of God in him?" Genuine community means being attuned to each other's needs and being willing to act in love and compassion. It's about more than just spiritual support; it's about practical, tangible expressions of care and generosity.

Jesus Himself modeled perfect community with His disciples. He shared His life with them, taught them, corrected them, and loved them deeply. In John 15:15, He says, "Henceforth I call you not servants; for the servant knoweth not what his lord doeth: but I have called you friends; for all things that I have heard of my Father I have made known unto you." This friendship and openness exemplify the depth of relationship we should strive for in our church communities. Jesus' example teaches us that

CHAPTER 39: SCRIPTURAL ENCOURAGEMENT TO BUILD A STRONG CHURCH COMMUNITY

community involves sharing not just our victories but also our struggles and failures.

In considering the future of our church communities, let us be guided by the wisdom of Colossians 3:16, "Let the word of Christ dwell in you richly in all wisdom; teaching and admonishing one another in psalms and hymns and spiritual songs, singing with grace in your hearts to the Lord." This scripture not only invites us to keep Christ's word at the center of our interactions but also to express our faith communally through worship that uplifts and educates. The power of a community united in worship cannot be overstated. It creates an atmosphere where the Holy Spirit can move freely, bringing healing, inspiration, and growth.

By embracing these scriptural truths and recommitting to the biblical model of community, our churches can counter the prevailing winds of individualism and become, once again, places of profound fellowship and transformative spiritual power. This is not just a nostalgic return to the past but a necessary advance toward a future where the church stands as a true community, united in Christ and effective in its mission. The journey towards a vibrant, scripturally-grounded community is ongoing, requiring dedication, humility, and love. As we move forward, let us do so with the assurance that in fostering true biblical community, we are fulfilling God's design for His church and making His love visible to the world.

Chapter 40: Success Stories

In the journey to restore the vibrant life of church community against the encroaching shadows of individualism, let us turn our attention to some inspiring success stories. These narratives not only offer hope but serve as beacons, guiding us back to the biblical model of fellowship and mutual edification. Take, for instance, the vibrant community of Brookdale Church, a place where Hebrews 10:24-25—"And let us consider one another to provoke unto love and to good works: Not forsaking the assembling of ourselves together, as the manner of some is; but exhorting one another: and so much the more, as ye see the day approaching"—is lived out with heartfelt sincerity. At Brookdale, every member is deeply engaged in one another's lives, from sharing meals to sharing burdens, reflecting the early church's spirit where believers held all things in common and grew daily in faith together.

Brookdale's success hinges on its small group ministries, which are more than just weekly meetings; they are a family system. Each group operates on the principle found in Acts 2:46, "And they, continuing daily with one accord in the temple, and breaking bread from house to house, did eat their meat with gladness and singleness of heart." The result? A community where isolation is dispelled by the warmth of genuine relationships and shared purpose. These small groups have become a fundamental building block for the church, fostering an environment where every voice is heard and every heart is nurtured.

CHAPTER 40: SUCCESS STORIES

Then there is the story of Summit Life Church, which triumphantly models the integration of diverse cultures and backgrounds into a harmonious community. Here, Galatians 3:28 comes alive: "There is neither Jew nor Greek, there is neither bond nor free, there is neither male nor female: for ye are all one in Christ Jesus." Summit Life celebrates this divine tapestry by hosting multicultural worship services and community festivals that showcase the beauty of its congregation's varied heritages, promoting understanding and appreciation among its members. Their approach not only enriches their worship experience but also strengthens the bonds of fellowship, making it a sanctuary of acceptance and love.

At the heart of these success stories is the commitment to biblical principles of community. For example, Valley Fellowship focuses intensely on the command of 1 Thessalonians 5:11, "Wherefore comfort yourselves together, and edify one another, even as also ye do." This church has developed a robust support network where experienced believers mentor new followers, creating a nurturing environment that encourages spiritual growth and personal development. Through these mentoring relationships, members experience firsthand the joy and strength that comes from walking together in faith, proving that the church is not just a gathering but a growing, thriving family.

Crossway Community Church provides yet another compelling example. Their outreach programs are based on Matthew 25:35-36, where Jesus calls us to feed the hungry, clothe the naked, and visit those in prison. Crossway has taken this call to heart, establishing numerous outreach initiatives that not only meet physical needs but also build deep, lasting connections within the community. These programs are not just about providing services; they are about creating spaces where people can come together, share their stories, and find a place of belonging. This active engagement in one another's lives is the essence of what it means to live out the gospel together.

The transformation seen in these communities is profound. They remind us that when we commit to living out the one-another commands of Scripture—like those found in Romans 12:10, "Be kindly affectioned one to another with brotherly love; in honour preferring one another;"—we witness the church not as an institution, but as a living organism, vibrant and dynamic. This transformation is not merely about adding numbers to church rolls but about deepening the quality of our collective faith and fellowship. It's about reviving the heart of what it means to be the Body of Christ.

Moreover, these stories teach us the importance of patience and persistence in building community. As in the case of Cedar Grove Community Church, their commitment to the principle of Isaiah 40:31—"But they that wait upon the LORD shall renew their strength; they shall mount up with wings as eagles; they shall run, and not be weary; and they shall walk, and not faint"—has allowed them to slowly, yet surely, build a community that reflects God's kingdom. Their journey was not without challenges, but their steadfast faith and commitment to God's timing have borne fruit in ways that exceed human expectations.

These examples serve not only as inspiration but as a call to action. They beckon us to rethink how we engage with our own church communities. Are we fostering environments where Ephesians 4:32—"And be ye kind one to another, tenderhearted, forgiving one another, even as God for Christ's sake hath forgiven you"—is the norm? Are we creating spaces where people feel valued, loved, and connected? If we aspire to see a revival of true biblical community in our churches, then these stories show us that it is not only possible, but it is imperative.

Consider the impact of Agape Church, where their focus on relational discipleship has transformed their congregation into a closely-knit family. Rooted in the words of John 13:35, "By this shall all men know that ye are my disciples, if ye have love one to another," Agape Church emphasizes love in action. Their discipleship program pairs new believers with seasoned saints who walk with them through life's challenges and victories. This mentorship has fostered deep, personal connections and cultivated a culture of mutual care and accountability, demonstrating the powerful impact of living out Christ's command to love one another.

The story of Harmony Baptist Church further illustrates the beauty of a community-centered church. Here, the guiding principle is found in Colossians 3:14-15, "And above all these things put on charity, which is the bond of perfectness. And let the peace of God rule in your hearts, to the which also ye are called in one body; and be ye thankful." Harmony Baptist has created various ministries that address the holistic needs of their members, from youth programs to senior care, ensuring that everyone feels included and valued. This intentional approach has cultivated an atmosphere of gratitude and peace, making the church a refuge for those seeking community and spiritual growth.

Another shining example is Grace Fellowship Church, which prioritizes prayer and intercession as the foundation of their community life. Echoing James 5:16, "Confess your faults one to another, and pray one for another, that ye may be healed. The effectual fervent prayer of a righteous man availeth much," Grace Fellowship has established prayer groups that meet regularly to intercede for the needs of the congregation and the community. These prayer groups have become lifelines for many, offering support and fostering deep spiritual bonds that transcend the superficial interactions often seen in larger congregations.

The impact of these success stories extends beyond the walls of the church, influencing the broader community as well. For instance, Faith Community Church's outreach initiatives, inspired by Acts 1:8, "But ye shall receive power, after that the Holy Ghost is come upon you: and ye shall be witnesses unto me both in Jerusalem, and in all Judaea, and in Samaria, and unto the uttermost part of the earth," have transformed their local community. Through acts of service, evangelism, and social justice, Faith Community has become a beacon of hope and a tangible representation of Christ's love in action. Their commitment to living out the Great Commission has drawn many to the faith, demonstrating the transformative power of a united and mission-focused church.

As we reflect on these narratives, let us be motivated to replicate such success in our own congregations. Let us be the church that does not merely grow in numbers but grows deeper in love, stronger in unity, and richer in diversity. May these stories inspire us to embrace the fullness of community life that God has envisioned for His church, where every member is cherished, and every relationship honors Him.

The testimony of Living Waters Church also offers valuable lessons. This congregation has embraced the principle of Philippians 2:3-4, "Let nothing be done through strife or vainglory; but in lowliness of mind let each esteem other better than themselves. Look not every man on his own things, but every man also on the things of others." By prioritizing humility and service, Living Waters has cultivated a culture where members actively seek to serve one another, creating an environment of mutual respect and support. Their approach has fostered a sense of belonging and unity that is palpable to anyone who walks through their doors.

These stories also remind us of the power of forgiveness and reconciliation in building strong communities. At New Hope Church, the teachings of Matthew 18:21-22, "Then came Peter to him, and said, Lord, how oft shall my brother sin against me, and I forgive him? till seven times? Jesus saith unto him, I say not unto thee, Until seven times: but, Until seventy times seven," have been foundational. New Hope has developed a ministry specifically focused on conflict resolution and reconciliation, helping members navigate interpersonal conflicts in a Christ-like manner. This emphasis on forgiveness has healed many wounds and restored relationships, strengthening the fabric of their community.

The dedication to continuous spiritual growth and discipleship is another common thread among these successful churches. At Cornerstone Fellowship, the focus on 2 Timothy 2:2, "And the things that thou hast heard of me among many witnesses, the same commit thou to faithful men, who shall be able to teach others also," has led to the establishment of a comprehensive discipleship program. This program encourages members to grow in their faith and equips them to disciple others, creating a multiplying effect that has profoundly impacted their community.

As we ponder these success stories, let us remember that the principles they embody are not beyond our reach. By committing to biblical community, prioritizing relationships, and fostering environments of mutual support and accountability, we can witness similar transformations in our own congregations. These stories are testaments to the power of the Holy Spirit working through believers who are dedicated to living out their faith in tangible ways.

Thus, my dear brothers and sisters, as we consider these success stories, let us renew our commitment to the biblical command in 1 Peter 3:8, "Finally, be ye all of one mind, having compassion one of another, love as brethren, be pitiful, be courteous." Let us strive to embody these virtues in our daily interactions and church activities. By doing so, we can ensure that our churches are not merely houses of worship but homes of enduring fellowship and love.

The journey to building strong, vibrant church communities is ongoing, but the rewards are immeasurable. As we follow the examples set by these successful churches, we can create spaces where individuals are not only welcomed but are deeply known and loved. Let us be inspired by their stories and challenged to cultivate communities that reflect the heart of God, where every member can thrive and grow in their faith.

These success stories provide a roadmap for us. They show us that with dedication, prayer, and a commitment to biblical principles, we can overcome the individualistic tendencies of our culture and build communities that honor God and support one another. As we seek to follow in their footsteps, let us do so with the assurance that God is with us, guiding and empowering us every step of the way.

In conclusion, the success stories of these churches remind us that true community is not a product of human effort alone but a work of the Holy Spirit. As we lean into His guidance and commit to living out His commands, we can witness the miraculous transformation of our churches into vibrant, loving communities that shine as beacons of hope in a dark world. Let us take up this mantle with courage and faith, knowing that in Him, all things are possible.

Section 9: The Influence of Culture on Church

Chapter 41: Cultural Trends vs. Eternal Truths

In today's fast-paced world, the church finds itself at a critical crossroads, caught between the enduring truths of scripture and the shifting sands of cultural trends. As believers, we must carefully discern our path, ensuring that our practices are rooted in the eternal, unchanging word of God rather than the fleeting preferences of society. The Apostle Paul reminds us in Romans 12:2, "And be not conformed to this world: but be ye transformed by the renewing of your mind, that ye may prove what is that good, and acceptable, and perfect, will of God." This scripture is not merely a suggestion; it's a divine directive to resist the pressure to conform to worldly standards and instead pursue transformation through Christ.

The influence of modern culture on the church is pervasive and often subtle, making it all the more dangerous. We see trends that promote a gospel of convenience and comfort, which starkly contrasts with the challenging truths Christ presented in His teachings. Jesus Himself declared in Matthew 7:14, "Because strait is the gate, and narrow is the way, which leadeth unto life, and few there be that find it." The reality is that the gospel is not meant to be comfortable or convenient; it is meant to transform us, which often means going against the grain of contemporary culture.

Moreover, the pursuit of cultural relevance can lead churches to compromise on scriptural truths. In the quest to be 'relevant,' many have embraced doctrines that align more with societal norms than with biblical teachings. This is not a new challenge. The early church faced similar pressures but was admonished by the Apostle Peter, who wrote in 1 Peter 1:14, "As obedient children, not fashioning yourselves according to the former lusts in your ignorance." We are called to be set apart, maintaining our distinctiveness as followers of Christ in a world that often stands in opposition to His teachings.

It is crucial, then, for church leaders and believers alike to critically evaluate how culture might be shaping our understanding and expression of the gospel. The church must serve as the pillar and ground of the truth, as stated in 1 Timothy 3:15. This role is not passive; it involves active engagement and sometimes resistance to cultural influences that do not align with biblical principles. Our mission is not to reflect the culture but to influence it, to be light and salt in a world that desperately needs the savory truth of the gospel and the bright hope of Christ's love.

In engaging with culture, we must do so from a position of strength, grounded in our understanding of scripture. The wisdom of Proverbs 4:23 exhorts us, "Keep thy heart with all diligence; for out of it are the issues of life." Our engagement must not lead to our assimilation but rather should come from a heart firmly anchored in scriptural truth, ensuring that we do not drift away from the core of our faith.

The challenge is significant, as cultural pressures are not only external but often arise within the congregation. Believers influenced by worldly perspectives may advocate for a church that mirrors these views, rather than one that transforms them through the gospel. Here, the wisdom of Ephesians 4:14 becomes pertinent:

CHAPTER 41: CULTURAL TRENDS VS. ETERNAL TRUTHS

"That we henceforth be no more children, tossed to and fro, and carried about with every wind of doctrine, by the sleight of men, and cunning craftiness, whereby they lie in wait to deceive." Stability in our doctrinal foundation enables us to weather the storms of cultural change without capsizing.

This stability comes from a deep, abiding knowledge of God's word and a commitment to prayer. The Psalmist declared in Psalm 119:11, "Thy word have I hid in mine heart, that I might not sin against thee." By embedding scripture in our hearts and minds, we build a bulwark against the encroachment of cultural norms that conflict with biblical directives. Our defense against cultural assimilation is not ignorance of cultural trends but an intimate knowledge of God and His statutes.

Furthermore, in our dialogue with the world around us, we must be wise as serpents and harmless as doves, as instructed by Jesus in Matthew 10:16. This means engaging with culture thoughtfully and respectfully, presenting the truth in love but also with unwavering clarity. We are ambassadors for Christ, tasked with representing Him faithfully in every interaction, whether it challenges cultural norms or not.

In the age of social media and digital communication, the pressure to conform to cultural trends has intensified. Churches are now more visible than ever, and the temptation to curate an image that aligns with popular culture is strong. Yet, we must remember the words of Galatians 1:10, "For do I now persuade men, or God? or do I seek to please men? for if I yet pleased men, I should not be the servant of Christ." Our primary allegiance is to Christ and His teachings, not to the shifting opinions of the world.

The allure of cultural acceptance can lead to a subtle but dangerous erosion of doctrinal purity. When churches prioritize cultural relevance over scriptural fidelity, they risk losing the transformative power of the gospel. Jesus warned in Matthew 15:9, "But in vain they do worship me, teaching for doctrines the commandments of men." True worship and faithful teaching must always be grounded in the unchanging truth of God's word, not the ever-changing trends of society.

This erosion can manifest in various ways, from the dilution of difficult truths to the outright rejection of biblical principles that conflict with contemporary values. The Apostle Paul foresaw this, warning in 2 Timothy 4:3-4, "For the time will come when they will not endure sound doctrine; but after their own lusts shall they heap to themselves teachers, having itching ears; And they shall turn away their ears from the truth, and shall be turned unto fables." This prophetic warning is a sobering reminder of the importance of holding fast to sound doctrine, even when it is unpopular.

It is not enough to simply resist cultural trends; we must actively cultivate a culture within the church that is rooted in biblical truth. This requires intentional discipleship and teaching that equips believers to discern truth from error. Colossians 2:8 warns, "Beware lest any man spoil you through philosophy and vain deceit, after the tradition of men, after the rudiments of the world, and not after Christ." Our teaching must always point back to Christ and His teachings, providing a firm foundation upon which believers can stand.

One of the most insidious effects of cultural influence is the temptation to measure success by worldly standards. Churches

CHAPTER 41: CULTURAL TRENDS VS. ETERNAL TRUTHS

may be tempted to prioritize numerical growth, financial prosperity, and social influence over spiritual depth and faithfulness to the gospel. Jesus addressed this in Mark 8:36, "For what shall it profit a man, if he shall gain the whole world, and lose his own soul?" The true measure of a church's success is not found in its size or wealth but in its faithfulness to Christ and its commitment to making disciples.

As we navigate these cultural pressures, it is essential to remain anchored in the truth of God's word. Hebrews 4:12 reminds us, "For the word of God is quick, and powerful, and sharper than any twoedged sword, piercing even to the dividing asunder of soul and spirit, and of the joints and marrow, and is a discerner of the thoughts and intents of the heart." The word of God is our ultimate authority, guiding us in truth and exposing the lies of the enemy.

Engaging with culture from a biblical perspective does not mean disengaging from the world. On the contrary, it means engaging thoughtfully and intentionally, bringing the light of Christ into every sphere of influence. Jesus prayed in John 17:15, "I pray not that thou shouldest take them out of the world, but that thou shouldest keep them from the evil." We are called to be in the world but not of it, living out our faith in a way that testifies to the transformative power of the gospel.

This call to engage with culture from a position of strength requires courage and conviction. It means standing firm in our faith even when it is unpopular or countercultural. The Apostle Paul exemplified this courage in 2 Timothy 1:7, "For God hath not given us the spirit of fear; but of power, and of love, and of a sound mind." We must rely on the Holy Spirit to empower us, to give us the boldness to speak the truth in love and the wisdom to navigate the complexities of our cultural moment.

In this endeavor, prayer is our greatest ally. Ephesians 6:18 exhorts us, "Praying always with all prayer and supplication in the Spirit, and watching thereunto with all perseverance and supplication for all saints." Through prayer, we seek God's guidance, strength, and discernment, ensuring that our engagement with culture is led by the Spirit and grounded in His word.

The ultimate goal of our engagement with culture is to glorify God and advance His kingdom. Matthew 5:16 instructs us, "Let your light so shine before men, that they may see your good works, and glorify your Father which is in heaven." Our lives and our churches should be a testament to the power and grace of God, drawing others to Him through our witness.

As we reflect on the cultural trends that influence the church, let us commit to holding fast to the eternal truths of scripture. Let us be vigilant in guarding against the subtle encroachments of worldly values and steadfast in our dedication to the teachings of Christ. Philippians 4:8 provides a powerful guideline for our thoughts and actions: "Finally, brethren, whatsoever things are true, whatsoever things are honest, whatsoever things are just, whatsoever things are pure, whatsoever things are lovely, whatsoever things are of good report; if there be any virtue, and if there be any praise, think on these things." By focusing on these virtues, we align ourselves with God's will and stand firm against the shifting tides of culture.

In conclusion, dear reader, as we navigate the intersection of cultural trends and eternal truths, let us be anchored in the word of

God. Let us resist the temptation to conform to the world and instead be transformed by the renewing of our minds. Let us engage with culture thoughtfully and intentionally, always pointing back to Christ and His teachings. And let us do so with courage, conviction, and an unwavering commitment to the truth of the gospel. For in doing so, we fulfill our calling as followers of Christ, shining His light in a world that desperately needs His truth.

Chapter 42: Scriptural Integrity

In the midst of an ever-evolving cultural landscape, maintaining scriptural integrity is a vital endeavor for the modern church. The pressures to conform to societal norms and to gain cultural relevance can often lead to compromises that dilute the powerful truths of Scripture. Yet, as we navigate these challenges, we must remain steadfast in our commitment to uphold the divine truths entrusted to us. The Apostle Paul's exhortation in Romans 12:2 resonates profoundly: "And be not conformed to this world: but be ye transformed by the renewing of your mind, that ye may prove what is that good, and acceptable, and perfect, will of God." This verse calls us not only to personal transformation but also to a corporate identity that resists the pressures of cultural conformity, standing firm in the immutable Word of God.

As the church, our engagement with the world should be marked by a clear distinction between embracing cultural practices that align with biblical principles and rejecting those that contradict the teachings of Scripture. The allure of adapting to cultural trends for the sake of relevance and growth is strong, but such adaptations can come at the expense of our core beliefs. In 2 Timothy 3:16-17, we are reminded, "All scripture is given by inspiration of God, and is profitable for doctrine, for reproof, for correction, for instruction in righteousness: That the man of God may be perfect, thoroughly furnished unto all good works." These verses underscore that Scripture is not a mere historical document but the living, breathing Word of God, designed to guide us through every cultural challenge.

CHAPTER 42: SCRIPTURAL INTEGRITY

Jesus Himself provides a profound perspective on engaging with the world without compromising our faith. In John 17:15-16, He prays, "I pray not that thou shouldest take them out of the world, but that thou shouldest keep them from the evil. They are not of the world, even as I am not of the world." This prayer highlights that while we are in the world, we are not of it. We are called to be distinct, to stand apart from the cultural currents that seek to undermine our faith. Our task is to engage with the world, to influence it for Christ, without allowing it to shape our beliefs and practices contrary to God's Word.

Engagement without compromise requires a discerning spirit, one that critically evaluates cultural influences through the lens of Scripture. When societal movements and trends promote values or ideologies that conflict with biblical teachings, our response should be grounded in love yet firm in truth. The Apostle Paul's words in Ephesians 4:14-15 guide us in this delicate balance: "That we henceforth be no more children, tossed to and fro, and carried about with every wind of doctrine, by the sleight of men, and cunning craftiness, whereby they lie in wait to deceive; But speaking the truth in love, may grow up into him in all things, which is the head, even Christ." We are called to speak the truth in love, to be mature in our faith, and to avoid being swayed by deceptive doctrines.

Maintaining scriptural integrity also means fostering environments within our churches where open and honest conversations about culture and doctrine can occur. These discussions are essential for addressing sensitive issues such as social justice, political involvement, and moral ethics in a way that is faithful to Scripture.

James 1:5 reassures us of divine guidance in these endeavors: "If any of you lack wisdom, let him ask of God, that giveth to all men liberally, and upbraideth not; and it shall be given him." We are promised wisdom from above, wisdom that equips us to navigate complex cultural issues with clarity and godly insight.

As leaders and shepherds of God's flock, it is our responsibility to educate and equip our congregations to discern cultural influences that may subtly undermine biblical truths. This is especially crucial for young believers and new converts who may be more susceptible to the allure of cultural acceptance. 1 Peter 5:2-3 instructs us, "Feed the flock of God which is among you, taking the oversight thereof, not by constraint, but willingly; not for filthy lucre, but of a ready mind; Neither as being lords over God's heritage, but being ensamples to the flock." This passage calls us to lead by example, to nurture our congregations with sound doctrine, and to protect them from the encroachments of worldly philosophies.

In a world where cultural trends are constantly shifting, the church must anchor itself in the unchanging Word of God. The teachings of Jesus, the apostles, and the prophets provide a timeless foundation that transcends cultural fads and societal shifts. In Matthew 24:35, Jesus assures us, "Heaven and earth shall pass away, but my words shall not pass away." This promise is a testament to the enduring nature of God's Word, a solid rock upon which we can build our lives and ministries, regardless of the cultural storms that may arise.

Scriptural integrity also involves a commitment to truth over popularity. The temptation to water down the gospel to make it

CHAPTER 42: SCRIPTURAL INTEGRITY

more palatable to a broader audience is a significant challenge facing the church today. However, our calling is to proclaim the full counsel of God, even when it is countercultural or unpopular. In Galatians 1:10, Paul writes, "For do I now persuade men, or God? or do I seek to please men? for if I yet pleased men, I should not be the servant of Christ." Our allegiance must be to God and His truth, not to the approval of men.

One of the critical areas where the church must maintain scriptural integrity is in its approach to moral and ethical issues. Cultural shifts in views on sexuality, marriage, and family life challenge the church to uphold biblical standards while showing Christ-like love and compassion. The Bible provides clear guidance on these matters, and we are called to stand firm in these truths. Ephesians 5:31-32 reminds us of the sanctity of marriage: "For this cause shall a man leave his father and mother, and shall be joined unto his wife, and they two shall be one flesh. This is a great mystery: but I speak concerning Christ and the church." Upholding these truths requires courage and conviction, particularly in a culture that often promotes contrary views.

As we strive to maintain scriptural integrity, we must also be vigilant in our personal lives, ensuring that our actions align with our professed beliefs. Hypocrisy within the church undermines our witness to the world and weakens our credibility. Jesus' rebuke of the Pharisees in Matthew 23:27 serves as a sobering reminder: "Woe unto you, scribes and Pharisees, hypocrites! for ye are like unto whited sepulchres, which indeed appear beautiful outward, but are within full of dead men's bones, and of all uncleanness."

Authenticity in our walk with God is crucial for maintaining the integrity of our witness.

Furthermore, scriptural integrity involves a commitment to the unity of the body of Christ. In an age of division and polarization, the church must be a model of unity and love. Paul's appeal in 1 Corinthians 1:10 is particularly relevant: "Now I beseech you, brethren, by the name of our Lord Jesus Christ, that ye all speak the same thing, and that there be no divisions among you; but that ye be perfectly joined together in the same mind and in the same judgment." Our unity is rooted in our shared commitment to the truth of Scripture, and it is this unity that will enable us to stand firm against cultural pressures.

The influence of culture on the church is an ongoing challenge that requires constant vigilance and discernment. As we engage with the world, we must do so with a firm grasp of the truths of Scripture, allowing them to guide our actions and decisions. In Psalm 119:105, we are reminded, "Thy word is a lamp unto my feet, and a light unto my path." The Word of God illuminates our way, helping us to navigate the complexities of modern culture without compromising our faith.

In addition to discernment, maintaining scriptural integrity requires a deep and abiding love for God's Word. Our commitment to Scripture must be more than intellectual assent; it must be a heartfelt devotion that shapes every aspect of our lives. The psalmist's words in Psalm 119:11 capture this devotion: "Thy word have I hid in mine heart, that I might not sin against thee." When God's Word is treasured in our hearts, it influences our thoughts, words, and actions, enabling us to live in a way that honors Him.

CHAPTER 42: SCRIPTURAL INTEGRITY

As we reflect on the need for scriptural integrity, it is essential to remember that we do not stand alone in this endeavor. We are part of a global body of believers, united by our faith in Christ and our commitment to His Word. Hebrews 10:24-25 encourages us to support one another in this journey: "And let us consider one another to provoke unto love and to good works: Not forsaking the assembling of ourselves together, as the manner of some is; but exhorting one another: and so much the more, as ye see the day approaching." Together, we can hold each other accountable, encourage one another, and stand firm in our commitment to the truths of Scripture.

In conclusion, maintaining scriptural integrity in the face of cultural pressure is a challenging but essential task for the church. As we engage with the world, we must do so with a firm commitment to the unchanging truths of God's Word, allowing them to guide our actions and decisions. This commitment requires discernment, courage, and a deep love for Scripture. By standing firm in our faith and upholding the truths of God's Word, we can influence the world for Christ without compromising our beliefs. Let us move forward with confidence, knowing that our labor in the Lord is not in vain, and that His Word will endure forever.

Chapter 43: Strategies for Resistance

In "Chapter 43: Strategies for Resistance" of our exploration of the cultural influences on the church, we embark on a journey to safeguard our faith against the subtle yet pervasive encroachments of secular values. The world's relentless push to conform can often lead the church away from its divine mandate. As we confront these challenges, we are reminded of Romans 12:2, which commands us not to conform to this world but to be transformed by the renewing of our minds. This transformation is not just a personal endeavor but a communal call to action, urging the church to steadfastly uphold its principles amidst the shifting sands of societal norms.

Resisting cultural assimilation requires a discernment deeply rooted in Scripture. We must engage with the world through a lens crafted by the Word of God, evaluating every cultural message and movement against the backdrop of biblical truth. The Apostle Paul's counsel in 1 Thessalonians 5:21 to test everything and hold on to what is good becomes our guiding principle. This testing is not a passive exercise but an active, prayerful examination of what aligns with Scripture and what does not. It ensures that our engagement with the world does not dilute our commitment to Christ's teachings but instead reinforces it.

This discernment is further strengthened by a culture of biblical literacy within the church. Empowering believers with a deep and comprehensive knowledge of Scripture acts as a safeguard against the subtle infiltrations of secular ideologies. Just as Jesus countered the devil's temptations by quoting Scripture (Matthew

CHAPTER 43: STRATEGIES FOR RESISTANCE

4:1-11), we too must equip ourselves and our fellow believers with the ability to respond to cultural pressures with biblical truth. This approach not only fortifies our individual faith but also solidifies the collective resolve of our church community.

Moreover, we must cultivate robust Christian fellowship that encourages accountability and mutual support. Hebrews 10:24-25 reminds us to consider how to spur one another on toward love and good deeds, not giving up meeting together, but encouraging one another. In a culture that often promotes individualism and self-gratification, the biblical model of community challenges us to live out our faith collectively and sacrificially, providing a stark contrast to the prevailing ethos of society. This fellowship acts as a haven where believers can support one another in resisting cultural conformity.

Engagement rather than isolation is also crucial. While it might seem counterintuitive, engaging with the culture provides opportunities to demonstrate the transformative power of the gospel. As Christ's ambassadors, we are called to be in the world, sharing the hope and truth of Jesus (John 17:15-18). This engagement should be strategic and intentional, focusing on areas where the gospel can shine its light into the darkness. By being present in various cultural arenas—whether in media, arts, education, or politics—we can influence these spaces with the truth of Christ, rather than retreating from them.

Our engagement must be accompanied by prayer. Every strategy and action must be steeped in prayer, aligning our hearts with God's will and empowering us with His Spirit. Ephesians 6:18 urges us to pray in the Spirit on all occasions with all kinds of prayers and requests. Prayer is the engine of our resistance, providing strength and wisdom to stand firm against cultural pressures while remaining effective witnesses of Christ's kingdom. It is through prayer that we receive the guidance and power necessary to navigate the complexities of cultural engagement.

In implementing these strategies, we must cultivate a spirit of grace and truth. As Jesus exemplified, we are to love truthfully and engage graciously (John 1:14). Our resistance to cultural conformity should not alienate those we are called to reach; rather, it should invite them into a deeper understanding of the joy and freedom found in following Christ. This dual commitment to grace and truth will guide our interactions, ensuring that our engagement is both loving and uncompromising in its adherence to biblical principles.

Remaining steadfast in our hope and trust in God's sovereignty is another crucial aspect of our resistance. The cultural tides will shift, but the Lord remains the same yesterday, today, and forever (Hebrews 13:8). This eternal perspective helps us resist despair and maintain our joy and hope, knowing that our labor in the Lord is not in vain. Our ultimate victory is secured in Christ, and this truth should motivate our every effort to resist cultural assimilation.

Building a strong, counter-cultural identity within the church is also essential. This identity should be rooted in our shared beliefs, values, and practices as followers of Christ. By fostering a sense of belonging and purpose within the church, we create an environment where believers are encouraged to stand firm in their faith. This identity acts as a buffer against the pressures to conform, providing a clear and compelling vision of what it means to live as citizens of God's kingdom.

Another key strategy is to emphasize the importance of personal holiness. In a culture that often blurs the lines between right and wrong, the call to be holy as God is holy (1 Peter 1:16) is more relevant than ever. Personal holiness involves a commitment to live according to God's standards in every area of our lives. It requires us to be vigilant against the subtle influences that can lead us away from God's will. By prioritizing holiness, we set ourselves apart from the world and reflect the character of Christ to those around us.

Equipping believers with apologetics is another vital strategy. Apologetics provides the tools to defend our faith against the intellectual challenges posed by secular ideologies. 1 Peter 3:15 encourages us to always be prepared to give an answer to everyone who asks us to give the reason for the hope that we have. This readiness involves understanding the core tenets of our faith and being able to articulate them clearly and confidently. Apologetics empowers us to engage in meaningful conversations with those who hold different worldviews, demonstrating the rational and compelling nature of the Christian faith.

Fostering a culture of discipleship within the church is also critical. Discipleship involves mentoring and nurturing believers to grow in their faith and live out their calling. This process is relational and transformative, helping believers to become more like Christ in their thoughts, actions, and attitudes. Matthew 28:19-20 commands us to make disciples of all nations, teaching them to obey everything Jesus has commanded us. By prioritizing discipleship, we create a strong foundation for spiritual growth and maturity, equipping believers to resist cultural pressures and stand firm in their faith.

Encouraging believers to pursue their God-given purpose is another effective strategy. Each of us has been uniquely gifted and called by God to fulfill a specific role within His kingdom. Ephesians 2:10 reminds us that we are God's handiwork, created in Christ Jesus to do good works, which God prepared in advance for us to do. By helping believers to discover and pursue their purpose, we empower them to live with intention and impact, contributing to the overall mission of the church and resisting the pull of cultural conformity.

In addition to these strategies, it is essential to foster a culture of worship that is centered on God. Worship is a powerful expression of our love and devotion to God, and it serves as a reminder of His greatness and goodness. John 4:24 tells us that true worshipers will worship the Father in spirit and truth. By cultivating a culture of genuine worship, we create an atmosphere where believers are continually reminded of God's presence and power, strengthening their resolve to live for Him and resist the influences of the world.

Another important aspect of our resistance is to engage in acts of service and compassion. Jesus taught us that the greatest among us would be those who serve (Matthew 20:26-28). By serving others and demonstrating Christ's love in practical ways, we embody the gospel and challenge the self-centered values of our culture. Service and compassion not only impact those we serve but also deepen our own faith and commitment to living out the gospel.

CHAPTER 43: STRATEGIES FOR RESISTANCE

Maintaining a prophetic voice is also crucial in our resistance. The prophets of the Old Testament were called to speak God's truth to a wayward people, often confronting the cultural norms and practices of their time. Similarly, the church today must be willing to speak out against the injustices and moral failures of our society. This prophetic voice should be rooted in love and truth, offering a vision of God's kingdom that challenges the status quo and calls people to repentance and renewal.

As we navigate these strategies, we must remember that our ultimate goal is to glorify God in all that we do. Colossians 3:17 exhorts us to do everything in the name of the Lord Jesus, giving thanks to God the Father through Him. This focus on God's glory helps to keep our motives pure and our actions aligned with His will. It reminds us that our resistance to cultural conformity is not just about maintaining our own integrity but about honoring God and advancing His kingdom.

Lastly, we must remain vigilant and persevere in our resistance. The pressures to conform will not cease, and the challenges we face may become more intense. However, we are reminded in Galatians 6:9 not to become weary in doing good, for at the proper time we will reap a harvest if we do not give up. Our perseverance is a testimony to our faith and trust in God, and it serves as an encouragement to others who are also striving to live faithfully in a challenging world.

In summary, the strategies for resisting cultural assimilation are multi-faceted and require a concerted effort from the entire church community. By grounding ourselves in Scripture, fostering a culture of biblical literacy, engaging in robust fellowship, and equipping believers with the tools they need to stand firm, we can navigate the cultural currents without losing our distinctiveness. As we do so, let us remain steadfast in our hope and trust in God's sovereignty, knowing that He is faithful and will sustain us as we seek to honor Him in all that we do.

Chapter 44: Scriptural Guidance on Cultural Influence

In "Church Gone Wild: A Call to Renewal and Restoration," we delve into the profound implications of cultural influence on the church and the paramount importance of adhering to scriptural guidance to navigate these turbulent waters. Romans 12:2 speaks directly to our situation today, urging us not to conform to this world but to be transformed by the renewing of our minds, so that we may prove what is that good and acceptable and perfect will of God. This transformation is not merely an individual endeavor but a collective necessity for the body of Christ to remain steadfast in its divine mission.

The modern church finds itself at a crossroads, often tempted to adopt worldly methods and ideologies to increase its appeal and relevance. Yet, as faithful stewards of Christ's teachings, we must remember our primary call is to influence culture rather than be influenced by it. The Apostle Paul's challenge in 1 Corinthians 1:20-21 is as relevant today as it was then: "Where is the wise? Where is the scribe? Where is the disputer of this age? Hath not God made foolish the wisdom of this world?" This rhetorical question underscores the futility of seeking approval from a world whose wisdom is often at odds with God's truth.

Engaging with culture does not necessitate isolation or withdrawal; rather, it requires a transformed perspective. We are called to be in the world but not of it. Jesus' prayer in John 17:15-16 encapsulates this dual reality: "I pray not that thou shouldest take them out of the world, but that thou shouldest keep them from the evil. They are not of the world, even as I am not of the world." This divine intercession highlights our mission to be lights in a dark world, illuminating the path to salvation through our distinctiveness, not through conformity.

Our engagement with culture must be strategic and intentional. Philippians 2:15 encourages us to be blameless and harmless, children of God without fault in the midst of a crooked and perverse generation, shining as lights in the world. This scripture calls us to more than mere moral excellence; it compels us to be beacons of hope and truth in a world that desperately needs both. Our distinctiveness should be evident, characterized by love, peace, and unwavering adherence to truth, thus drawing others to Christ through the compelling contrast we present to worldly norms.

Cultural engagement must be approached with wisdom and discernment. Colossians 2:8 warns us: "Beware lest any man spoil you through philosophy and vain deceit, after the tradition of men, after the rudiments of the world, and not after Christ." In a culture that often exalts self and marginalizes God, it is imperative that we anchor our actions and decisions in the teachings of Christ. Our engagement with culture should not signify a departure from our faith but rather a demonstration of it, highlighting the transformative power of living in alignment with God's Word.

Daniel's example in the Bible serves as a powerful illustration of maintaining faithfulness amidst cultural pressure. Daniel 1:8 recounts how Daniel resolved not to defile himself with the king's food and wine, seeking permission to avoid this cultural

CHAPTER 44: SCRIPTURAL GUIDANCE ON CULTURAL INFLUENCE

compromise. His commitment to his faith, even in a foreign land, stands as a testament to the power of unwavering adherence to God's commands over societal expectations. Daniel's story encourages us to prioritize spiritual integrity over cultural integration, demonstrating that faithfulness can lead to divine favor and influence.

The integrity displayed by Shadrach, Meshach, and Abednego further underscores the importance of steadfast faith. In Daniel 3, these three young men refused to bow to Nebuchadnezzar's golden image, despite the threat of a fiery furnace. Their courageous stand not only saved them but also served as a powerful testimony to God's glory, prompting the king to acknowledge their God. Their story vividly reminds us that our faithfulness in resisting cultural pressures can lead to profound opportunities for witness and transformation, not just within us but also in those who observe our steadfastness.

As we cultivate a culture of scriptural adherence and divine focus within the church, it is crucial to teach and disciple others about the importance of biblical precedence over cultural trends. 2 Timothy 2:15 exhorts us to "study to shew thyself approved unto God, a workman that needeth not to be ashamed, rightly dividing the word of truth." This directive emphasizes the need for biblical literacy, equipping us to discern and effectively navigate cultural challenges. By grounding ourselves in scripture, we fortify our faith and ensure our engagement with culture is rooted in divine wisdom.

Maintaining scriptural integrity requires courage and conviction, qualities epitomized by early Christian martyrs who chose to stand for their faith despite severe persecution. Hebrews 11:36-38 recounts the trials and tribulations faced by these faithful ones, who "had trial of cruel mockings and scourgings, yea, moreover of bonds and imprisonment: they were stoned, they were sawn asunder, were tempted, were slain with the sword: they wandered about in sheepskins and goatskins; being destitute, afflicted, tormented; (of whom the world was not worthy)." Their unwavering faith amidst such hardships inspires us to hold fast to our beliefs, even when cultural pressures mount.

In today's context, maintaining this kind of unwavering faith might not always involve physical persecution but can manifest in various forms of social and ideological pressure. The subtle yet pervasive influence of cultural trends can sometimes lead us away from the core tenets of our faith. Proverbs 4:23 advises, "Keep thy heart with all diligence; for out of it are the issues of life." Guarding our hearts ensures that we remain aligned with God's truth, resisting the subtle encroachments of cultural conformity.

As the church engages with culture, it is vital to remember the ultimate authority of Scripture. 2 Timothy 3:16-17 declares, "All scripture is given by inspiration of God, and is profitable for doctrine, for reproof, for correction, for instruction in righteousness: that the man of God may be perfect, throughly furnished unto all good works." This foundational truth underscores the necessity of grounding all cultural engagement in the inspired Word of God, ensuring that our actions and decisions reflect divine wisdom rather than human philosophy.

The story of the Bereans in Acts 17:11 provides a model for this kind of engagement. They were more noble than those in

CHAPTER 44: SCRIPTURAL GUIDANCE ON CULTURAL INFLUENCE

Thessalonica, in that they received the word with all readiness of mind, and searched the scriptures daily, whether those things were so. Their diligent examination of scripture ensured that their beliefs were rooted in truth, setting an example for us to follow as we navigate cultural influences. By emulating the Bereans, we can critically engage with cultural ideas while steadfastly upholding scriptural integrity.

Moreover, the call to be salt and light, as expressed in Matthew 5:13-16, emphasizes our role in the world. "Ye are the salt of the earth: but if the salt have lost his savour, wherewith shall it be salted? It is thenceforth good for nothing, but to be cast out, and to be trodden under foot of men. Ye are the light of the world. A city that is set on a hill cannot be hid." Our distinctiveness as believers is our greatest asset in influencing culture. When we lose our distinctiveness by conforming to the world, we lose our effectiveness in fulfilling our divine mission.

This distinctiveness is further highlighted by the metaphor of the narrow gate in Matthew 7:13-14. "Enter ye in at the strait gate: for wide is the gate, and broad is the way, that leadeth to destruction, and many there be which go in thereat: because strait is the gate, and narrow is the way, which leadeth unto life, and few there be that find it." The path of cultural conformity is broad and alluring, but it leads to spiritual compromise. The narrow way, though challenging, leads to life and must be our chosen path as followers of Christ.

Scriptural guidance is not merely about resisting cultural influences but about actively shaping culture through the transformative power of the Gospel. Romans 1:16 declares, "For I am not ashamed of the gospel of Christ: for it is the power of God unto salvation to every one that believeth." Our engagement with culture should be characterized by a bold proclamation of the Gospel, demonstrating its power to bring salvation and transformation. This active engagement, rooted in scriptural truth, positions the church as a catalyst for divine change in society.

In resisting cultural pressures, we must also cultivate a deep and abiding relationship with God through prayer. Jesus' example in Luke 5:16, where He often withdrew to lonely places to pray, underscores the importance of communion with God in maintaining spiritual strength. Prayer equips us with the discernment and fortitude needed to navigate cultural challenges, ensuring that our actions are guided by divine wisdom rather than human inclination.

The promise of God's presence, as articulated in Joshua 1:9, offers profound assurance: "Have not I commanded thee? Be strong and of a good courage; be not afraid, neither be thou dismayed: for the Lord thy God is with thee whithersoever thou goest." This divine assurance encourages us to stand firm in our faith, confident that God is with us as we engage with and influence culture. His presence empowers us to be bold and courageous, knowing that we are never alone in our efforts to uphold His truth.

Finally, as we embrace scriptural guidance in our cultural engagement, we must do so with humility and love. Colossians 3:12-14 exhorts us to "put on therefore, as the elect of God, holy and beloved, bowels of mercies, kindness, humbleness of mind, meekness, longsuffering; forbearing one another, and forgiving one another... And above all these things put on charity, which is

CHAPTER 44: SCRIPTURAL GUIDANCE ON CULTURAL INFLUENCE

the bond of perfectness." Our approach to cultural engagement must reflect the character of Christ, marked by love and humility, drawing others to Him through our godly example.

By integrating these scriptural truths into our daily walk and communal church life, we embody the renewal and restoration that "Church Gone Wild" calls for. Let us move forward, equipped and inspired by the Word, to reclaim the church's influence in the world, transforming it from within, one heart, one mind, at a time.

Chapter 45: Balancing Engagement and Separation

Balancing engagement and separation in our Christian walk is akin to walking a tightrope. It requires not only skill and awareness but also a deep trust in the Lord who guides our steps. The Apostle Paul reminds us in Romans 12:2, "And be not conformed to this world: but be ye transformed by the renewing of your mind, that ye may prove what is that good, and acceptable, and perfect, will of God." This transformation is the foundation of our engagement with the world—an engagement that must be rooted in our distinctiveness as followers of Christ.

Engaging with culture is not about assimilating into it but rather influencing it with the values of the Kingdom. Jesus tells us in Matthew 5:13-14 that we are the salt of the earth and the light of the world. Salt, in its essence, preserves and flavors, while light dispels darkness. Our presence in the world should bring preservation against moral decay and illuminate the path to righteousness. However, our effectiveness hinges on maintaining our distinctiveness, much like salt losing its flavor becomes useless.

The church today faces the temptation to seek cultural acceptance and relevance, often at the expense of doctrinal purity and spiritual fervor. This pursuit can lead to a form of godliness that denies its power, as warned in 2 Timothy 3:5. We must guard against this, ensuring that our engagement with culture does not dilute the transformative power of the Gospel. The challenge is to engage

CHAPTER 45: BALANCING ENGAGEMENT AND SEPARATION

without compromising, to influence without being influenced, and to stand firm without standing apart in isolation.

Consider the words of Jesus in John 17:15-16, where He prays to the Father, "I pray not that thou shouldest take them out of the world, but that thou shouldest keep them from the evil. They are not of the world, even as I am not of the world." Jesus acknowledges our presence in the world but calls for our protection from its corrupting influences. This divine balance is our model—being in the world but not of it.

Cultural engagement must be intentional and purposeful, driven by a mission to reflect Christ in all we do. The early church thrived in a hostile environment by living out their faith boldly and unapologetically. They did not seek to blend in but to stand out as a testimony to the life-changing power of Jesus Christ. Acts 4:13 recounts the boldness of Peter and John, who were recognized as having been with Jesus. Their engagement with the culture was marked by a distinctiveness that pointed others to Christ.

However, this does not mean we retreat into holy huddles, disconnected from the world around us. We are called to be witnesses, as Jesus commissioned in Acts 1:8, "But ye shall receive power, after that the Holy Ghost is come upon you: and ye shall be witnesses unto me both in Jerusalem, and in all Judaea, and in Samaria, and unto the uttermost part of the earth." Witnessing requires presence and interaction, yet always under the guidance and power of the Holy Spirit.

Engagement also involves understanding and addressing the issues that the culture grapples with, providing biblical perspectives and solutions. This demands a deep grounding in Scripture and a sensitivity to the leading of the Holy Spirit. As we navigate social, political, and moral landscapes, we must do so with wisdom and discernment. James 1:5 encourages us, "If any of you lack wisdom, let him ask of God, that giveth to all men liberally, and upbraideth not; and it shall be given him." Godly wisdom is our anchor as we engage the complexities of our world.

Yet, there are times when separation becomes necessary to preserve the purity and witness of the church. Paul's instruction in 2 Corinthians 6:17 is clear, "Wherefore come out from among them, and be ye separate, saith the Lord, and touch not the unclean thing; and I will receive you." This call to separation is not a retreat but a strategic withdrawal from influences that threaten our faith and witness. It is a proactive stance to maintain holiness and integrity.

The church's challenge is to discern when to engage and when to separate. This requires a deep intimacy with God, a sensitivity to His Spirit, and a commitment to His Word. Psalm 1:1-2 provides a framework for this discernment, "Blessed is the man that walketh not in the counsel of the ungodly, nor standeth in the way of sinners, nor sitteth in the seat of the scornful. But his delight is in the law of the Lord; and in his law doth he meditate day and night." Meditating on God's Word day and night equips us to navigate the delicate balance of engagement and separation.

Engagement should always be undergirded by prayer. Jesus often withdrew to solitary places to pray, as noted in Luke 5:16. This practice of communion with the Father empowered Him to minister effectively and remain aligned with the Father's will. Similarly, our engagement with the world must be bathed in prayer,

CHAPTER 45: BALANCING ENGAGEMENT AND SEPARATION

seeking God's guidance and strength. Prayer is our lifeline, keeping us connected to the source of our power and purpose.

We must also cultivate a community of believers who support and encourage one another in this journey. Hebrews 10:24-25 urges us, "And let us consider one another to provoke unto love and to good works: Not forsaking the assembling of ourselves together, as the manner of some is; but exhorting one another: and so much the more, as ye see the day approaching." The community provides accountability, encouragement, and a shared mission as we engage the world together.

Our engagement with the world should be characterized by love and truth. Ephesians 4:15 calls us to speak the truth in love. This balance is critical—truth without love can be harsh and alienating, while love without truth can be permissive and compromising. Jesus exemplified this balance perfectly, showing compassion without compromising His message. As His followers, we are called to emulate this balance, engaging the world with a heart of love and a commitment to truth.

In all our engagements, we must remember that our ultimate goal is to glorify God. Colossians 3:17 reminds us, "And whatsoever ye do in word or deed, do all in the name of the Lord Jesus, giving thanks to God and the Father by him." Our actions, words, and interactions should reflect His character and bring Him honor. This perspective keeps our engagement focused and purposeful, avoiding the pitfalls of self-promotion or cultural conformity.

As we engage with the world, we must also be vigilant against the subtle influences that seek to conform us to its image. First John 2:15-17 warns, "Love not the world, neither the things that are in the world. If any man love the world, the love of the Father is not in him. For all that is in the world, the lust of the flesh, and the lust of the eyes, and the pride of life, is not of the Father, but is of the world. And the world passeth away, and the lust thereof: but he that doeth the will of God abideth for ever." This admonition calls us to a higher allegiance to the will of God over the fleeting attractions of the world.

Our separation is not isolation but a consecration. We are set apart for God's purposes, to be holy as He is holy (1 Peter 1:16). This holiness is not about withdrawing from the world but living distinctively within it. It is a witness to the transforming power of the Gospel and a testament to the hope we have in Christ. Our lives should reflect a different set of values, priorities, and purposes that draw others to the beauty of holiness.

In the journey of balancing engagement and separation, we must continually evaluate our hearts and motives. Psalm 139:23-24 is a prayer we should frequently echo, "Search me, O God, and know my heart: try me, and know my thoughts: And see if there be any wicked way in me, and lead me in the way everlasting." This introspection helps us remain aligned with God's will and responsive to His leading.

Ultimately, our engagement with the world is a mission field. Jesus' Great Commission in Matthew 28:19-20 commands us to go and make disciples of all nations. This mandate requires us to engage with culture, sharing the Good News of Jesus Christ. Yet, as we go, we do so with the understanding that we are ambassadors of another Kingdom, representing the values and truths of our heavenly homeland.

CHAPTER 45: BALANCING ENGAGEMENT AND SEPARATION

Balancing engagement and separation is a dynamic, ongoing process. It requires us to remain grounded in God's Word, guided by His Spirit, and connected to His community. It challenges us to be both bold and humble, firm and compassionate, distinct and relatable. In this balance, we find our true calling as the church, a beacon of hope and truth in a world desperately in need of both.

Section 10: The Call to Holiness

Chapter 46: Understanding Biblical Holiness

Understanding biblical holiness is essential for every believer who seeks to walk closely with God. Holiness is not a lofty, unattainable ideal but a foundational aspect of our Christian faith. As it is written, "Be ye holy; for I am holy" (1 Peter 1:16). This divine command is not merely an Old Testament relic but a present call for every disciple of Christ. God's holiness is the standard by which we are to live, and it encompasses every aspect of our being. Our journey towards holiness begins with a deep understanding of what it means to be set apart for God's purposes.

When we talk about holiness, we are not just referring to moral purity. Holiness, in its truest sense, means being consecrated, set apart for God. The vessels in the Temple were considered holy because they were dedicated to God's service. Similarly, our lives, once given to Christ, are to be wholly dedicated to Him. "Know ye not that ye are the temple of God, and that the Spirit of God dwelleth in you?" (1 Corinthians 3:16). This powerful truth reminds us that our bodies are not our own. We are the dwelling place of the Holy Spirit, and this calls for a life that reflects His presence within us.

Holiness is not just about avoiding sin; it is about actively pursuing righteousness. It is a proactive, not reactive, stance. "Follow peace with all men, and holiness, without which no man shall see the Lord" (Hebrews 12:14). This scripture underscores the necessity of holiness in our relationship with God. Without it, our spiritual vision is clouded, and our fellowship with the Lord is hindered.

Holiness is the lens through which we see God clearly, and it is through a holy life that we draw nearer to Him.

In today's world, the call to holiness can seem daunting. Society often promotes values and behaviors that are contrary to God's standards. However, the Bible reminds us, "And be not conformed to this world: but be ye transformed by the renewing of your mind" (Romans 12:2). This transformation is a continuous process, a daily renewal that aligns our thoughts and actions with God's will. Holiness requires a deliberate, conscious effort to resist conforming to worldly patterns and instead embrace the values of the Kingdom of God.

The pursuit of holiness affects every area of our lives. It is not limited to our actions but extends to our thoughts, intentions, and attitudes. Jesus taught, "Blessed are the pure in heart: for they shall see God" (Matthew 5:8). Purity of heart is a critical aspect of holiness. It is not enough to appear righteous outwardly; our inner life must reflect the holiness of God. This inner purity is what enables us to experience God more deeply and to see His hand at work in our lives.

Holiness also demands a separation from sin. This does not mean isolating ourselves from the world, but it does mean living distinctively within it. "Wherefore come out from among them, and be ye separate, saith the Lord, and touch not the unclean thing; and I will receive you" (2 Corinthians 6:17). This separation is about choosing God's ways over the world's ways, even when it is difficult or counter-cultural. It is a call to live in such a way that others can see the difference Christ makes in our lives.

CHAPTER 46: UNDERSTANDING BIBLICAL HOLINESS

Living a holy life also means walking in obedience to God's commands. Jesus said, "If ye love me, keep my commandments" (John 14:15). Obedience is the practical outworking of our love for God. It is through obedience that we demonstrate our commitment to holiness. Each act of obedience, no matter how small, is a step towards a life that is wholly pleasing to God. This obedience is not burdensome but is a joy and delight as we align our will with God's perfect will.

The Holy Spirit plays a crucial role in our journey toward holiness. We cannot achieve holiness through our own efforts; it is the work of the Spirit within us. "But the fruit of the Spirit is love, joy, peace, longsuffering, gentleness, goodness, faith, meekness, temperance: against such there is no law" (Galatians 5:22-23). These fruits are evidence of the Holy Spirit's sanctifying work in our lives. As we yield to the Spirit, He produces these characteristics within us, shaping us to be more like Christ.

Holiness also involves a commitment to community. The church, as the body of Christ, is called to be a holy people. "That he might present it to himself a glorious church, not having spot, or wrinkle, or any such thing; but that it should be holy and without blemish" (Ephesians 5:27). Our personal holiness contributes to the holiness of the church. When we live holy lives, we build up the body of Christ, encouraging one another to pursue righteousness and godliness.

A holy life is marked by humility. "Humble yourselves in the sight of the Lord, and he shall lift you up" (James 4:10). Humility is recognizing our need for God and depending on Him completely. It is not thinking less of ourselves, but thinking of ourselves less.

It is about putting God and others first, seeking to serve rather than to be served. This humble posture allows God's grace to flow through us, making us vessels of His holiness.

Holiness brings us into a deeper relationship with God. "Draw nigh to God, and he will draw nigh to you" (James 4:8). As we pursue holiness, we experience a greater intimacy with our Creator. We become more attuned to His voice, more sensitive to His leading, and more aware of His presence in our lives. This closeness with God is the ultimate reward of a holy life.

The pursuit of holiness also protects us from the snares of the enemy. "Put on the whole armour of God, that ye may be able to stand against the wiles of the devil" (Ephesians 6:11). Holiness is our defense against the temptations and attacks of Satan. It equips us to stand firm in our faith and to resist the lure of sin. When we are clothed in holiness, we are fortified against the enemy's schemes.

Moreover, holiness is a witness to the world. "Ye are the light of the world. A city that is set on a hill cannot be hid" (Matthew 5:14). Our holy lives shine brightly in a world darkened by sin. They testify to the transformative power of the gospel and point others to Christ. Our holiness is not for our glory but for God's glory, drawing others to Him through the testimony of our lives.

Holiness also leads to personal fulfillment and joy. "In thy presence is fulness of joy; at thy right hand there are pleasures for evermore" (Psalm 16:11). When we live in holiness, we experience the fullness of life that God intends for us. We find satisfaction and contentment in His presence, and our lives are marked by peace and joy that the world cannot give.

CHAPTER 46: UNDERSTANDING BIBLICAL HOLINESS

The journey towards holiness is ongoing. It is not a destination but a continual process of growth and transformation. "Being confident of this very thing, that he which hath begun a good work in you will perform it until the day of Jesus Christ" (Philippians 1:6). God is faithful to complete the work of holiness in us. As we remain faithful to Him, He continues to shape and mold us into the image of His Son.

In pursuing holiness, we must also be aware of the cost. Jesus said, "If any man will come after me, let him deny himself, and take up his cross daily, and follow me" (Luke 9:23). Holiness requires sacrifice and self-denial. It involves laying down our desires and ambitions for the sake of God's will. This path is not easy, but it is the path that leads to life.

Holiness ultimately prepares us for eternity. "Follow peace with all men, and holiness, without which no man shall see the Lord" (Hebrews 12:14). Our pursuit of holiness is not just for this life but for the life to come. It readies us for the presence of God, where we will dwell in perfect holiness forever. This eternal perspective motivates us to live holy lives now, in anticipation of the glorious future that awaits us.

In conclusion, understanding biblical holiness is crucial for every believer. It is a call to be set apart for God's purposes, to live in purity, obedience, and humility. It is a journey marked by the Holy Spirit's work within us, transforming us to be more like Christ. As we pursue holiness, we draw closer to God, resist the enemy, and shine as witnesses to the world. Holiness is the path to true joy and fulfillment, both now and for eternity. Let us, therefore, heed the call to holiness, knowing that it is both our privilege and our duty as children of God.

Chapter 47: Practical Holiness

Living a life of practical holiness is both a profound privilege and a significant responsibility for every believer. It calls us to a higher standard, a divine invitation to reflect God's character in every aspect of our lives. The apostle Peter's words resonate deeply: "But as he which hath called you is holy, so be ye holy in all manner of conversation; Because it is written, Be ye holy; for I am holy" (1 Peter 1:15-16). This divine mandate is not limited to our spiritual practices but extends to our daily interactions, decisions, and behaviors.

Holiness is fundamentally about being set apart for God's purposes. It means making conscious choices that align with His will, even when they contradict societal norms. Joseph's refusal to succumb to Potiphar's wife's advances is a compelling example of practical holiness. Faced with intense temptation, Joseph fled, choosing to honor God above yielding to sin (Genesis 39:12). His actions teach us that practical holiness often requires courage and a commitment to uphold God's standards, no matter the cost.

Our journey towards holiness begins with our hearts and minds. The Psalmist wisely declares, "Thy word have I hid in mine heart, that I might not sin against thee" (Psalm 119:11). Immersing ourselves in God's Word is essential for nurturing a holy life. As we meditate on Scripture, the Holy Spirit transforms our thoughts, aligning them with God's truth. This renewal empowers us to resist temptation and make choices that honor Him.

Holiness also encompasses how we treat others. It calls us to embody Christ's love, patience, and kindness in our relationships. The apostle Paul exhorts us in Ephesians 4:32 to "be kind one to another, tenderhearted, forgiving one another, even as God for Christ's sake hath forgiven you." Forgiveness and grace are powerful expressions of holiness that reflect God's heart. When we forgive, we mirror the divine forgiveness we have received, fostering an environment where healing and reconciliation can flourish.

Integrity is a hallmark of practical holiness. It involves being truthful and transparent in all our dealings. Proverbs 10:9 reminds us, "He that walketh uprightly walketh surely: but he that perverteth his ways shall be known." Living a life of integrity honors God and builds trust with those around us. Our words and actions should consistently reflect our commitment to truth, demonstrating the transformative power of God's work in our lives.

In an age dominated by media and technology, guarding our hearts and minds is crucial. The content we consume shapes our values and perceptions. Paul's counsel in Philippians 4:8 is particularly relevant: "Finally, brethren, whatsoever things are true, whatsoever things are honest, whatsoever things are just, whatsoever things are pure, whatsoever things are lovely, whatsoever things are of good report; if there be any virtue, and if there be any praise, think on these things." Choosing to engage with media that uplifts and edifies helps us maintain a holy focus, protecting us from influences that desensitize us to sin.

Serving others is a tangible expression of holiness. Jesus, the epitome of holiness, came not to be served but to serve (Matthew

CHAPTER 47: PRACTICAL HOLINESS

20:28). Serving others shifts our focus from self-centeredness to Christ-centeredness. Whether it's volunteering in our local community or offering support to those in need, acts of service reflect God's love and compassion. They also provide opportunities for us to share the gospel and demonstrate the reality of Christ's transformative power.

Financial stewardship is another critical aspect of practical holiness. How we handle our resources reflects our priorities and integrity. Jesus taught that "where your treasure is, there will your heart be also" (Matthew 6:21). Faithful stewardship means managing our finances in a way that honors God, supports His work, and meets the needs of others. It involves generosity, integrity, and a reliance on God's provision, demonstrating our trust in His faithfulness.

Living a life of holiness also means making ethical choices in our professional lives. Colossians 3:23 instructs us, "And whatsoever ye do, do it heartily, as to the Lord, and not unto men." Our work should be done with excellence and integrity, reflecting our commitment to God. This principle applies whether we are in positions of leadership or serving in seemingly mundane roles. Our professional conduct can be a powerful testimony of our faith, influencing others and glorifying God.

The pursuit of holiness is not a solitary journey. It thrives in the context of community, where we can encourage and support one another. Hebrews 10:24-25 urges us to "consider one another to provoke unto love and to good works: Not forsaking the assembling of ourselves together, as the manner of some is; but exhorting one another: and so much the more, as ye see the day approaching." Being part of a vibrant, supportive Christian community strengthens our resolve to live holy lives and provides accountability and encouragement.

Prayer is the lifeblood of practical holiness. Through prayer, we draw near to God, seek His guidance, and receive His strength. Jesus frequently withdrew to pray, setting an example for us to follow (Luke 5:16). In our busy lives, setting aside time for prayer cultivates a deeper relationship with God and aligns our hearts with His. It is in these moments of communion that we are transformed and empowered to live holy lives.

Holiness also involves a commitment to purity in our thoughts and actions. Jesus taught that sin begins in the heart and mind (Matthew 5:28). Therefore, we must be vigilant in guarding our thoughts and intentions. This vigilance requires us to reject sinful desires and cultivate purity, seeking God's help to overcome temptation and live in a way that pleases Him.

Our speech is another area where holiness should be evident. Ephesians 4:29 advises, "Let no corrupt communication proceed out of your mouth, but that which is good to the use of edifying, that it may minister grace unto the hearers." Our words should build up and encourage others, reflecting the grace and truth of Christ. By speaking with kindness and integrity, we demonstrate the transformative impact of God's holiness in our lives.

Holiness in the home is foundational for a godly life. Our families should see our commitment to God in how we love, serve, and lead. Deuteronomy 6:6-7 instructs us to diligently teach God's commandments to our children, integrating them into our daily routines. Modeling holiness at home creates a nurturing

CHAPTER 47: PRACTICAL HOLINESS

environment where faith can grow and thrive, influencing future generations.

Holiness requires a continual examination of our lives in light of Scripture. Psalm 139:23-24 invites us to ask God to "search me, O God, and know my heart: try me, and know my thoughts: And see if there be any wicked way in me, and lead me in the way everlasting." This ongoing self-examination and repentance keep us aligned with God's will, ensuring that we remain on the path of holiness.

Fasting is another discipline that fosters practical holiness. By denying ourselves physical sustenance, we focus more intently on spiritual nourishment. Jesus fasted and taught about its importance (Matthew 6:16-18). Fasting helps us to break the hold of worldly desires, draw closer to God, and seek His guidance and power in our lives.

In our pursuit of holiness, we must remain humble and dependent on God's grace. James 4:10 reminds us, "Humble yourselves in the sight of the Lord, and he shall lift you up." Recognizing our need for God's help keeps us from pride and self-righteousness. It is His grace that enables us to live holy lives, transforming us into His likeness.

As we strive to live holy lives, we must also be mindful of the spiritual battles we face. Ephesians 6:12-13 tells us that "we wrestle not against flesh and blood, but against principalities, against powers, against the rulers of the darkness of this world, against spiritual wickedness in high places." To stand firm, we must put on the full armor of God, relying on His strength to overcome the enemy's attacks.

Finally, our journey towards practical holiness is a continual process of growth and transformation. Philippians 1:6 assures us that "he which hath begun a good work in you will perform it until the day of Jesus Christ." God is faithful to complete the work He has started in us. As we remain committed to living holy lives, we can trust that He will guide and empower us, transforming us into vessels of His glory.

Living a life of practical holiness is a profound expression of our love for God and our desire to reflect His character. It requires daily decisions to honor Him in every aspect of our lives. By immersing ourselves in Scripture, engaging in prayer, and seeking the support of a Christian community, we can cultivate a holy lifestyle that glorifies God and impacts those around us. As we pursue holiness, we fulfill our calling to be set apart for His purposes, shining as lights in a world that desperately needs to see the reality of Christ's transformative power.

Chapter 48: The Challenges of Holiness in Modern Society

In our contemporary world, the pursuit of holiness often feels like swimming against a powerful current. We live in a society that increasingly values convenience, instant gratification, and self-indulgence, which can make the call to holiness seem counterintuitive and even burdensome. Yet, the Bible clearly instructs us to strive for holiness, for without it, "no man shall see the Lord" (Hebrews 12:14). This divine mandate challenges us to rise above the prevailing cultural norms and align our lives with God's sacred standards.

The pressure to conform to societal expectations is immense. Everywhere we turn, we are bombarded with messages that encourage us to blend in rather than stand out. The Apostle Paul's exhortation to the Romans is particularly relevant today: "And be not conformed to this world: but be ye transformed by the renewing of your mind" (Romans 12:2). This transformation requires a deliberate and continuous effort to renew our minds with the truths of Scripture, resisting the allure of worldly patterns that seek to dilute our faith.

One significant challenge in pursuing holiness today is the pervasive influence of media. From television and movies to social media and advertising, the content we consume can subtly shape our values and priorities. Often, what is celebrated in media is at odds with the virtues of purity, humility, and self-control that define a holy life. Jesus warns us to be mindful of what we allow into our hearts and minds: "The light of the body is the eye: if therefore thine eye be single, thy whole body shall be full of light" (Matthew 6:22). By guarding our eyes and ears against unwholesome influences, we protect the sanctity of our inner lives.

Social media, in particular, poses a unique challenge to our pursuit of holiness. The constant stream of updates and images can lead to a culture of comparison, where our worth is measured by likes, shares, and followers rather than our identity in Christ. This environment can foster envy, pride, and a desire for approval that distracts us from our spiritual journey. The Apostle John cautions us against loving the world and its enticements: "For all that is in the world, the lust of the flesh, and the lust of the eyes, and the pride of life, is not of the Father, but is of the world" (1 John 2:16). By focusing on our relationship with God rather than the approval of others, we maintain our commitment to holiness.

The relentless pursuit of material success is another obstacle to living a holy life. Society often equates success with wealth, status, and possessions, leading many to prioritize these over spiritual growth. However, Scripture reminds us that our true treasure lies not in earthly riches but in our relationship with God. Jesus teaches, "Lay not up for yourselves treasures upon earth, where moth and rust doth corrupt, and where thieves break through and steal: but lay up for yourselves treasures in heaven" (Matthew 6:19-20). By prioritizing spiritual wealth over material gain, we align our lives with God's eternal purposes.

Moreover, the culture of individualism prevalent in modern society can undermine our sense of community and accountability, both of which are essential for fostering holiness. The Bible emphasizes

CHAPTER 48: THE CHALLENGES OF HOLINESS IN MODERN SOCIETY

the importance of mutual encouragement and support within the body of Christ: "And let us consider one another to provoke unto love and to good works" (Hebrews 10:24). When we isolate ourselves, we become more susceptible to temptation and less accountable to living out our faith. Engaging actively in a faith community helps us to stay committed to our holy calling.

The entertainment industry also exerts a powerful influence over how we perceive and practice holiness. Often, the content that is glorified does not align with the values of purity, integrity, and reverence for God that holiness demands. As believers, we must exercise discernment, remembering the advice given in Philippians 4:8 to focus on whatever is true, noble, right, pure, lovely, admirable, excellent, or praiseworthy. This scripture guides us in choosing entertainment that enriches rather than detracts from our spiritual health.

In addition to external challenges, our internal struggles with sin and temptation can hinder our pursuit of holiness. The Apostle Paul candidly shares his own battle with sin: "For the good that I would, I do not: but the evil which I would not, that I do" (Romans 7:19). This honest admission reminds us that even the most devoted believers face ongoing struggles. However, we are not left to fight these battles alone. Through the power of the Holy Spirit, we are given the strength to overcome our sinful tendencies and grow in holiness. "This I say then, Walk in the Spirit, and ye shall not fulfill the lust of the flesh" (Galatians 5:16).

The challenge of maintaining sexual purity in an increasingly permissive society cannot be overlooked. With pervasive sexual content and liberal attitudes toward sex, adhering to biblical standards of purity requires intentional effort and vigilance. Paul's advice to the Thessalonians is clear: "For this is the will of God, even your sanctification, that ye should abstain from fornication" (1 Thessalonians 4:3). Upholding sexual purity honors God and protects us from the emotional and spiritual consequences of sexual immorality.

Another significant barrier to holiness is the pressure to conform to modern ethical standards that often conflict with biblical teachings. Issues such as abortion, marriage, and gender identity are hotly debated in society, with many voices urging the church to adapt its stance to align with contemporary views. However, as followers of Christ, we are called to stand firm on the truths of Scripture, regardless of societal pressure. Paul's instruction to Timothy is a timely reminder: "Preach the word; be instant in season, out of season; reprove, rebuke, exhort with all longsuffering and doctrine" (2 Timothy 4:2). By faithfully proclaiming God's word, we uphold His standards in a world that often seeks to undermine them.

The call to holiness also involves how we handle our relationships and interactions with others. Jesus calls us to love our neighbors as ourselves and to forgive those who wrong us. This call to love and forgiveness is central to living a holy life, yet it can be incredibly challenging in a world where resentment, division, and hostility are prevalent. The apostle Peter exhorts us, "Above all things have fervent charity among yourselves: for charity shall cover the multitude of sins" (1 Peter 4:8). By practicing love and forgiveness, we reflect God's holiness in our relationships and contribute to a more compassionate and just society.

CHAPTER 48: THE CHALLENGES OF HOLINESS IN MODERN SOCIETY

Our pursuit of holiness must also extend to our thoughts and intentions. Jesus emphasized the importance of inner purity when He taught, "Blessed are the pure in heart: for they shall see God" (Matthew 5:8). Holiness is not merely about external actions but also about cultivating a heart that is aligned with God's will. This requires regular self-examination and repentance, allowing the Holy Spirit to convict and cleanse us from any impure thoughts or motives.

Furthermore, the pursuit of holiness involves a commitment to justice and righteousness. In a world plagued by inequality and injustice, believers are called to be agents of change, reflecting God's love and justice in their actions. Micah 6:8 encapsulates this calling: "He hath shewed thee, O man, what is good; and what doth the Lord require of thee, but to do justly, and to love mercy, and to walk humbly with thy God?" By actively seeking justice and showing mercy, we demonstrate the holiness of God in a tangible way.

In addition to personal challenges, systemic issues within the church can also hinder our pursuit of holiness. When church leadership prioritizes growth and popularity over spiritual integrity, it can lead to a dilution of the gospel message and a compromise of biblical standards. Jesus warned about the dangers of false prophets and teachers who lead the flock astray: "Beware of false prophets, which come to you in sheep's clothing, but inwardly they are ravening wolves" (Matthew 7:15). Upholding holiness within the church requires discernment and a commitment to maintaining doctrinal purity.

Prayer and worship are vital components of a holy life. Through prayer, we communicate with God, seeking His guidance and strength to live according to His will. Worship, both corporate and personal, aligns our hearts with God's and reinforces our commitment to holiness. Jesus highlighted the importance of sincere worship when He said, "God is a Spirit: and they that worship him must worship him in spirit and in truth" (John 4:24). By making prayer and worship central to our lives, we draw closer to God and fortify our resolve to live holy lives.

The pursuit of holiness is a lifelong journey that requires perseverance and resilience. There will be times when we stumble and fall, but God's grace is sufficient to lift us up and set us back on the right path. The apostle Paul's words offer encouragement: "And he said unto me, My grace is sufficient for thee: for my strength is made perfect in weakness" (2 Corinthians 12:9). By relying on God's grace and strength, we can overcome the challenges we face and continue striving for holiness.

Ultimately, the pursuit of holiness is about reflecting the character of God in our lives. It is about being set apart for His purposes and living in a way that brings glory to His name. As Peter writes, "But ye are a chosen generation, a royal priesthood, an holy nation, a peculiar people; that ye should shew forth the praises of him who hath called you out of darkness into his marvelous light" (1 Peter 2:9). Embracing our identity as God's holy people empowers us to live distinctively and purposefully in a world that desperately needs the light of Christ.

In conclusion, while the challenges to holiness in modern society are significant, they are not insurmountable. By grounding

CHAPTER 48: THE CHALLENGES OF HOLINESS IN MODERN SOCIETY

ourselves in Scripture, remaining vigilant against worldly influences, and relying on the Holy Spirit, we can navigate these challenges and live lives that are pleasing to God. Holiness is not about perfection, but about a sincere and ongoing commitment to align our lives with God's will. Let us, therefore, embrace the call to holiness with courage and conviction, knowing that "he which hath begun a good work in you will perform it until the day of Jesus Christ" (Philippians 1:6).

Chapter 49: Scriptural Exhortation to Pursue Holiness

The pursuit of holiness is a sacred call that resonates deeply within the soul of every believer. When Peter exhorts us, "Be ye holy; for I am holy" (1 Peter 1:16), he is echoing the divine expectation that our lives reflect the very character of God. This command is not a suggestion or an ideal to strive for on special occasions; it is the core of our Christian identity. Holiness is the manifestation of God's presence in our lives, showing the world that we are set apart for His purposes. It is a journey, a daily commitment to living in accordance with God's will and letting His light shine through us.

Living a holy life in today's world presents unique challenges. We are constantly bombarded by influences that seek to distract us from our spiritual path. The Apostle Paul understood these challenges when he wrote, "Having therefore these promises, dearly beloved, let us cleanse ourselves from all filthiness of the flesh and spirit, perfecting holiness in the fear of God" (2 Corinthians 7:1). This call to cleanse ourselves encompasses every aspect of our lives, urging us to rid ourselves of anything that tarnishes our relationship with God. It is an ongoing process of sanctification, one that requires vigilance and a sincere desire to draw nearer to God.

Our journey towards holiness begins with a heart of repentance and a desire for transformation. King David's heartfelt plea, "Create in me a clean heart, O God; and renew a right spirit within me"

CHAPTER 49: SCRIPTURAL EXHORTATION TO PURSUE HOLINESS

(Psalm 51:10), captures the essence of this transformation. It is a prayer that acknowledges our need for God's cleansing power and a renewed spirit. Daily, we must examine our hearts and seek God's forgiveness, allowing Him to remove the impurities that hinder our spiritual growth. This continual renewal is vital for maintaining a heart that is aligned with God's will.

Holiness is not merely an internal transformation; it profoundly impacts our relationships with others. Jesus teaches in the Beatitudes, "Blessed are the pure in heart: for they shall see God" (Matthew 5:8). Purity of heart influences how we interact with the world around us. It affects our thoughts, our words, and our actions. When our hearts are pure, we begin to see others through God's eyes, with love and compassion. This purity guides us to act justly, love mercy, and walk humbly with our God (Micah 6:8), embodying the essence of true Christian living.

In a world where cultural values often conflict with biblical principles, maintaining holiness requires a firm commitment to God's Word. Romans 12:2 instructs us, "And be not conformed to this world: but be ye transformed by the renewing of your mind, that ye may prove what is that good, and acceptable, and perfect, will of God." This transformation is essential for living a life that honors God. It involves renewing our minds daily with Scripture, allowing God's truth to shape our thoughts and actions rather than the fleeting trends of society. This steadfast commitment to biblical principles sets us apart and enables us to stand firm in our faith.

The pursuit of holiness is intrinsically linked to our love for God and for others. Jesus encapsulates the essence of the law with the commandment, "Thou shalt love the Lord thy God with all thy heart, and with all thy soul, and with all thy mind. This is the first and great commandment. And the second is like unto it, Thou shalt love thy neighbour as thyself" (Matthew 22:37-39). Our love for God is expressed through our obedience to His commandments and our love for others. True holiness cannot be separated from this divine love. It compels us to act in ways that reflect God's love and justice in the world.

Holiness is also marked by a distinct separation from worldly values and pursuits. The Apostle Paul admonishes us in 2 Corinthians 6:17, "Wherefore come out from among them, and be ye separate, saith the Lord, and touch not the unclean thing; and I will receive you." This call to separation is not a retreat from the world but a call to live differently within it. It is a rejection of values and practices that are contrary to God's Word and an embrace of a lifestyle that honors Him. This separation is a testament to our commitment to living a life that is pleasing to God.

One of the most profound aspects of a holy life is the peace that accompanies it. Philippians 4:7 speaks of "the peace of God, which passeth all understanding, shall keep your hearts and minds through Christ Jesus." This peace is not dependent on external circumstances but is a reflection of our trust in God. It is a peace that guards our hearts and minds, allowing us to remain steadfast in our faith even in the midst of trials. This inner peace is a powerful testimony to the transforming power of a life dedicated to holiness.

The journey towards holiness is not without its trials and challenges. Hebrews 12:14 exhorts us to "follow peace with all men, and holiness, without which no man shall see the Lord." The

CHAPTER 49: SCRIPTURAL EXHORTATION TO PURSUE HOLINESS

pursuit of holiness requires perseverance and endurance. It is a path marked by discipline and sacrifice, but it is also a path of profound joy and fulfillment. The trials we face are opportunities for growth and refinement, drawing us closer to God and shaping us into His likeness.

God's call to holiness is a call to be His ambassadors in the world. As 1 Peter 2:9 reminds us, "But ye are a chosen generation, a royal priesthood, an holy nation, a peculiar people; that ye should shew forth the praises of him who hath called you out of darkness into his marvellous light." Our lives are meant to reflect His light and draw others to Him. When we live holy lives, we become living testimonies of God's grace and power, demonstrating the transformative impact of His presence in our lives.

The foundation of our call to holiness is our relationship with God. John 15:4-5 emphasizes the importance of abiding in Christ: "Abide in me, and I in you. As the branch cannot bear fruit of itself, except it abide in the vine; no more can ye, except ye abide in me. I am the vine, ye are the branches: He that abideth in me, and I in him, the same bringeth forth much fruit: for without me ye can do nothing." Our ability to live holy lives is rooted in our connection to Jesus. As we remain in Him, we draw strength, wisdom, and grace to live in a way that honors God.

Our pursuit of holiness is also fueled by the hope of eternity. In 1 John 3:2-3, we are reminded of this hope: "Beloved, now are we the sons of God, and it doth not yet appear what we shall be: but we know that, when he shall appear, we shall be like him; for we shall see him as he is. And every man that hath this hope in him purifieth himself, even as he is pure." Our hope in Christ's return and our future with Him motivates us to purify ourselves and live lives that are pleasing to Him. This hope keeps us focused on our ultimate goal and helps us endure the challenges of the present.

In our daily walk, the Holy Spirit is our guide and helper in the pursuit of holiness. Romans 8:26 assures us, "Likewise the Spirit also helpeth our infirmities: for we know not what we should pray for as we ought: but the Spirit itself maketh intercession for us with groanings which cannot be uttered." The Holy Spirit empowers us to overcome our weaknesses and live in accordance with God's will. He convicts us of sin, leads us into truth, and enables us to produce the fruit of the Spirit, which is essential for a holy life.

The call to holiness is also a call to vigilance. 1 Peter 5:8 warns us, "Be sober, be vigilant; because your adversary the devil, as a roaring lion, walketh about, seeking whom he may devour." We must be watchful and alert, recognizing the enemy's attempts to lead us astray. Vigilance in prayer, study of the Word, and fellowship with other believers helps us stay grounded in our faith and resistant to the schemes of the enemy. This vigilance is a crucial aspect of maintaining a holy life in a world that constantly tries to pull us away from God.

Holiness is reflected in our speech as well. Ephesians 4:29 instructs, "Let no corrupt communication proceed out of your mouth, but that which is good to the use of edifying, that it may minister grace unto the hearers." Our words should build others up and reflect the grace and truth of Christ. Speech that is seasoned with love and wisdom is a powerful testimony of the transformation God has wrought in our lives. It is through our words that we can bless others and bring glory to God.

CHAPTER 49: SCRIPTURAL EXHORTATION TO PURSUE HOLINESS

The community of believers plays a vital role in our pursuit of holiness. Hebrews 10:24-25 encourages us, "And let us consider one another to provoke unto love and to good works: Not forsaking the assembling of ourselves together, as the manner of some is; but exhorting one another: and so much the more, as ye see the day approaching." Fellowship with other believers provides accountability, encouragement, and support. Together, we can spur one another on towards love and good deeds, helping each other grow in holiness and faithfulness to God.

Holiness is also demonstrated through our service to others. Galatians 5:13-14 exhorts us, "For, brethren, ye have been called unto liberty; only use not liberty for an occasion to the flesh, but by love serve one another. For all the law is fulfilled in one word, even in this; Thou shalt love thy neighbour as thyself." Our freedom in Christ is not a license for selfishness but an opportunity to serve others in love. Service that is motivated by love is a reflection of God's holiness in us, showing the world His compassion and grace.

In all these aspects, the pursuit of holiness is a journey that requires dedication, perseverance, and a deep dependence on God. It is a call that encompasses every area of our lives, transforming us from the inside out. As we heed the scriptural exhortation to be holy, we experience the fullness of life that God intends for us. Our lives become a powerful testimony of His grace and a beacon of hope to a world in desperate need of His love and truth.

As we conclude this reflection on holiness, let us be reminded of the words in Philippians 2:12-13, "Wherefore, my beloved, as ye have always obeyed, not as in my presence only, but now much more in my absence, work out your own salvation with fear and trembling. For it is God which worketh in you both to will and to do of his good pleasure." Our pursuit of holiness is a cooperative effort with God, who works within us to accomplish His purposes. Let us embrace this divine partnership with reverence and joy, striving to live lives that glorify Him in all we do.

Chapter 50: Fostering a Culture of Holiness

Fostering a culture of holiness within the church is an urgent and vital task for any congregation seeking to live in alignment with God's will. The call to holiness is not a suggestion but a divine imperative, as stated in 1 Peter 1:16, "Be ye holy; for I am holy." This command reverberates through the ages, reminding us that our lives should reflect the sanctity of our Creator. The church, as the body of Christ, must embody this holiness in every aspect of its existence, serving as a beacon of light in a world often shrouded in darkness.

To foster such a culture, we must first understand that holiness is not merely an external display of piety but a deep, internal transformation. Ephesians 4:24 exhorts us to "put on the new self, created after the likeness of God in true righteousness and holiness." This new self is characterized by a heart and mind transformed by the Holy Spirit, continually seeking to emulate Christ in thought, word, and deed. It is a profound metamorphosis that begins within and manifests outwardly, influencing every interaction and decision.

Leadership plays a crucial role in cultivating a culture of holiness. Leaders are called to set an example, living lives that are visibly aligned with biblical principles. Paul's instruction in 1 Corinthians 11:1, "Be ye followers of me, even as I also am of Christ," highlights the responsibility of leaders to model Christ-like behavior. When leaders walk in integrity, humility, and righteousness, they inspire their congregation to pursue similar paths. The authenticity of leadership, marked by transparency and accountability, becomes a powerful catalyst for communal holiness.

Holiness also flourishes in an environment of mutual accountability. Galatians 6:1 teaches us, "Brethren, if a man be overtaken in a fault, ye which are spiritual, restore such an one in the spirit of meekness; considering thyself, lest thou also be tempted." This scripture underscores the importance of gentle correction and support within the church. When members feel safe to confess their struggles and receive compassionate guidance, it fosters an atmosphere where growth and repentance are encouraged. It is within this context of loving accountability that true holiness can take root and thrive.

Worship is another critical component in fostering a culture of holiness. Jesus declares in John 4:24, "God is a Spirit: and they that worship him must worship him in spirit and in truth." Worship that is genuine and heartfelt draws us closer to God, aligning our hearts with His. It transcends mere rituals and becomes a profound expression of adoration and submission. When worship is infused with reverence and sincerity, it transforms not only our relationship with God but also our interactions with each other, promoting a collective pursuit of holiness.

Discipleship is essential in nurturing holiness within the church. The Great Commission in Matthew 28:19-20 commands us to "go and make disciples of all nations... teaching them to observe all things that I have commanded you." Discipleship goes beyond imparting knowledge; it involves guiding individuals towards a deeper relationship with Christ, helping them to integrate biblical principles into their daily lives. Effective discipleship programs

CHAPTER 50: FOSTERING A CULTURE OF HOLINESS

provide structured opportunities for spiritual growth, fostering an environment where holiness is both taught and lived out.

Holiness is also reflected in our outreach and engagement with the community. Micah 6:8 instructs us to "act justly, love mercy, and walk humbly with your God." This scripture encapsulates the essence of living a holy life. Our interactions with the world should reflect the justice, mercy, and humility that characterize a life dedicated to God. When the church embodies these virtues, it becomes a powerful witness to the transformative power of Christ, drawing others to the faith through the authenticity of its love and service.

Prayer is the lifeline of a holy culture. James 5:16 reminds us, "The effectual fervent prayer of a righteous man availeth much." Regular, fervent prayer unites the church in its dependence on God, fostering a spirit of humility and submission. Prayer meetings, personal devotions, and communal intercessions are vital practices that reinforce the church's commitment to holiness. Through prayer, we invite God's presence into our lives and communities, seeking His guidance and strength to live out our holy calling.

Building a culture of holiness also involves embracing the challenges and opposition that may arise. Ephesians 6:13 exhorts us to "take up the whole armour of God, that ye may be able to withstand in the evil day, and having done all, to stand." The pursuit of holiness often runs counter to societal norms and values, inviting resistance both from within and outside the church. Yet, we are called to stand firm, clothed in the armor of God, steadfast in our commitment to His truth. This resilience in the face of adversity strengthens our resolve and deepens our reliance on God.

Scripture plays a foundational role in nurturing holiness. Psalm 119:11 declares, "Thy word have I hid in mine heart, that I might not sin against thee." Immersing ourselves in the Word of God grounds us in His truth, providing a solid foundation upon which to build our lives. Regular study, meditation, and application of scripture cultivate a mindset that seeks to honor God in all things. When the Word of God is central to the life of the church, it guides our actions, shapes our character, and transforms our community.

Holiness must also be reflected in our relationships. Romans 12:10 exhorts us to "be kindly affectioned one to another with brotherly love; in honour preferring one another." The way we treat each other within the church is a testament to our commitment to holiness. Genuine love, respect, and honor create an environment where everyone feels valued and supported. This culture of mutual care and consideration nurtures spiritual growth and fosters a deeper sense of unity within the body of Christ.

The pursuit of holiness is a communal journey. Hebrews 10:24-25 encourages us to "consider one another to provoke unto love and to good works: not forsaking the assembling of ourselves together, as the manner of some is; but exhorting one another." Regular fellowship and communal activities strengthen our bonds and provide opportunities for mutual encouragement. Through corporate worship, small groups, and fellowship events, we support each other in our spiritual walk, collectively striving towards greater holiness.

Our speech is another area where holiness must be evident. Colossians 4:6 advises, "Let your speech be alway with grace, seasoned with salt, that ye may know how ye ought to answer

CHAPTER 50: FOSTERING A CULTURE OF HOLINESS

every man." The words we speak reflect the condition of our hearts. When our speech is gracious and edifying, it builds up the body of Christ and exemplifies the purity and love that should characterize a holy life. Encouraging a culture of wholesome and uplifting communication within the church fosters an environment of respect and spiritual growth.

Holiness is also about stewardship. 1 Peter 4:10 teaches us, "As every man hath received the gift, even so minister the same one to another, as good stewards of the manifold grace of God." We are called to use our gifts and resources for the glory of God and the edification of His church. This involves being responsible and generous with our time, talents, and treasures, recognizing that everything we have is a gift from God. Faithful stewardship reflects our commitment to living a life set apart for His purposes.

Service is a practical expression of holiness. Jesus' example in Mark 10:45, "For even the Son of man came not to be ministered unto, but to minister, and to give his life a ransom for many," calls us to a life of selfless service. When we serve others with humility and love, we demonstrate the heart of Christ and embody the holiness to which we are called. Service within the church and the broader community is a tangible way to live out our faith and impact the world for God's kingdom.

Faith and obedience are central to a life of holiness. Hebrews 11:6 reminds us, "But without faith it is impossible to please him." Our journey towards holiness is marked by trust in God and adherence to His commands. Faith propels us to step out in obedience, even when it challenges our comfort or understanding. Obedience, in turn, deepens our faith, creating a dynamic cycle of spiritual growth and maturity. As we walk in faith and obedience, we draw closer to God and become more like Him.

Fostering a culture of holiness involves a continual process of repentance and renewal. 2 Corinthians 7:1 urges us to "cleanse ourselves from all filthiness of the flesh and spirit, perfecting holiness in the fear of God." This process requires ongoing self-examination and a willingness to turn away from sin. It is through repentance that we experience God's grace and the transformative power of His Spirit. By regularly confessing our sins and seeking God's forgiveness, we maintain a posture of humility and dependence on Him.

Ultimately, fostering a culture of holiness is about reflecting the character of God in every aspect of our lives. Ephesians 5:1-2 calls us to "be ye therefore followers of God, as dear children; and walk in love, as Christ also hath loved us, and hath given himself for us." As we imitate God's love, grace, and holiness, we become a living testament to His glory. Our lives, individually and collectively, serve as a powerful witness to the world, demonstrating the transformative power of a holy God.

The journey towards holiness is not easy, but it is profoundly rewarding. As we commit to fostering a culture of holiness within our churches, we invite God's presence and power into our midst. We create an environment where spiritual growth is nurtured, and lives are transformed. Let us, therefore, embrace this holy calling with determination and joy, knowing that as we pursue holiness, we fulfill our divine purpose and bring glory to our Heavenly Father.

Section 11: The Prophetic Warning of Separation

Chapter 51: The Biblical Basis for Separation

Separation, as mandated by scripture, is not merely a physical distancing but a profound spiritual stance that we, as believers, must embrace with unwavering commitment. In 2 Corinthians 6:17, we are called to "come out from among them, and be ye separate, saith the Lord, and touch not the unclean thing; and I will receive you." This call to separation is a divine command that underscores our identity as God's chosen people, set apart for His holy purposes. It is a call that beckons us to stand distinct in a world increasingly blending the sacred with the secular.

The concept of separation begins with the holiness of God. In 1 Peter 1:16, we are reminded, "Because it is written, Be ye holy; for I am holy." Holiness is not just about moral purity but about being wholly dedicated to God, distinct from the world in our thoughts, actions, and desires. This separation is a reflection of God's own nature and His desire for us to mirror that sanctity in every aspect of our lives. It is not a call to arrogance or self-righteousness, but to a humble recognition of our need to be different because we belong to a holy God.

The Old Testament is replete with instances where God commanded His people to be separate from the nations around them. Leviticus 20:26 declares, "And ye shall be holy unto me: for I the Lord am holy, and have severed you from other people, that ye should be mine." The Israelites were to be distinct in their worship, their conduct, and their societal structures. This was not to isolate them but to make them a beacon of God's truth and

CHAPTER 51: THE BIBLICAL BASIS FOR SEPARATION

righteousness in a world darkened by idolatry and immorality. Similarly, the church today is called to be a light, not by blending in but by standing out, by living out the radical differences that come from a life transformed by Christ.

Yet, the drift towards cultural assimilation is a real and present danger. Many churches today face the temptation to conform to societal norms and values, often at the expense of biblical truth. Romans 12:2 warns us, "And be not conformed to this world: but be ye transformed by the renewing of your mind, that ye may prove what is that good, and acceptable, and perfect, will of God." The pressure to conform can lead to a dilution of the gospel, where the desire to be relevant overshadows the need to be faithful. But transformation, not conformity, is our calling—transforming our minds through the truth of God's Word and thereby transforming our communities through the power of the gospel.

Jesus' prayer for His disciples encapsulates the delicate balance of being in the world but not of it. In John 17:15-16, He prays, "I pray not that thou shouldest take them out of the world, but that thou shouldest keep them from the evil. They are not of the world, even as I am not of the world." This prayer highlights our mission—to be actively engaged in the world, bringing the light of Christ into every dark corner, while remaining untouched by its corruption. This separation is not about physical isolation but about a spiritual and moral distinctiveness that testifies to the transformative power of Christ in us.

The call to separation is also a call to deeper fellowship with God. James 4:8 invites us, "Draw nigh to God, and he will draw nigh to you. Cleanse your hands, ye sinners; and purify your hearts, ye double minded." As we separate ourselves from worldly influences, we draw closer to God, experiencing a deeper intimacy and fellowship with Him. This separation is both a privilege and a responsibility. It requires us to cleanse our hands and purify our hearts, to rid ourselves of anything that hinders our relationship with God and our witness to the world.

Our separation from the world is also a testimony to those around us. In Philippians 2:15, Paul exhorts believers to "be blameless and harmless, the sons of God, without rebuke, in the midst of a crooked and perverse nation, among whom ye shine as lights in the world." Our distinctiveness is a beacon that points others to the truth and hope found in Christ. It is not about withdrawing from the world but about living in such a way that our lives reflect the character and love of Christ, drawing others to Him through our example.

This call to be separate is also a prophetic warning. Throughout scripture, God has used separation as a means of preserving the purity of His people and as a precursor to His judgment. The parable of the wheat and tares in Matthew 13:24-30 illustrates this vividly. Jesus speaks of the final separation at the end of the age, where the wheat (the righteous) will be gathered into His barn, and the tares (the wicked) will be burned. This parable is a sobering reminder that there will come a time when God will separate those who are His from those who are not. Our current separation is both a preparation for that final separation and a means of preserving the purity of the church.

As we heed this call to separation, we must also recognize the cost. In Luke 14:27-28, Jesus warns, "And whosoever doth not bear his

CHAPTER 51: THE BIBLICAL BASIS FOR SEPARATION

cross, and come after me, cannot be my disciple. For which of you, intending to build a tower, sitteth not down first, and counteth the cost, whether he have sufficient to finish it?" The cost of separation may include persecution, misunderstanding, and even rejection by those who do not understand our commitment to God's standards. But the reward is far greater—intimacy with God, a powerful witness to the world, and the assurance of eternal life with Him.

Separation also involves a proactive stance against the encroaching influence of false doctrines and teachings. In 2 Timothy 4:3-4, Paul warns, "For the time will come when they will not endure sound doctrine; but after their own lusts shall they heap to themselves teachers, having itching ears; and they shall turn away their ears from the truth, and shall be turned unto fables." The proliferation of false teachings requires that we be vigilant, grounding ourselves in the truth of God's Word and discerning what is of God and what is not. This vigilance is part of our calling to be separate, to guard the purity of the gospel against all attempts to distort it.

The act of separation is also an act of obedience. In 1 John 2:15-17, we are commanded, "Love not the world, neither the things that are in the world. If any man love the world, the love of the Father is not in him. For all that is in the world, the lust of the flesh, and the lust of the eyes, and the pride of life, is not of the Father, but is of the world. And the world passeth away, and the lust thereof: but he that doeth the will of God abideth forever." Our obedience to this command is a testament to our love for God and our desire to do His will. It is a rejection of the temporal pleasures and pursuits of this world in favor of the eternal promises of God.

As we pursue this path of separation, we must do so with a spirit of humility and grace. Ephesians 4:2-3 instructs us to walk "with all lowliness and meekness, with longsuffering, forbearing one another in love; endeavoring to keep the unity of the Spirit in the bond of peace." Our separation should never be a source of pride or division within the body of Christ but a humble commitment to live according to God's standards while loving and encouraging one another in our respective journeys.

Furthermore, our separation from the world is not an end in itself but a means to a greater end—the glorification of God. In Matthew 5:16, Jesus tells us, "Let your light so shine before men, that they may see your good works, and glorify your Father which is in heaven." Our distinctiveness should lead others to glorify God, recognizing that our good works are a reflection of His work in us. This is the ultimate purpose of our separation—that through our lives, others may see and come to know the God we serve.

The church's drift towards cultural conformity must be met with a renewed commitment to biblical separation. This commitment requires courage, discernment, and an unwavering focus on the truth of God's Word. As Hebrews 12:1-2 exhorts us, "Let us lay aside every weight, and the sin which doth so easily beset us, and let us run with patience the race that is set before us, looking unto Jesus the author and finisher of our faith." Our eyes must be fixed on Jesus, our hearts committed to His ways, and our lives aligned with His truth.

Separation is not a rejection of the world but a demonstration of the transformative power of the gospel. It is a testament to the reality that in Christ, we are new creations, called to live in a way

CHAPTER 51: THE BIBLICAL BASIS FOR SEPARATION

that reflects His holiness and love. As 2 Corinthians 5:17 declares, "Therefore if any man be in Christ, he is a new creature: old things are passed away; behold, all things are become new." Our new identity in Christ calls for a new way of living, one that is marked by separation from the old ways of the world and a dedication to the new life we have in Him.

In conclusion, the biblical basis for separation is clear and compelling. It is a divine mandate that calls us to live distinctly and purposefully for God's glory. This separation is not about isolation but about transformation, about living out the reality of our faith in a world that desperately needs to see the light of Christ. As we embrace this call, let us do so with confidence and conviction, knowing that in our separation, we are fulfilling God's purpose and advancing His kingdom.

Chapter 52: The Necessity of Separation for Renewal

In the divine journey toward spiritual renewal, the church must first recognize the necessity of separation from worldliness—a principle deeply rooted in the Word of God. As the Apostle Paul instructs us in 2 Corinthians 6:17, "Wherefore come out from among them, and be ye separate, saith the Lord, and touch not the unclean thing; and I will receive you." This call to separation is not merely about physical or emotional distance, but a profound spiritual shift that enables us to refocus on God's purposes without the distractions of contemporary culture that so often lead us astray.

Consider the metaphor of pruning in John 15:2, where Jesus says, "Every branch in me that beareth not fruit he taketh away: and every branch that beareth fruit, he purgeth it, that it may bring forth more fruit." Just as a gardener prunes the branches to ensure a healthier plant, God calls for His church to cut away the unfruitful parts of its life. This pruning is painful yet necessary. It challenges us to let go of practices, traditions, and alliances that do not contribute to our spiritual health or advance the Kingdom of God. This divine pruning process ensures that we remain in Him and bear much fruit, aligning our lives with His divine purpose.

The history of God's people demonstrates that times of great renewal often follow acts of decisive separation. Look to the revival movements throughout the ages, where a return to doctrinal purity often necessitated a bold departure from the religious norms

CHAPTER 52: THE NECESSITY OF SEPARATION FOR RENEWAL

of the times. These movements were marked not just by a rediscovery of neglected truths but by a determined rejection of the syncretism that had diluted their spiritual potency. Separation, in this context, is not an act of elitism but a necessary step toward reclaiming the purity and power of the early church.

In our modern context, the allure of cultural acceptance has muddied the waters of true doctrine. The church often fears the reproach of Christ more than it fears the dilution of its message. Yet, Hebrews 13:13 exhorts us, "Let us go forth therefore unto him without the camp, bearing his reproach." To truly seek renewal, we must be willing to bear the discomfort of disapproval from the world, knowing that our reward in Christ far outweighs the fleeting pleasures of human acceptance. This willingness to endure reproach is a testament to our commitment to Christ and His unchanging truth.

The process of separation for renewal also involves the individual believer's heart and mind, aligning them more closely with God's will. Romans 12:2 urges us not to be conformed to this world but to be transformed by the renewing of our minds, that we may prove what is that good, and acceptable, and perfect, will of God. This transformation is critical; it requires us to reject the patterns of thinking and behaving that the world champions and to adopt a godly perspective that cherishes obedience over convenience. By allowing the Holy Spirit to renew our minds, we gain clarity and strength to live out our faith authentically.

Practically speaking, separation can manifest in various aspects of church life, from the messages preached from the pulpit to the partnerships formed with external organizations. Each decision must be weighed against the unerring truth of Scripture, not the shifting sands of societal norms. We must ask ourselves, are we mirroring the world to draw its members, or are we reflecting Christ to transform the world? This introspection calls for a courageous re-evaluation of our motives and methods, ensuring they align with God's directives.

True renewal necessitates a return to the first love, a concept beautifully illustrated in Revelation 2:4-5, where the church in Ephesus is admonished for having forsaken its first love. The text calls for repentance and doing the works as at first. Here lies the essence of renewal – it is not only about what we avoid but also about what we embrace. It is about rekindling the passion for the Great Commission, for prayer, for worship, and for community that characterizes the early church. This return to foundational practices ignites a genuine and powerful revival.

As the church heeds this call to separate from worldliness, it must also guard against the danger of isolationism. The goal of separation is not to remove ourselves from the world entirely but to engage with it on God's terms. Jesus prayed not for His disciples to be taken out of the world but that they would be protected from the evil one (John 17:15). Our engagement should be preservative, like salt, and illuminative, like light, always pointing back to Christ. This balance between separation and engagement ensures that our witness remains effective and authentic.

Embracing separation for renewal will undoubtedly lead to resistance, both from within and without. Yet, as we align more closely with God's Word and His ways, we find that His grace is sufficient for us, His power made perfect in weakness (2

CHAPTER 52: THE NECESSITY OF SEPARATION FOR RENEWAL

Corinthians 12:9). It is in this divine strength that we can stand firm against the tides of cultural compromise and hold fast to the unchanging truth of the gospel. This reliance on God's strength rather than our own enables us to navigate the challenges of a faith-filled life with confidence and hope.

In this endeavor, the church must continually seek the guidance of the Holy Spirit, who convicts, counsels, and comforts, leading us into all truth (John 16:13). By heeding His promptings, the church can navigate the complexities of modernity without forsaking the timeless truths that have sustained it through centuries. The Holy Spirit's role in this process is indispensable, providing wisdom and discernment that surpass human understanding.

Separation for renewal also involves a communal aspect, where the church collectively seeks a deeper relationship with God. Acts 2:42 describes the early church as devoted to the apostles' teaching, fellowship, the breaking of bread, and prayer. This communal pursuit of holiness and unity forms a strong foundation for renewal, fostering an environment where God's presence is manifest and His will is pursued. This communal commitment to God's ways creates a fertile ground for spiritual growth and revival.

Moreover, the necessity of separation for renewal is highlighted by the parable of the wheat and the tares in Matthew 13:24-30. Jesus explains that the enemy sows tares among the wheat, but at the time of harvest, the wheat will be gathered into the barn, and the tares will be burned. This parable underscores the inevitability of separation as part of God's divine plan. The church must recognize that this process, though difficult, is essential for maintaining the purity and integrity of the faith community.

In times of renewal, God often raises up prophetic voices to call His people back to righteousness. These voices, like John the Baptist crying in the wilderness, prepare the way for the Lord by calling for repentance and separation from sin. As Amos 3:7 states, "Surely the Lord God will do nothing, but he revealeth his secret unto his servants the prophets." The church must heed these prophetic warnings, understanding that they are given out of God's love and desire for His people to return to Him wholeheartedly.

Furthermore, the call to separation is a call to holiness. Leviticus 20:26 declares, "And ye shall be holy unto me: for I the Lord am holy, and have severed you from other people, that ye should be mine." This divine separation marks us as God's own, setting us apart for His purposes. Holiness is not an optional extra but a fundamental aspect of our identity in Christ. It signifies our total dedication to God's will and our rejection of anything that detracts from His glory.

The church's response to this call must be characterized by humility and obedience. James 4:10 urges, "Humble yourselves in the sight of the Lord, and he shall lift you up." Humility opens our hearts to God's correction and guidance, enabling us to align more closely with His will. This posture of humility allows us to receive God's grace and power, essential for navigating the challenges of a life set apart for Him.

Ultimately, the necessity of separation for renewal is about drawing closer to God and experiencing His transformative power. As we distance ourselves from worldly influences and embrace

CHAPTER 52: THE NECESSITY OF SEPARATION FOR RENEWAL

His ways, we create space for His Spirit to work in and through us. This process of sanctification is ongoing, requiring daily commitment and surrender. Philippians 1:6 reassures us, "Being confident of this very thing, that he which hath begun a good work in you will perform it until the day of Jesus Christ." God's faithful work in our lives continues as we remain committed to His call.

In this season of renewal, let us be vigilant and discerning, ready to separate from anything that hinders our relationship with God. Let us embrace His call to holiness and purity, knowing that it is through this separation that we experience true spiritual renewal. The journey may be challenging, but the reward is great—a deeper, more intimate relationship with our Creator and a powerful witness to the world of His transforming grace.

Chapter 53: Prophetic Voices in Scripture

Throughout the ages, the prophetic voices in Scripture have served as divine heralds, calling God's people back to the paths of righteousness and separation from the world. These prophets did not speak of their own accord but were moved by the Holy Spirit to deliver messages that were often as challenging as they were necessary. In the book of Ezekiel, we find the prophet speaking forth boldly: "And I sought for a man among them, that should make up the hedge, and stand in the gap before me for the land, that I should not destroy it: but I found none" (Ezekiel 22:30). This poignant declaration reveals the heart of God—a desire for intercessors, for those who would embody the call to holiness and separation amidst a culture of compromise.

In reflecting on the prophet Ezekiel's experiences, we see a clear and recurring theme: the dire consequences of Israel's failure to heed God's commands. The prophet's life was a vivid tableau of these divine warnings, exemplifying through action and word the severity of God's judgment upon those who stray from His statutes. Yet, within this narrative of judgment, there lies a profound message of hope. For just as Ezekiel was called to be a "watchman unto the house of Israel" (Ezekiel 3:17), today's church is called to a similar vigilance. We are urged to watch, pray, and stand firm in our commitment to the truths of Scripture, resisting the cultural currents that seek to erode the bedrock of our faith.

Jeremiah, another stalwart prophet, lamented the spiritual adultery of his people, who exchanged their glorious God for worthless idols. "For my people have committed two evils; they have

CHAPTER 53: PROPHETIC VOICES IN SCRIPTURE

forsaken me the fountain of living waters, and hewed them out cisterns, broken cisterns, that can hold no water" (Jeremiah 2:13). This imagery is not merely historical; it mirrors the modern church's dalliance with the ideologies of secularism and materialism. Just as Jeremiah called for Israel to return to the Lord, we too are summoned to abandon the broken cisterns of contemporary culture and return to the living waters of Christ.

The call of Isaiah to the people of Judah rings with equal urgency today. "Wash you, make you clean; put away the evil of your doings from before mine eyes; cease to do evil; Learn to do well; seek judgment, relieve the oppressed, judge the fatherless, plead for the widow" (Isaiah 1:16-17). Isaiah's admonition is a clarion call to the church to cleanse itself from the impurities of worldly entanglements and injustices. It is a summons not merely to avoid evil but to actively pursue righteousness and justice. As followers of Christ, we are compelled to mirror this prophetic zeal in our congregations, promoting a faith that acts justly and loves mercy.

Consider the boldness of John the Baptist, a voice crying out in the wilderness, preparing the way for the Lord by calling for repentance and spiritual renewal. His message, though direct, was imbued with the hope of redemption: "Bring forth therefore fruits meet for repentance" (Matthew 3:8). John's life and ministry exemplify the prophetic call to separation and readiness, a theme that is profoundly relevant to us today. As modern believers, we are to prepare the way for the Lord in our hearts and communities, fostering environments where repentance and holiness are pursued with vigor.

The minor prophets, too, offer rich insights into God's requirements for His people. Micah succinctly captures the essence of what God deems good, coupled with what He requires: "He hath shewed thee, O man, what is good; and what doth the LORD require of thee, but to do justly, and to love mercy, and to walk humbly with thy God?" (Micah 6:8). This rhetorical question challenges the church to embody these virtues—justice, mercy, and humility—not as lofty ideals, but as practical realities within our daily walk with God.

Hosea's life was a dramatic portrayal of God's relentless love and pursuit of His wayward people. His personal story—a prophet commanded to marry a woman prone to wander—symbolizes the heartbreaking unfaithfulness of God's people and His unyielding commitment to restore them. "I will heal their backsliding, I will love them freely: for mine anger is turned away from him" (Hosea 14:4). Hosea's prophetic ministry encourages us to recognize God's readiness to forgive and renew those who turn back to Him in genuine repentance.

In the narrative of Jonah, we find a prophet reluctant to deliver God's message of repentance to the city of Nineveh. Yet, the eventual submission of Jonah to God's command and the subsequent repentance of the Ninevites serve as a powerful testament to the transformative impact of heeding God's call. This story prompts us to reflect on our own willingness to embrace God's directives, even when they challenge us deeply. The repentance of Nineveh, where even the king humbled himself, stands as a timeless reminder of the power of repentance and God's mercy.

CHAPTER 53: PROPHETIC VOICES IN SCRIPTURE

The prophetic voices of Amos and Obadiah also resonate with clarity today. Amos, a shepherd turned prophet, spoke against the injustices and complacency of Israel, declaring, "Let judgment run down as waters, and righteousness as a mighty stream" (Amos 5:24). His call for justice and righteousness cuts through the noise of contemporary culture, reminding us that true worship of God is inseparable from our commitment to justice. Obadiah, though his book is brief, delivers a powerful message against the pride and violence of Edom, emphasizing that God will not tolerate arrogance and cruelty.

Daniel's life and prophecies offer a profound example of steadfast faith in the midst of a pagan culture. Despite the pressures to conform, Daniel and his friends remained resolute in their devotion to God, even when faced with death. Daniel's unwavering commitment is encapsulated in his prayer life, where he continued to pray three times a day despite the king's decree. His prophecies, such as the vision of the seventy weeks, foretell both judgment and restoration, pointing to God's ultimate sovereignty over history and His people.

Zechariah's prophecies are rich with visions of restoration and the coming of the Messiah. "Rejoice greatly, O daughter of Zion; shout, O daughter of Jerusalem: behold, thy King cometh unto thee: he is just, and having salvation; lowly, and riding upon an ass, and upon a colt the foal of an ass" (Zechariah 9:9). This prophetic vision, fulfilled in Jesus' triumphal entry into Jerusalem, highlights the ultimate hope and restoration found in Christ. Zechariah's call to return to the Lord and his visions of a restored

Jerusalem encourage us to look beyond present trials to the future glory promised by God.

Malachi, the last prophet of the Old Testament, confronts the laxity and corruption of the priests and people. His call for pure worship and integrity in service to God is encapsulated in his declaration, "For I am the LORD, I change not; therefore ye sons of Jacob are not consumed" (Malachi 3:6). Malachi's prophecies also point forward to the coming of John the Baptist, the forerunner of Christ, and the ultimate refinement and purification that Christ would bring.

The prophetic voices of the New Testament also call us to a higher standard of living and faithfulness. Jesus Himself, the greatest prophet, priest, and king, warns and encourages His followers to live in readiness for His return. "Watch therefore, for ye know neither the day nor the hour wherein the Son of man cometh" (Matthew 25:13). His parables, such as the wise and foolish virgins, serve as stark reminders of the importance of spiritual vigilance and preparedness.

The apostle Paul, though primarily an apostle, often spoke with a prophetic voice, warning the early churches of false teachings and urging them to remain steadfast in the truth. "For I know this, that after my departing shall grievous wolves enter in among you, not sparing the flock" (Acts 20:29). Paul's letters are filled with exhortations to purity, faithfulness, and the avoidance of worldly entanglements, reflecting the timeless need for the church to guard against compromise.

Peter's letters also carry a prophetic tone, particularly his warnings about the end times and the call to holy living. "But the day of the

CHAPTER 53: PROPHETIC VOICES IN SCRIPTURE

Lord will come as a thief in the night; in the which the heavens shall pass away with a great noise, and the elements shall melt with fervent heat, the earth also and the works that are therein shall be burned up. Seeing then that all these things shall be dissolved, what manner of persons ought ye to be in all holy conversation and godliness" (2 Peter 3:10-11). Peter's urgent call to holiness in light of impending judgment underscores the importance of living with eternal perspectives.

The book of Revelation, written by the apostle John, is the culmination of prophetic revelation. Its vivid imagery and powerful messages to the seven churches serve as both a warning and an encouragement. To the church in Laodicea, John delivers a stern rebuke for their lukewarmness: "I know thy works, that thou art neither cold nor hot: I would thou wert cold or hot. So then because thou art lukewarm, and neither cold nor hot, I will spue thee out of my mouth" (Revelation 3:15-16). This call to fervent and sincere faith is a timely reminder for us to examine our own spiritual temperature.

The prophetic voices of Scripture collectively serve as both a warning and a guide for the church today. They remind us of the importance of standing firm in our faith, maintaining our distinctiveness as followers of Christ, and heeding the call to separation and holiness. As we consider these ancient warnings and teachings, let us be moved to a deeper commitment to live out our faith authentically and courageously, embodying the truth of God's Word in every aspect of our lives.

In conclusion, the role of the church today is not merely to exist within society but to transform it. By revisiting the messages of the prophets, we are reminded of the crucial balance between being in the world but not of it. Let this prophetic wisdom inspire us to renew our dedication to God's unchanging standards, ensuring that our churches do not merely survive but thrive as beacons of His truth and love in a world gone wild.

Chapter 54: Scriptural Warning About Separation

The call for separation is not a foreign concept in the Scriptures; rather, it is a recurring theme that echoes the heart of God for His people. When we look at the teachings of Jesus, we see an unwavering commitment to holiness and purity, encapsulated in the poignant words of Matthew 3:12: "Whose fan is in his hand, and he will thoroughly purge his floor, and gather his wheat into the garner; but he will burn up the chaff with unquenchable fire." This vivid imagery serves as a divine reminder that God is not indifferent to the condition of His church. He is actively involved in purifying His people, separating the genuine from the counterfeit.

In today's world, the church faces a multitude of pressures to conform to societal norms and cultural trends. The temptation to blend in rather than stand out is ever-present. Yet, Paul's exhortation to the Romans remains as relevant as ever: "And be not conformed to this world: but be ye transformed by the renewing of your mind, that ye may prove what is that good, and acceptable, and perfect, will of God" (Romans 12:2). This transformation requires a deliberate and conscious effort to renew our minds, aligning our thoughts and actions with the truths of Scripture rather than the shifting sands of popular opinion.

The process of separation is neither easy nor comfortable. It involves a refining fire, a divine purification that removes impurities and prepares us for greater purposes. The prophet

Malachi captures this process beautifully: "And he shall sit as a refiner and purifier of silver: and he shall purify the sons of Levi, and purge them as gold and silver, that they may offer unto the Lord an offering in righteousness" (Malachi 3:3). This purification is both an act of divine love and a necessity for those who seek to serve the Lord with integrity and righteousness.

One of the most profound aspects of separation is its basis in love. God's call for us to be set apart is not a form of punishment, but a demonstration of His deep love for us. It is a call to protect us from the corrupting influences of the world and to draw us closer to His heart. Jesus, in His prayer for His disciples, expressed this protective desire: "I pray not that thou shouldest take them out of the world, but that thou shouldest keep them from the evil" (John 17:15). This prayer highlights the delicate balance of being in the world but not of it, living out our faith without succumbing to the world's corruptions.

As we heed the call to separation, we must also understand the importance of doctrinal purity. The Bereans were commended for their diligence in verifying the teachings they received: "These were more noble than those in Thessalonica, in that they received the word with all readiness of mind, and searched the scriptures daily, whether those things were so" (Acts 17:11). In a time where false teachings can easily infiltrate the church, it is imperative that we, like the Bereans, remain vigilant, testing every doctrine against the unchanging Word of God.

The church of Ephesus serves as a sobering example of what happens when we stray from our first love. Jesus' message to them was clear: "Nevertheless I have somewhat against thee, because

CHAPTER 54: SCRIPTURAL WARNING ABOUT SEPARATION

thou hast left thy first love. Remember therefore from whence thou art fallen, and repent, and do the first works; or else I will come unto thee quickly, and will remove thy candlestick out of his place, except thou repent" (Revelation 2:4-5). The warning is stark, yet it is filled with hope. It calls us to repentance, to return to the fervor and purity of our initial commitment to Christ.

Separation also involves a departure from behaviors and practices that contradict the teachings of Scripture. Paul's instruction to the Corinthians is a call to holiness: "Wherefore come out from among them, and be ye separate, saith the Lord, and touch not the unclean thing; and I will receive you, and will be a Father unto you, and ye shall be my sons and daughters, saith the Lord Almighty" (2 Corinthians 6:17-18). This command is not merely about physical separation but involves a spiritual and moral distancing from sin and compromise.

In this journey of separation, we must also embrace the call to live differently. Peter's exhortation captures the essence of our distinct identity: "But ye are a chosen generation, a royal priesthood, an holy nation, a peculiar people; that ye should shew forth the praises of him who hath called you out of darkness into his marvellous light" (1 Peter 2:9). Our lives, set apart by God, should reflect His glory and draw others towards His light. This identity as God's peculiar people is both a privilege and a responsibility.

The path of separation is marked by a continuous refining process. Just as gold is refined in the fire, our faith is tested and purified through trials and challenges. James encourages us with these words: "My brethren, count it all joy when ye fall into divers temptations; knowing this, that the trying of your faith worketh patience" (James 1:2-3). These trials are not meant to break us but to strengthen and purify our faith, making us more resilient and more like Christ.

As we navigate the complexities of living in a world that often stands in opposition to our faith, we are called to stand firm in the truth. Paul's charge to Timothy resonates with this call: "Preach the word; be instant in season, out of season; reprove, rebuke, exhort with all longsuffering and doctrine" (2 Timothy 4:2). Our commitment to God's Word must remain unwavering, even when it is inconvenient or unpopular. It is through steadfastness in the truth that we fulfill our calling and remain separate unto God.

The prophetic call to separation also serves as a warning against complacency. Jesus' parable of the ten virgins in Matthew 25 underscores the importance of being prepared and vigilant. The wise virgins, who kept their lamps filled with oil, were ready when the bridegroom arrived, while the foolish ones, who neglected their preparation, were left outside. This parable is a stark reminder that we must remain spiritually alert and prepared for the return of Christ.

In embracing the call to separation, we must also cultivate a heart of humility and repentance. The psalmist's plea should be our constant prayer: "Search me, O God, and know my heart: try me, and know my thoughts: and see if there be any wicked way in me, and lead me in the way everlasting" (Psalm 139:23-24). This openness to God's examination and guidance is crucial in our journey towards holiness and purity.

As we reflect on the scriptural warnings about separation, it becomes clear that this call is rooted in God's desire for a holy and

CHAPTER 54: SCRIPTURAL WARNING ABOUT SEPARATION

pure church. Paul's letter to the Ephesians highlights the ultimate goal of this divine process: "That he might present it to himself a glorious church, not having spot, or wrinkle, or any such thing; but that it should be holy and without blemish" (Ephesians 5:27). This vision of a spotless church is what we strive towards, through the process of separation and sanctification.

It is important to recognize that the call to separation is not a call to isolation. Jesus' commission to His disciples was to go into all the world and make disciples of all nations (Matthew 28:19-20). While we are called to be distinct and set apart, we are also called to engage with the world, sharing the gospel and extending the love of Christ. Our separation is meant to empower us for effective ministry, not to remove us from the mission field.

The journey of separation is ultimately about drawing closer to God. As we distance ourselves from worldly influences, we are invited into a deeper and more intimate relationship with our Creator. James encourages us with this promise: "Draw nigh to God, and he will draw nigh to you" (James 4:8). This promise is the heartbeat of our call to separation—a call to experience the fullness of God's presence and to be transformed by His holiness.

In conclusion, as we heed the prophetic warning of separation, we must do so with hearts fully surrendered to God. This journey is not about legalism or self-righteousness, but about a passionate pursuit of holiness and a desire to honor God with our lives. Let us embrace this call with humility and courage, knowing that it is through separation that we become vessels fit for the Master's use, ready to reflect His glory in a world that desperately needs His light. As we commit to this path, may we be inspired by the words of Paul: "Having therefore these promises, dearly beloved, let us cleanse ourselves from all filthiness of the flesh and spirit, perfecting holiness in the fear of God" (2 Corinthians 7:1). This is our sacred call—to be a holy people, set apart for God's glory and purpose.

Chapter 55: Heeding the Call

Heeding the call to separate from the worldly influences that have crept into the church is a matter of utmost urgency. As we look around, it becomes clear that the church has often sought to blend in with the culture rather than stand apart in holiness. Jesus warned us in Matthew 3:12 that He would clear His threshing floor, gathering His wheat into the barn and burning the chaff with unquenchable fire. This vivid imagery compels us to examine our lives and churches, identifying and removing anything that does not align with His holy standards.

The first step in responding to this divine mandate is a heartfelt introspection. Each believer must look deeply into their own heart and practices. Are our actions driven by a desire for cultural acceptance, or are they rooted in a desire to please God? James 4:4 starkly reminds us that friendship with the world is enmity with God. We must choose our allegiance carefully, for a divided heart cannot serve the Lord fully. This self-examination is not a one-time event but a continuous process of aligning our lives with God's word.

Returning to the core doctrines of our faith is essential in this process. These doctrines are not merely historical relics but living truths that connect us to God. Hebrews 4:12 tells us that the word of God is living and active, sharper than any two-edged sword. It discerns the thoughts and intentions of the heart, cutting through our pretenses and leading us back to the paths of righteousness. By immersing ourselves in scripture, we can rediscover the foundational truths that have sustained the church through centuries of trials and triumphs.

True repentance is at the heart of heeding this prophetic call. Repentance is not just feeling sorry for our sins but a radical turning away from them and a returning to God. Acts 3:19 encourages us to repent and turn back, so that our sins may be blotted out and times of refreshing may come from the presence of the Lord. These times of refreshing are promised to those who genuinely turn to God, forsaking the seductive paths of secular conformity. This turning back involves both personal and corporate repentance, as the church collectively seeks God's face.

The church must also stand firm against the tides of cultural and moral relativism. In a world that constantly seeks to redefine truth, we must boldly proclaim the unchanging truth of the gospel. Ephesians 4:15 urges us to speak the truth in love, growing up in every way into Him who is the head, into Christ. This growth is both individual and communal, as we strengthen each other in faith and hold fast to the truth amidst a culture of shifting morals and values. We are called to be beacons of light, illuminating the darkness with the truth of God's word.

Accountability is crucial in this journey of separation and renewal. The church must cultivate a culture where leaders and members hold each other to the high standards of scripture. Galatians 6:1 teaches us that if anyone is caught in a transgression, those who are spiritual should restore them in a spirit of gentleness. We must keep watch on ourselves as well, lest we too be tempted. This mutual accountability ensures that we remain faithful to our calling and supports one another in the pursuit of holiness.

CHAPTER 55: HEEDING THE CALL

Prayer is the lifeline of the church in this endeavor. We must become a house of prayer, where believers fervently seek God's direction and empowerment. As 2 Chronicles 7:14 promises, if God's people humble themselves, pray, seek His face, and turn from their wicked ways, He will hear from heaven, forgive their sin, and heal their land. Prayer is not just a religious duty but a powerful means of drawing near to God, receiving His guidance, and interceding for our communities and nations. It is through prayer that we align our hearts with God's will and find the strength to carry out His mandates.

Education and discipleship are essential for sustaining this renewed commitment. We must invest in teaching the next generations the truths of scripture, equipping them to discern and withstand the pressures to conform to the world. Deuteronomy 6:6-7 commands us to keep God's words in our hearts and diligently teach them to our children, talking about them in our daily lives. This diligent instruction ensures that the faith is passed on intact and that future generations are prepared to stand firm in their beliefs.

As we embark on this journey, we must be motivated by love for our Savior, who has called us out of darkness into His marvelous light. The path ahead may be challenging, but the rewards are eternal. Revelation 2:5 calls us to remember from where we have fallen, repent, and do the works we did at first. If we do not, our lampstand will be removed. This call to action is urgent and non-negotiable. The health of the church and the salvation of the world depend on our response to God's prophetic warning of separation and renewal.

In practical terms, this means making tangible changes in our personal lives and church practices. It might involve reevaluating the content of our sermons, ensuring they are rooted in scripture and not merely appealing to cultural trends. It could mean restructuring church activities to focus more on discipleship and less on entertainment. Romans 12:2 reminds us not to be conformed to this world but to be transformed by the renewal of our minds. This transformation requires deliberate effort and a willingness to make sacrifices for the sake of holiness.

Another crucial aspect is fostering a spirit of unity within the church. Ephesians 4:3 exhorts us to maintain the unity of the Spirit in the bond of peace. This unity is not based on superficial agreement but on a shared commitment to God's truth. As we strive for purity and renewal, we must do so with humility and grace, recognizing that we are all in need of God's mercy. By supporting and encouraging one another, we create a strong, resilient community that can withstand external pressures.

We must also be vigilant in guarding against false teachings. Acts 20:29-30 warns that after Paul's departure, fierce wolves would come in among the flock, not sparing it, and that from among their own selves men would arise, speaking twisted things to draw away the disciples. This warning is as relevant today as it was in the early church. We must be discerning, testing every teaching against the word of God, and rejecting anything that deviates from the truth.

In our personal lives, heeding the call means making daily choices that reflect our commitment to God. Colossians 3:17 encourages us to do everything in the name of the Lord Jesus, giving thanks to God the Father through Him. This encompasses every aspect of our lives, from our work and relationships to our thoughts and attitudes. By living in a way that honors God, we become living testimonies of His transforming power.

We must also be bold in our witness. Matthew 5:14-16 calls us the light of the world, a city set on a hill that cannot be hidden. We are to let our light shine before others so that they may see our good works and give glory to our Father in heaven. This involves sharing the gospel with those around us, not just through words but through our actions. By demonstrating the love and truth of Christ, we can draw others to Him.

As we pursue this path of separation and renewal, we can expect opposition. John 15:18-19 reminds us that if the world hates us, it hated Jesus first. We are not of the world, and therefore the world will oppose us. This opposition is a sign that we are on the right track. We must stand firm, knowing that our reward is in heaven. God has promised to be with us, and His grace is sufficient for every challenge we face.

Ultimately, our goal is to glorify God and advance His kingdom. Matthew 6:33 urges us to seek first the kingdom of God and His righteousness, and all these things will be added to us. By prioritizing God's kingdom, we align our lives with His purposes and experience His provision and blessing. This requires a shift in focus from earthly concerns to eternal priorities.

In conclusion, heeding the call to separation and renewal is a comprehensive, ongoing process that involves introspection, repentance, adherence to sound doctrine, prayer, discipleship, and bold witness. It is motivated by a deep love for Christ and a desire to see His church reflect His holiness and truth. As we respond to this prophetic call, we are assured of God's presence and power to guide and sustain us. Let us embrace this call with courage and commitment, knowing that in doing so, we honor our Savior and fulfill our divine mandate.

Section 12: The Road to Renewal

Chapter 56: Steps to Spiritual Renewal

Spiritual renewal is the lifeline that sustains the vitality of the church. In these times when the church is often distracted by worldly pursuits and diluted doctrines, a return to the core of our faith is crucial. Romans 12:2 calls us to "be not conformed to this world: but be ye transformed by the renewing of your mind, that ye may prove what is that good, and acceptable, and perfect, will of God." This transformation is not a one-time event but an ongoing journey, an ever-deepening process of aligning ourselves with the will and purposes of God.

The journey towards spiritual renewal begins with a sincere self-assessment. This is more than a superficial glance at our lives; it is a deep, honest examination of our hearts and our relationship with God. King David's prayer in Psalm 139:23-24, "Search me, O God, and know my heart: try me, and know my thoughts: And see if there be any wicked way in me, and lead me in the way everlasting," serves as a profound template for this introspection. We must invite God to reveal the hidden areas of our lives where we have strayed, allowing His light to expose the darkness within us.

True repentance follows genuine self-assessment. Repentance is not merely feeling sorry for our sins; it is a deliberate turning away from them and turning back to God. Acts 3:19 urges us, "Repent ye therefore, and be converted, that your sins may be blotted out, when the times of refreshing shall come from the presence of the Lord." This promise of refreshing and renewal from God's presence is contingent upon our repentance. As we confess and

CHAPTER 56: STEPS TO SPIRITUAL RENEWAL

forsake our sins, we experience a renewed sense of God's grace and mercy washing over us, bringing healing and restoration.

Prayer is the vital breath of the Christian life and a cornerstone of spiritual renewal. It is through prayer that we communicate with God, express our deepest desires, and align our will with His. James 5:16 reminds us, "The effectual fervent prayer of a righteous man availeth much." Prayer is powerful not because of the words we say but because of the God who hears and responds. In the quiet place of prayer, we draw near to God, and He draws near to us, transforming our hearts and minds.

The study of God's Word is equally critical in the process of renewal. Hebrews 4:12 declares, "For the word of God is quick, and powerful, and sharper than any two-edged sword, piercing even to the dividing asunder of soul and spirit, and of the joints and marrow, and is a discerner of the thoughts and intents of the heart." As we immerse ourselves in scripture, we allow the Holy Spirit to speak to us, convict us, and guide us into all truth. The Word of God becomes a mirror, reflecting our true condition and pointing us to the way of righteousness.

Fellowship with other believers plays a transformative role in our spiritual lives. The early church thrived on a vibrant community where believers regularly gathered for teaching, fellowship, breaking of bread, and prayers, as seen in Acts 2:42. In these gatherings, they found encouragement, accountability, and mutual edification. Our spiritual vitality is significantly enhanced when we connect with others who share our faith, spurring one another on towards love and good deeds. Hebrews 10:24-25 emphasizes the importance of this, urging us to "consider one another to provoke unto love and to good works: Not forsaking the assembling of ourselves together, as the manner of some is; but exhorting one another: and so much the more, as ye see the day approaching."

Serving others is a natural outflow of a renewed spirit. Galatians 5:13 encourages us, "For, brethren, ye have been called unto liberty; only use not liberty for an occasion to the flesh, but by love serve one another." Service is a tangible expression of our love for God and our neighbors. It shifts our focus from ourselves to others, mirroring the example of Christ who came not to be served but to serve. In serving, we participate in God's redemptive work, bringing His love and compassion to a hurting world.

Worship is an essential aspect of renewal. Worship is more than singing songs; it is a lifestyle of honoring and glorifying God in all that we do. Jesus said in John 4:23-24, "But the hour cometh, and now is, when the true worshippers shall worship the Father in spirit and in truth: for the Father seeketh such to worship him. God is a Spirit: and they that worship him must worship him in spirit and in truth." True worship aligns our spirit with the Holy Spirit, creating an environment where God's presence dwells and transforms us from the inside out.

Forgiveness is another crucial step in the path of spiritual renewal. Holding onto grudges and harboring unforgiveness can be a significant barrier to experiencing God's renewal. Ephesians 4:32 instructs us, "And be ye kind one to another, tenderhearted, forgiving one another, even as God for Christ's sake hath forgiven you." When we forgive, we release the burden of bitterness and

CHAPTER 56: STEPS TO SPIRITUAL RENEWAL

allow God's healing to flow through us, bringing freedom and restoration.

Humility is a hallmark of a renewed spirit. James 4:10 exhorts us, "Humble yourselves in the sight of the Lord, and he shall lift you up." Humility involves recognizing our dependence on God and submitting our will to His. It is through humility that we are positioned to receive God's grace and empowerment. As we humble ourselves, we open the door for God to work mightily in and through us.

Obedience to God's Word is the natural outcome of a renewed spirit. Jesus said in John 14:23, "If a man love me, he will keep my words: and my Father will love him, and we will come unto him, and make our abode with him." Obedience is not about legalistic adherence to rules but a loving response to God's love for us. It reflects our trust in His goodness and our desire to live in a way that pleases Him. As we walk in obedience, we experience the fullness of God's blessings and favor.

Gratitude is another essential component of spiritual renewal. 1 Thessalonians 5:18 urges us, "In every thing give thanks: for this is the will of God in Christ Jesus concerning you." A heart of gratitude recognizes God's hand in every aspect of our lives and cultivates a spirit of joy and contentment. Gratitude shifts our focus from what we lack to what we have, fostering a deeper appreciation for God's provision and grace.

Silence and solitude are often overlooked but vital practices for spiritual renewal. Psalm 46:10 invites us to "Be still, and know that I am God." In the busyness of life, it is crucial to carve out time for quiet reflection and communion with God. In these moments of stillness, we tune our hearts to hear God's voice, allowing Him to speak and minister to our deepest needs.

Faith is the foundation upon which spiritual renewal is built. Hebrews 11:6 reminds us, "But without faith it is impossible to please him: for he that cometh to God must believe that he is, and that he is a rewarder of them that diligently seek him." Faith is trusting in God's promises and stepping out in obedience, even when we do not see the full picture. It is through faith that we access God's power and experience His supernatural intervention in our lives.

Joy is a hallmark of a renewed spirit. Nehemiah 8:10 declares, "The joy of the Lord is your strength." Joy is not dependent on our circumstances but on our relationship with God. It is a deep-seated confidence in His sovereignty and goodness. As we cultivate joy, we find strength and resilience to face life's challenges, knowing that God is with us and for us.

Love is the ultimate evidence of spiritual renewal. 1 Corinthians 13:13 concludes, "And now abideth faith, hope, charity, these three; but the greatest of these is charity." Love is the highest expression of our faith and the most compelling witness to the world. It is through love that we fulfill God's greatest commandments: to love Him with all our heart, soul, mind, and strength, and to love our neighbor as ourselves.

Patience is another virtue that marks a renewed spirit. James 1:4 encourages us, "But let patience have her perfect work, that ye may be perfect and entire, wanting nothing." Patience is the ability to endure trials and waiting periods with grace and trust in God's

CHAPTER 56: STEPS TO SPIRITUAL RENEWAL

timing. It is through patience that our faith is tested and strengthened, leading us to maturity and completeness in Christ.

Generosity is a natural outflow of a renewed spirit. 2 Corinthians 9:7 reminds us, "Every man according as he purposeth in his heart, so let him give; not grudgingly, or of necessity: for God loveth a cheerful giver." Generosity reflects the heart of God, who gave His only Son for our redemption. As we give freely and joyfully, we participate in God's kingdom work, blessing others and being blessed in return.

Hope is a sustaining force in the journey of spiritual renewal. Romans 15:13 prays, "Now the God of hope fill you with all joy and peace in believing, that ye may abound in hope, through the power of the Holy Ghost." Hope anchors our soul in the promises of God, giving us the confidence to face the future with assurance. It is through hope that we persevere, knowing that God's plans for us are good and His purposes will prevail.

In this journey towards spiritual renewal, we must remember that it is not by our might nor by power, but by the Spirit of the Lord, as Zechariah 4:6 declares. Each step taken in dependence on Him ensures our path is not just a return to form but a deeper, richer, and more vibrant walk with God. Let us then move forward, renewed in spirit and truth, eager to manifest the glory of God in and through our lives. As we embrace these steps towards renewal, may we become the vessels through which God's light shines brightly in a world desperately in need of His love and grace.

Chapter 57: Revival Histories

In the rich tapestry of church history, revivals stand out as vivid threads, moments when God dramatically intervened to revitalize His people and reclaim lost ground. As we seek renewal within our churches today, the echoes of these spiritual awakenings serve as both guide and inspiration. Consider the profound Great Awakening of the 18th century, which swept through the American colonies. This revival was marked by an intense reaffirmation of the gospel, piercing the hardest hearts and reviving the complacent. Jonathan Edwards, a preacher of that era, observed the hand of God moving mightily, much like the promise in Acts 3:19-20: "Repent ye therefore, and be converted, that your sins may be blotted out, when the times of refreshing shall come from the presence of the Lord." This scriptural promise fueled transformative fires that reshaped the spiritual landscape of an emerging nation.

The Second Great Awakening, which followed some years later, further exemplifies how revivals can shape not only church life but also societal structures. This period witnessed the burgeoning of social reform movements, from abolitionism to advances in women's rights, all rooted in a renewed zeal for biblical truths and righteousness. The spirit of revival infused believers with a fervor that transcended the walls of the church, spilling over into passionate societal engagement. As Galatians 5:1 exhorts, "Stand fast therefore in the liberty wherewith Christ hath made us free, and be not entangled again with the yoke of bondage." This scripture animated the hearts of those who fought for freedom and

CHAPTER 57: REVIVAL HISTORIES

dignity against societal injustices, demonstrating that revival often extends beyond personal piety to include active communal transformation.

In more recent history, the Welsh Revival of the early 20th century further illustrates the unpredictability and sovereignty of God in renewal movements. Within a short span, hundreds of thousands were added to the church, and entire communities were transformed by the power of the Holy Spirit. The revival fires in Wales were marked by spontaneous and overwhelming senses of God's presence, aligning with Zechariah 4:6, which declares, "Not by might, nor by power, but by my spirit, saith the Lord of hosts." This underscores a pivotal lesson: true revival is not manufactured by human effort but is a sovereign move of God, where His Spirit orchestrates a divine dance of restoration.

The Azusa Street Revival in Los Angeles, beginning in 1906, stands as a testament to God's desire to break down racial and denominational barriers through the outpouring of His Spirit. Led by William J. Seymour, a humble African American preacher, this revival was characterized by fervent prayer, spontaneous worship, and miraculous healings. People of diverse backgrounds gathered in a small, rundown mission to experience the Holy Spirit's power, embodying Ephesians 2:14: "For he is our peace, who hath made both one, and hath broken down the middle wall of partition between us." This revival birthed the modern Pentecostal movement, demonstrating that God's Spirit transcends human divisions and unites believers in a powerful, supernatural fellowship.

These historical revivals share common threads, one of which is fervent prayer. Before each of these movements, believers were found on their knees, crying out in unity for a visitation from heaven, reflective of 2 Chronicles 7:14's call to prayer: "If my people, which are called by my name, shall humble themselves, and pray, and seek my face, and turn from their wicked ways; then will I hear from heaven, and will forgive their sin, and will heal their land." The fervent, effectual prayers of the righteous have always been the precursor to the outpouring of spiritual renewal. Thus, as we seek a fresh revival in our time, we must also commit to a posture of deep, earnest intercession.

Moreover, each revival brought about a profound return to the Word of God. As believers increasingly turned to scripture, they found not only personal edification but also a blueprint for expanding the Kingdom of God. Just as Hebrews 4:12 describes, "For the word of God is quick, and powerful, and sharper than any two-edged sword," the rediscovery of scriptural truths cut through apathy and sin during these revivals, igniting a passion for holiness and mission. Today, as we face the challenge of cultural drift and doctrinal dilution, a return to the diligent study and application of scripture is non-negotiable for genuine renewal.

Another hallmark of revival is the emphasis on repentance. During the Great Awakening, preachers like George Whitefield and Jonathan Edwards emphasized the necessity of turning away from sin and returning to God with a contrite heart. This call to repentance aligns with Isaiah 55:7, which declares, "Let the wicked forsake his way, and the unrighteous man his thoughts: and let him return unto the Lord, and he will have mercy upon him; and

CHAPTER 57: REVIVAL HISTORIES

to our God, for he will abundantly pardon." True revival always begins with a deep, personal acknowledgment of sin and a sincere turning back to God, paving the way for divine forgiveness and renewal.

In examining the Asbury Revival of 1970, we see the impact of sustained, heartfelt worship and confession. What began as a routine chapel service at Asbury College in Wilmore, Kentucky, extended into days of continuous prayer, worship, and public confession of sins. This revival spread across college campuses and churches, drawing thousands into a deeper relationship with God. The spontaneous and organic nature of this revival echoes the sentiment of Psalm 85:6, "Wilt thou not revive us again: that thy people may rejoice in thee?" The joy and renewal experienced at Asbury remind us that God often chooses the unexpected places and times to pour out His Spirit.

The revival histories also teach us that genuine moves of God often come with opposition and controversy. As the light of God's truth shines brighter, it exposes sin and convicts hearts, which can lead to discomfort and resistance both within and outside the church. Yet, as Jesus taught in John 15:18-19, "If the world hate you, ye know that it hated me before it hated you. If ye were of the world, the world would love his own: but because ye are not of the world, but I have chosen you out of the world, therefore the world hateth you." This stark reminder calls us to brace for resistance but also to rejoice, knowing that our alignment with Christ's kingdom sets us apart for His sacred purposes.

Reflecting on these revivals, we see a pattern of communal impact. The revival in the Hebrides, off the coast of Scotland, during the late 1940s and early 1950s, is a powerful example. It began with two elderly sisters who prayed fervently for revival. Soon, the entire community was engulfed in a spiritual awakening. Churches overflowed, prayer meetings multiplied, and countless lives were transformed. The entire island experienced a tangible sense of God's presence, akin to Habakkuk 3:2, "O Lord, I have heard thy speech, and was afraid: O Lord, revive thy work in the midst of the years, in the midst of the years make known; in wrath remember mercy." This revival underscores the profound impact that dedicated prayer and faith can have on a community, transforming not just individual lives but entire regions.

One cannot overlook the transformative power of youth in revival history. The Jesus Movement of the late 1960s and early 1970s saw a wave of young people turning to Christ in the midst of cultural upheaval. Emerging from the countercultural movements of the time, this revival was characterized by a raw, unpolished enthusiasm for Jesus and a rejection of traditional church formalities. Matthew 18:3 captures this spirit well: "Verily I say unto you, Except ye be converted, and become as little children, ye shall not enter into the kingdom of heaven." The simplicity and sincerity of faith displayed by the youth in this movement brought about a refreshing wave of renewal that reshaped contemporary Christian worship and evangelism.

As we contemplate these revival histories, it becomes clear that God's methods may vary, but His purposes remain the same: to glorify His name and to draw people into a deeper relationship with Him. Isaiah 43:19 declares, "Behold, I will do a new thing; now it shall spring forth; shall ye not know it? I will even make a way in

CHAPTER 57: REVIVAL HISTORIES

the wilderness, and rivers in the desert." This promise assures us that God is always at work, even in the most barren seasons, crafting streams of revival that refresh and restore.

Each of these historical accounts highlights the crucial role of humility in revival. Revival does not come to the proud or self-sufficient but to those who recognize their desperate need for God. James 4:10 exhorts, "Humble yourselves in the sight of the Lord, and he shall lift you up." This humility is not just a personal virtue but a collective posture that invites God's presence and power into the church. As we seek renewal, cultivating a spirit of humility will be essential for experiencing God's transformative work.

The lessons from revival histories also remind us of the importance of unity. Divisions and strife within the body of Christ can quench the Spirit and hinder revival. Psalm 133:1 states, "Behold, how good and how pleasant it is for brethren to dwell together in unity!" Unity among believers, despite differences, creates an environment where the Holy Spirit can move freely. As we strive for renewal, fostering unity within our churches will be paramount in welcoming God's revival presence.

Furthermore, these revivals teach us that revival is not a one-time event but a continual process. The fervor and passion ignited during a revival must be nurtured and sustained through ongoing discipleship and obedience to God's word. Philippians 1:6 encourages us with these words: "Being confident of this very thing, that he which hath begun a good work in you will perform it until the day of Jesus Christ." Maintaining the fruits of revival requires commitment and perseverance, ensuring that the initial outpouring of God's Spirit leads to lasting transformation.

In considering the road to renewal for our time, let us draw inspiration from these histories of revival. They serve not only as reminders of what God has done but also as beacons of hope for what He can and will do again. As we stand on the threshold of potential revival, let our prayer echo that of Habakkuk 3:2, "O Lord, revive thy work in the midst of the years, in the midst of the years make known; in wrath remember mercy." In this plea, we find the synthesis of our desire for revival and our dependence on God's sovereign grace to bring it to fruition.

In each of these historical revivals, the Spirit of God moved uniquely, tailored to the needs and context of the time. As we seek renewal today, let us be open to the fresh and creative ways God might choose to revive His church, ensuring that our hearts are prepared, our motives are pure, and our eyes are fixed on Him—the author and finisher of our faith.

Chapter 58: Role of Prayer and Repentance

The road to renewal in the church is a journey paved with the stones of prayer and repentance. These twin pillars are foundational to the Christian faith and indispensable for any believer or congregation seeking to return to the heart of God. Prayer and repentance are not just religious activities; they are profound expressions of our relationship with the Divine, our recognition of His sovereignty, and our dependence on His grace. In 2 Chronicles 7:14, we are given a clear and powerful promise: if God's people humble themselves, pray, seek His face, and turn from their wicked ways, then He will hear from heaven, forgive their sin, and heal their land. This verse encapsulates the essence of the transformative power that lies in prayer and repentance.

Prayer is our lifeline to God, a direct line of communication that allows us to speak to Him and, just as importantly, to listen. It is in these moments of intimate conversation with our Creator that we find clarity, peace, and direction. James 4:8 encourages us with the promise that if we draw near to God, He will draw near to us. This is not a distant, impersonal deity but a loving Father eager to engage with His children. When we approach Him in prayer, we align our hearts with His, opening ourselves to His guidance and wisdom. The more we immerse ourselves in prayer, the more our desires and actions reflect His will, shaping us into instruments of His purpose.

Repentance, meanwhile, is the act of turning away from sin and realigning our lives with God's standards. It goes beyond mere remorse or regret; it is a decisive change of direction, a deliberate choice to forsake sin and pursue righteousness. Acts 3:19 implores us to repent so that our sins may be blotted out, leading to times of refreshing from the Lord. This refreshing is the renewal of our spirits, a rejuvenation that comes from being in right standing with God. Each act of repentance cleanses us, making us vessels through which God's Spirit can flow more freely and powerfully.

The combination of prayer and repentance creates a powerful dynamic in the life of a believer. Prayer without repentance can become hollow, while repentance without prayer lacks the relational aspect that brings us into deeper communion with God. Together, they foster a spiritual environment where growth and transformation can thrive. In Daniel 9:3, we see a profound example of this dynamic as Daniel turned to the Lord in prayer and fasting, confessing the sins of his people and seeking God's mercy. His earnest intercession and repentant heart moved God to reveal great insights and prophecies about the future.

Incorporating these disciplines into our daily lives is not merely about setting aside specific times for prayer and repentance but about cultivating a lifestyle where every moment is lived in awareness of God's presence and in alignment with His will. This continual interaction with the divine shapes us into people who are not just hearers but doers of the Word (James 1:22). It transforms our character, influences our decisions, and impacts our interactions with others. As we make prayer and repentance integral to our lives, we become more attuned to the leading of the Holy Spirit, more sensitive to His promptings, and more effective in our witness to the world.

CHAPTER 58: ROLE OF PRAYER AND REPENTANCE

For the church as a corporate body, the call to prayer and repentance is equally critical. When believers come together in unity to seek God's face and repent of their collective transgressions, it unleashes a powerful spiritual force. The early church in Acts 2:42 was devoted to the apostles' teaching, fellowship, the breaking of bread, and prayer. Their commitment to these practices created a community marked by signs and wonders, a place where the presence of God was palpably manifest. This is the model for us today: a church that prays together and repents together is a church that experiences God's power together.

But the effectiveness of our prayers and repentance depends on the sincerity of our hearts. God is not impressed by outward displays of piety but looks at the motives behind our actions (Jeremiah 17:10). True prayer and repentance come from a place of genuine humility and a deep desire to honor God above all else. It is in the secret place, away from the eyes of others, that our true spiritual condition is revealed. Matthew 6:6 reminds us that our Father who sees in secret will reward us openly. This is a call to authenticity, to ensure that our spiritual practices are not for show but are driven by a sincere longing for God.

The transformative power of prayer and repentance is not always immediate. There are times when it feels like our prayers go unanswered or our efforts at repentance fall short. In these moments, it is crucial to persevere, to continue seeking God with all our hearts. Jesus told His disciples a parable to show them that they should always pray and not give up (Luke 18:1). Persistence in prayer demonstrates our faith in God's goodness and His perfect timing. It is through this perseverance that we build spiritual resilience, deepening our trust in God even when we cannot see the immediate results of our prayers.

In fostering a culture of prayer and repentance within our churches, we must also encourage one another to engage earnestly in these practices. Hebrews 10:24-25 exhorts us to spur one another on toward love and good deeds, not giving up meeting together, but encouraging one another. This communal aspect of our faith is vital. As we support and challenge each other to grow in prayer and repentance, we create a spiritual environment that nurtures and sustains revival. It is a collective effort, a shared commitment to pursue God with all our hearts.

Imagine a church where prayer and repentance are woven into the very fabric of its existence, where every decision, every action, is bathed in prayer and aligned with God's will through continual repentance. Such a church would be a beacon of light in a dark world, a place where the presence of God is evident, and His power is at work. It would be a community marked by love, unity, and holiness, reflecting the beauty and purity of Christ to all who encounter it.

The promise of renewal through prayer and repentance is not just for the church as an institution but for each believer individually. As we commit to these disciplines, we open ourselves to the transformative work of the Holy Spirit. Our lives become testimonies of God's grace and power, drawing others to the hope and salvation found in Christ. The journey may be challenging, but the rewards are eternal. We are called to be a people set apart, holy and dedicated to God's purposes.

CHAPTER 58: ROLE OF PRAYER AND REPENTANCE

In times of difficulty or spiritual dryness, it is tempting to abandon our commitment to prayer and repentance. Yet it is precisely in these times that we must press in even more fervently. The psalmist declares in Psalm 42:1, "As the deer pants for streams of water, so my soul pants for you, my God." This deep longing for God, this thirst for His presence, is what sustains us through the dry seasons. It is in seeking Him earnestly, in praying without ceasing, and in continually repenting of our sins that we find the strength to persevere.

The impact of a praying and repentant church extends beyond its walls. It influences the community, the nation, and even the world. A church that prays and repents is a church that God can use mightily to advance His kingdom. It becomes a catalyst for change, a source of hope, and a conduit of God's love and power. As we heed the call to prayer and repentance, we position ourselves to be used by God in ways that we cannot even begin to imagine.

The journey to renewal is ongoing. It requires a steadfast commitment to the disciplines of prayer and repentance. It is a daily decision to seek God, to turn away from sin, and to pursue righteousness. But as we remain faithful, we will see the fruit of our labor. We will experience the joy of walking in close fellowship with God, the peace that comes from being in right standing with Him, and the power of His Spirit at work in and through us.

Let us, therefore, embrace the call to prayer and repentance with all our hearts. Let us commit to these practices not out of duty, but out of a deep desire to know God and to make Him known. As we do, we will find that the road to renewal is not just a path we walk but a journey we live, one that leads us ever closer to the heart of God.

Chapter 59: Scriptural Promise of Divine Restoration

In "Church Gone Wild: A Call to Renewal and Restoration," we come to a pivotal point in our journey, focusing on the scriptural promises that guide us towards renewal. As we navigate through the challenges of modern church dynamics, it is essential to hold firmly to the assurances found in God's Word. "If my people, which are called by my name, shall humble themselves, and pray, and seek my face, and turn from their wicked ways; then will I hear from heaven, and will forgive their sin, and will heal their land" (2 Chronicles 7:14). This verse is not just a call to action; it is a divine assurance that when we align our lives with God's will, healing and revival are inevitable.

The promise of healing our land is profound, speaking not just to physical restoration but to spiritual and moral renewal. In today's context, where the church often finds itself at crossroads with cultural and societal norms, this promise is more relevant than ever. Our surroundings reflect our spiritual state. When there is a disconnection from the foundational truths of the gospel, both our personal lives and our communities suffer. The healing of our land begins with repentance and revival within our hearts. It starts with the individual, extends to the church, and ultimately impacts the entire community. God's promise to hear from heaven is a literal assurance that He remains actively engaged in the lives of those who dedicate themselves wholly to His cause.

Renewal is not merely about external changes; it is about a transformation that begins within. True renewal and revival do not occur because we will them into existence but because we position ourselves in obedience to God. Humbling ourselves involves recognizing our limitations and surrendering to God's sovereignty. It is an acknowledgment that without Him, our efforts are in vain. This humility must be coupled with fervent prayer. Prayer is our lifeline to the divine, a direct communication channel that remains open regardless of our circumstances. When we seek His face with all our hearts, leaving behind our past transgressions, the intimacy of our relationship with God grows, and so does our capacity to receive His blessings and guidance.

Seeking God's face is more than a simple act; it is a pursuit of His presence and His will. It involves a deep, personal engagement with Him, moving beyond superficial religious activities into a profound relational depth. This is where we find the strength and the courage to turn from our wicked ways. Turning from our wicked ways is perhaps the most challenging aspect, yet it is the most crucial. It involves a thorough examination of our actions, thoughts, and motivations. Are they aligned with the character and commands of Christ? This is not about achieving perfection but about a sincere effort to live out the gospel in every aspect of our lives. It is a continuous journey of repentance where each step taken in obedience is a step towards renewal.

The promise that God will hear from heaven is not a mere formality. It is a profound truth that underscores His attentiveness to our genuine efforts of transformation. He doesn't ignore the cries of the repentant; He leans close, listens intently, and acts

CHAPTER 59: SCRIPTURAL PROMISE OF DIVINE RESTORATION

sovereignly. His forgiveness is a powerful catalyst for healing, not just spiritually but also materially and socially within our communities. This healing is comprehensive, touching every wound and restoring every breach. The impact of God's forgiveness and healing extends beyond individual lives, permeating communities, and restoring broken relationships and systems.

Our human efforts alone can only take us so far; it is the Spirit of the Lord that must lead the charge in this renewal. "Not by might, nor by power, but by my spirit, saith the LORD of hosts" (Zechariah 4:6). We are called to be vessels, conduits through which His power flows to effect real change. This involves a steadfast faith in His ability to perform that which He has promised. Embracing God's promises requires patience and endurance. The healing of our land is a gradual process. Just as the farmer waits for the precious fruit of the earth, being patient about it, until it receives the early and latter rain, so must we be patient (James 5:7). Our anticipation for revival must be tempered with the understanding that God's timing is perfect, and His ways are higher than ours.

Scriptural promises provide a solid foundation for our faith. God's words are unchanging and reliable, offering us the assurance we need to face uncertainties and challenges. "For all the promises of God in him are yea, and in him Amen, unto the glory of God by us" (2 Corinthians 1:20). This means that every promise God has made is affirmed and fulfilled in Christ. This is the bedrock of our confidence as we seek renewal. It reminds us that God's promises are not empty words but guaranteed realities.

In seeking renewal, we must also remember the role of community. The scripture speaks to "my people"—a collective body of believers united in purpose and action. Renewal is not an isolated journey but a communal effort. As we humble ourselves, pray, seek God's face, and turn from our wicked ways, we must do so together, supporting and encouraging one another. The power of unity in the body of Christ cannot be underestimated. Jesus prayed for our unity, knowing that it would be a testament to the world of God's love and power (John 17:21).

Moreover, the scriptural promise of renewal calls us to a lifestyle of repentance. Repentance is not a one-time event but a continual turning back to God. It is a posture of the heart that acknowledges our need for His grace daily. "If we confess our sins, he is faithful and just to forgive us our sins, and to cleanse us from all unrighteousness" (1 John 1:9). This cleansing is part of the healing process, making us whole and preparing us to be effective vessels of God's love and power.

As we advocate for this renewal, let us remember that it is God's Spirit that brings about the change. Our role is to remain obedient, faithful, and responsive to His leading. The Holy Spirit empowers us to live out the promises of God, guiding us into all truth and enabling us to walk in His ways. This partnership with the Holy Spirit is crucial for sustained renewal and revival. We cannot do it in our own strength; we need the infilling and empowering presence of the Holy Spirit.

The journey to renewal also requires us to reclaim the spiritual disciplines that have been neglected or forgotten. Prayer, fasting, and the study of God's Word are essential practices that cultivate a

CHAPTER 59: SCRIPTURAL PROMISE OF DIVINE RESTORATION

deeper relationship with God and prepare our hearts for His work. These disciplines are not mere rituals but means of grace that God uses to transform us from the inside out. They help us to stay focused on His promises and to align our lives with His purposes.

As we delve deeper into the scriptural promise of renewal, we must also address the importance of faith. Faith is the key that unlocks the promises of God. "But without faith it is impossible to please him: for he that cometh to God must believe that he is, and that he is a rewarder of them that diligently seek him" (Hebrews 11:6). Faith moves us beyond our current realities and allows us to see the possibilities of what God can do. It is faith that sustains us through the waiting and the challenges, keeping our eyes fixed on the promise of renewal.

God's promise to heal our land is also a call to action. It requires us to step out in faith, to engage with our communities, and to be agents of change. This might mean addressing social injustices, caring for the poor, and standing up for righteousness. Our faith must be active, demonstrated through our works, as James reminds us, "Faith without works is dead" (James 2:26). True renewal is evident in transformed lives and communities that reflect the love and justice of God.

In this journey towards renewal, let us not lose sight of the ultimate goal: to glorify God. The purpose of renewal is not for our benefit alone but for the glory of God to be displayed in and through us. "Let your light so shine before men, that they may see your good works, and glorify your Father which is in heaven" (Matthew 5:16). As we pursue renewal, our lives should point others to God, showing them His goodness and faithfulness.

Finally, as we hold on to the scriptural promise of renewal, let us do so with hope and expectation. God is faithful, and He will fulfill His promises. "Being confident of this very thing, that he which hath begun a good work in you will perform it until the day of Jesus Christ" (Philippians 1:6). This assurance gives us the strength to persevere, knowing that God is at work, even when we do not see immediate results. Our hope is anchored in His faithfulness, and we can trust that He will bring about the renewal we long for.

In closing this chapter on the scriptural promise of renewal, let's hold fast to the assurance that God is not man, that He should lie; neither the son of man, that He should repent: hath He said, and shall He not do it? or hath He spoken, and shall He not make it good? (Numbers 23:19). With such a firm foundation, we stand on the threshold of revival, ready to step into the fullness of what God has prepared for those who love Him and are called according to His purpose.

Thus, dear reader, as we contemplate this path to renewal, let it be with a heart full of hope and a spirit willing to align with God's divine plan. Each step we take, grounded in the principles laid out in His Word, brings us closer to the realization of a church and a community that truly embodies the Kingdom of God on earth. As we endeavor to move forward, let us do so with the conviction that God's promises are yea and amen, and that our obedience and faith will indeed heal our land and bring about the renewal we so deeply desire.

Chapter 60: Envisioning the Future Church

Envisioning the future church is like gazing upon a horizon filled with the radiant light of dawn, where the promise of a new day in Christ stirs the spirit with hope and expectation. This vision of the church is not merely an exercise in imagination but a divine invitation to witness and partake in the manifest workings of God's kingdom on earth as it is in heaven. As we stand on the threshold of renewal, let us recall the words of the prophet Isaiah, who declared, "Behold, I will do a new thing; now it shall spring forth; shall ye not know it? I will even make a way in the wilderness, and rivers in the desert" (Isaiah 43:19). This scripture is a beacon for our journey forward, illuminating the path toward a church rejuvenated by its fidelity to Christ and animated by the Holy Spirit's power.

The future church we aspire to build must be deeply rooted in the truth of God's Word, resisting the shifting sands of cultural compromise. In this renewed church, the unchanging gospel of Jesus Christ is the cornerstone, and its teachings are not diluted but delivered with clarity and conviction. Imagine a church where the pulpit is ablaze with righteousness, and each message is steeped in the scriptural richness that Paul urged Timothy to hold fast to, saying, "Preach the word; be instant in season, out of season; reprove, rebuke, exhort with all longsuffering and doctrine" (2 Timothy 4:2). In such a church, the congregation is nurtured on solid doctrine, growing strong and steadfast in faith.

In the communion of this future church, the fellowship is marked by genuine love and selfless service, reflecting the early church's unity and fervor. As believers, our interactions should embody the love Christ commanded in John 13:34, "A new commandment I give unto you, That ye love one another; as I have loved you, that ye also love one another." This love is active, sacrificial, and transformative, knitting the body of Christ into a tight-knit community of believers who support, encourage, and edify one another in their walk with the Lord.

Worship in the future church will be a profound expression of our reverence and awe for God, transcending the superficial allure of entertainment-driven services. True worship, as Jesus described to the Samaritan woman at the well, must be "in spirit and in truth" (John 4:24). This worship is neither a weekly performance nor a routine gathering but a continuous outpouring of our hearts before God, recognizing His holiness and responding in adoration and thanksgiving.

Outreach and evangelism are the lifeblood of the future church, driven by an unquenchable zeal to share the gospel's hope with every corner of the earth. The Great Commission, which commands us to "Go ye therefore, and teach all nations, baptizing them in the name of the Father, and of the Son, and of the Holy Ghost" (Matthew 28:19), remains our mandate. This mission is carried out not only across seas and borders but also across streets and neighborhoods, reaching out with compassion and the message of redemption to the lost and hurting around us.

The future church recognizes the indispensable role of prayer as the engine of its ministry and the secret to its power. A church steeped in prayer is a church attuned to the will of God, fortified against the assaults of the enemy, and fertile ground for miracles

CHAPTER 60: ENVISIONING THE FUTURE CHURCH

and testimonies. As we are exhorted in 1 Thessalonians 5:17 to "pray without ceasing," so the future church integrates prayer into every aspect of its life, ensuring that every endeavor is birthed in and sustained by prayer.

Social justice and community service will be hallmarks of the future church, demonstrating the kingdom's values through practical, loving action. This church does not retreat from societal challenges but meets them head-on, embodying the spirit of Micah 6:8: "He hath shewed thee, O man, what is good; and what doth the Lord require of thee, but to do justly, and to love mercy, and to walk humbly with thy God?" Through initiatives that address poverty, injustice, and need, the future church acts as Christ's hands and feet on earth, bringing healing and hope.

Leadership in the future church is neither authoritarian nor aloof but exemplifies servant leadership modeled by Christ Himself. Leaders are shepherds, as Peter directed, "Feed the flock of God which is among you, taking the oversight thereof, not by constraint, but willingly; not for filthy lucre, but of a ready mind" (1 Peter 5:2). These leaders guide with humility, serve with integrity, and inspire their congregations to pursue God's heart in all things.

In the future church, discipleship is a continual journey of growth and learning, where every member is both a disciple and a discipler, engaging in the mutual edification and equipping of the saints. This dynamic of discipleship ensures that the church never stagnates but perpetually rejuvenates itself through the fresh insights and energies of its members, all growing in the grace and knowledge of our Lord and Savior Jesus Christ (2 Peter 3:18).

The culture of the future church is one of continuous renewal, where the Holy Spirit's presence is fervently sought and revered. This church values the Spirit's movements as essential to its life and growth, recognizing that "where the Spirit of the Lord is, there is liberty" (2 Corinthians 3:17). The atmosphere of this church is charged with expectancy, knowing that the Spirit is always at work to guide, to comfort, and to empower for greater works than we can imagine.

Education in the future church goes beyond doctrinal instruction to include teaching how to live out one's faith in the real world. This comprehensive approach ensures that believers are not only hearers of the Word but doers also, as James encourages us, "But be ye doers of the word, and not hearers only, deceiving your own selves" (James 1:22). In this future church, biblical truths are applied to everyday challenges, equipping believers to navigate complex social, ethical, and spiritual landscapes with wisdom and grace.

Mission and service in the future church are integral, not peripheral. The church does not exist for itself but is God's appointed agent for healing and transformation in the world. As Isaiah 58:10-11 teaches us, when we "pour out your soul to the hungry and satisfy the afflicted soul," then our "light shall rise in darkness, and thy obscurity be as the noonday." The future church actively engages in missions both locally and globally, driven by a profound commitment to embodying Christ's love and compassion to all people.

Financial stewardship in the future church reflects a profound trust in God's provision and a rejection of the consumerism that

CHAPTER 60: ENVISIONING THE FUTURE CHURCH

pervades our culture. With the wisdom of Proverbs 3:9, "Honour the LORD with thy substance, and with the firstfruits of all thine increase," the future church manages its resources with integrity, ensuring that God's work is not only sustained but flourishes. This stewardship extends to caring for the needy and supporting missions, reflecting a kingdom economy that prioritizes eternal investments over worldly gain.

As we imagine this future church, it becomes clear that such a community could transform the world. The ripples of its influence would extend far beyond its local setting, touching lives across nations and generations. The church's vibrant witness in word and deed would draw many to Christ, fulfilling the Great Commission in a manner that reverberates with the echoes of Matthew 24:14, "And this gospel of the kingdom shall be preached in all the world for a witness unto all nations; and then shall the end come."

The call to holiness will be a defining characteristic of the future church, embracing the command to "be ye holy; for I am holy" (1 Peter 1:16). Holiness is not merely a set of external behaviors but a heart posture of complete devotion to God, reflecting His purity in every aspect of our lives. This pursuit of holiness will stand in stark contrast to the moral relativism of our age, shining as a beacon of integrity and righteousness.

Relationships within the future church will be marked by genuine community, moving beyond superficial interactions to deep, authentic connections. As Hebrews 10:24-25 encourages us, "And let us consider one another to provoke unto love and to good works: not forsaking the assembling of ourselves together, as the manner of some is; but exhorting one another: and so much the more, as ye see the day approaching." This scripture highlights the importance of gathering together, not just physically but in spirit and purpose, to encourage and build one another up in love.

The future church will also be characterized by its unwavering commitment to truth, standing firm against the tides of deception and falsehood that seek to undermine the gospel. Ephesians 4:14 reminds us, "That we henceforth be no more children, tossed to and fro, and carried about with every wind of doctrine, by the sleight of men, and cunning craftiness, whereby they lie in wait to deceive." This commitment to truth will require discernment, courage, and a deep grounding in the Word of God.

Prayer will be the lifeblood of the future church, an ever-present source of power and guidance. As Jesus taught in Matthew 6:6, "But thou, when thou prayest, enter into thy closet, and when thou hast shut thy door, pray to thy Father which is in secret; and thy Father which seeth in secret shall reward thee openly." This emphasis on private, personal prayer will fuel the corporate prayer life of the church, creating a community that is continually seeking God's face and aligning itself with His will.

In the future church, there will be a renewed emphasis on the ministry of the Holy Spirit, recognizing His vital role in empowering believers for service and witness. Acts 1:8 declares, "But ye shall receive power, after that the Holy Ghost is come upon you: and ye shall be witnesses unto me both in Jerusalem, and in all Judaea, and in Samaria, and unto the uttermost part of the earth." This promise of power will be evident in the life of the church, as believers operate in the gifts and fruits of the Spirit, bringing transformation to their communities and beyond.

CHAPTER 60: ENVISIONING THE FUTURE CHURCH

Outreach will be strategic and intentional, driven by a passion to reach the lost and fulfill the Great Commission. As Paul writes in Romans 10:14-15, "How then shall they call on him in whom they have not believed? and how shall they believe in him of whom they have not heard? and how shall they hear without a preacher? And how shall they preach, except they be sent?" This sense of urgency will propel the church into action, sharing the gospel with clarity and compassion, and making disciples of all nations.

The future church will embrace technology as a tool for ministry, leveraging digital platforms to reach a global audience. However, this will be done with discernment, ensuring that technology enhances rather than detracts from the core mission of the church. As Proverbs 16:3 advises, "Commit thy works unto the LORD, and thy thoughts shall be established." This commitment will guide the church in using technology wisely, always seeking to glorify God and advance His kingdom.

Education in the future church will be holistic, addressing the spiritual, emotional, and intellectual needs of believers. Proverbs 4:7 emphasizes, "Wisdom is the principal thing; therefore get wisdom: and with all thy getting get understanding." This pursuit of wisdom will be evident in the church's teaching and discipleship programs, equipping believers to live out their faith in every area of life.

As we envision this future church, it is clear that it will be a community of transformation, both for its members and the world around it. This transformation will be rooted in a deep love for God and a commitment to His purposes, as expressed in Deuteronomy 6:5, "And thou shalt love the LORD thy God with all thine heart, and with all thy soul, and with all thy might." This all-encompassing love will drive the church to greater heights of faithfulness and impact.

In this future church, the role of the family will be strengthened, recognizing its importance as the foundational unit of society and the church. Ephesians 6:1-4 provides guidance, "Children, obey your parents in the Lord: for this is right. Honour thy father and mother; (which is the first commandment with promise;) That it may be well with thee, and thou mayest live long on the earth. And, ye fathers, provoke not your children to wrath: but bring them up in the nurture and admonition of the Lord." This scripture underscores the importance of nurturing and discipling the next generation within the context of loving, Christ-centered families.

Finally, the future church will be a place of healing and restoration, offering hope and wholeness to those who are broken and hurting. Isaiah 61:1-3 encapsulates this mission, "The Spirit of the Lord GOD is upon me; because the LORD hath anointed me to preach good tidings unto the meek; he hath sent me to bind up the brokenhearted, to proclaim liberty to the captives, and the opening of the prison to them that are bound; To proclaim the acceptable year of the LORD, and the day of vengeance of our God; to comfort all that mourn; To appoint unto them that mourn in Zion, to give unto them beauty for ashes, the oil of joy for mourning, the garment of praise for the spirit of heaviness; that they might be called trees of righteousness, the planting of the LORD, that he might be glorified." This vision of a church that brings healing and hope will inspire us to create spaces where God's love and power can bring transformation to all who enter.

CHAPTER 60: ENVISIONING THE FUTURE CHURCH

As we stand on the cusp of this new era, let us commit to being architects of this divine blueprint, laboring in faith and obedience to see it realized. The call to renewal is a call to action, a summons to align our churches with the kingdom's purposes and to rekindle the flame of our first love for Christ. May we respond with the zeal of those early believers who "continued stedfastly in the apostles' doctrine and fellowship, and in breaking of bread, and in prayers" (Acts 2:42). Thus, our churches will not only endure but thrive as beacons of light and truth in a world in desperate need of the gospel.

This is our mandate, this is our mission, and this is our moment. As co-laborers with Christ, let us embrace this vision with unwavering faith, knowing that our labor in the Lord is not in vain (1 Corinthians 15:58). Together, let us build the future church that God envisions, a church that stands as a testament to His glory, power, and love.

Amen and Beyond

As we draw near to the conclusion of "Church Gone Wild: A Call to Renewal and Restoration," it is essential to gather the threads of prophetic warnings, historical lessons, and the urgent need for renewal that we've explored together. The journey through these pages is more than a critique; it is a heartfelt invitation from the Lord to return to the purity and power of our foundational beliefs. As Revelation 2:5 implores us, "Remember therefore from whence thou art fallen, and repent, and do the first works." This is not merely an advisory; it is a divine mandate for those desiring to see the church thrive in authenticity and spiritual truth.

In the spirit of this call, let us consider our personal roles within the broader narrative of the church. Each of us holds the potential to influence our local congregations towards deeper spiritual integrity and biblical faithfulness. Just as Joshua declared unto the people, "Choose you this day whom ye will serve... but as for me and my house, we will serve the LORD" (Joshua 24:15), we too must decide daily to serve God with unwavering commitment and purity of heart.

This choice becomes particularly significant in an era where cultural currents sway many away from the gospel's truth. Our commitment to Christ must not be passive but active, engaging in constant self-examination and renewal. Paul's words to the Corinthians resonate deeply here: "Examine yourselves, whether ye be in the faith; prove your own selves" (2 Corinthians 13:5).

Such introspection ensures our faith is not only professed but also deeply rooted and flourishing in the soil of God's Word.

Moreover, the church's ability to navigate the complexities of modern society while holding fast to biblical principles is paramount. As we face social, moral, and ethical dilemmas, the wisdom of Scripture must be our guide. We are reminded of Paul's advice in Romans 12:2, "And be not conformed to this world: but be ye transformed by the renewing of your mind, that ye may prove what is that good, and acceptable, and perfect, will of God." Transformation through the renewal of our minds is crucial in discerning and accomplishing God's will in our lives and our congregations.

The call to renewal is also a call to unity and collective action within the body of Christ. The early church exemplified this as they "continued steadfastly in the apostles' doctrine and fellowship, and in breaking of bread, and in prayers" (Acts 2:42). Their unity was not just in belief but also in purpose and daily living, which propelled the gospel forward with remarkable power and grace. Our modern assemblies can see similar blessings when we unite in true biblical fellowship and purpose.

Yet, true renewal often requires difficult choices, including the willingness to separate from practices and influences that compromise our spiritual integrity. Jesus' parable of the wheat and the tares is instructive; the tares, representing elements contrary to the kingdom of God, grow alongside the wheat until the harvest (Matthew 13:24-30). The separation is inevitable and necessary, illustrating that purity in the church will ultimately be restored, though it requires patience and discernment.

The prophetic role within the church is not only to comfort but also to confront when necessary. As God's messengers, we must not shy away from proclaiming the full counsel of God, including the parts that challenge and convict. As Ezekiel was appointed as a watchman unto the house of Israel, so too are we called to be watchmen for our brothers and sisters, declaring, "Thus saith the Lord GOD; repent, and turn yourselves from your idols; and turn away your faces from all your abominations" (Ezekiel 14:6).

Heeding the call to renewal also involves embracing the disciplines of prayer and fasting, tools that foster spiritual strength and clarity. The early church leaders in Antioch ministered to the Lord and fasted before making significant decisions (Acts 13:2-3), a practice that can guide us through the complexities of church leadership and personal spiritual growth today.

As we aim to restore the church to its biblical foundations, we must also rekindle our passion for evangelism and discipleship. These are not optional activities but central to the mission Christ has given us. "Go ye therefore, and teach all nations, baptizing them in the name of the Father, and of the Son, and of the Holy Ghost" (Matthew 28:19). This Great Commission remains as relevant today as it was two thousand years ago.

The church's journey toward renewal is not merely about addressing external issues but involves a deep, internal transformation that begins in the hearts of each believer. As David prayed in Psalm 51:10, "Create in me a clean heart, O God; and renew a right spirit within me." This personal renewal is essential for the corporate health and spiritual vitality of the church.

In conclusion, let us not be disheartened by the challenges we face but be inspired by the possibilities of what our churches can become through divine renewal. The path forward involves returning to our first love, embracing our biblical heritage, and pursuing God's heart with relentless passion and purity. "And let us not be weary in well doing: for in due season we shall reap, if we faint not" (Galatians 6:9). Our efforts and faithfulness will bear fruit in due time, and our churches can indeed become beacons of light and truth in a world that desperately needs the transformative power of the gospel.

May this book serve as a catalyst for reflection, repentance, and renewal in your life and in your local church. As we close this chapter together, may your spirit be stirred to action, and may your heart be aligned with the profound and beautiful call of Christ. Together, let us work towards a church that truly embodies the principles and power of the kingdom of God, transforming not only individual lives but whole communities for His glory. Amen and beyond.

A Prayer for You

Heavenly Father, in the name of Jesus, I come before You with a heart full of gratitude and a spirit eager to intercede for the precious soul reading these words. Lord, You know their innermost thoughts, their deepest desires, and the challenges they face. I pray that as they journey through the pages of this book, they will not only gain knowledge but experience a profound spiritual awakening that draws them closer to Your heart.

Lord, as Your Scripture reminds us in James 4:8, "Draw nigh to God, and he will draw nigh to you." I ask that You draw near to this reader. Wash their hands, purify their hearts, and let them not be double-minded but wholly committed to Your purpose and Your ways. Let Your presence envelop them, providing comfort and stirring up a passionate pursuit of holiness and truth.

Father, I pray against any force that seeks to distract or pull them away from the foundational truths of Your Word. In a world where many have strayed towards the seduction of cultural acceptance and material gains, I ask that You anchor this reader in the truth of Your Word. May they be like the wise man who built his house upon the rock, steadfast amid storms (Matthew 7:24-25).

Holy Spirit, breathe on them anew. Fill them with a renewed love for the Gospel, which is the power of God unto salvation to everyone that believeth (Romans 1:16). Let this love not be superficial but deeply rooted in a profound understanding of the grace and mercy bestowed upon us through Christ Jesus.

Father, guide them in all wisdom and understanding as they seek to apply what they have learned to their daily lives. May Your Word be a lamp unto their feet and a light unto their path (Psalm 119:105), guiding them in every decision and illuminating their steps in righteousness. Help them to not conform to the patterns of this world but to be transformed by the renewing of their mind, proving what is that good, and acceptable, and perfect, will of God (Romans 12:2).

I pray for the courage and boldness for this reader to stand against the tide of popular opinion and societal norms that contradict Your commands. Grant them the strength to uphold Your statutes, not for the sake of tradition but as a true expression of their love and reverence for You.

Lord, Your Word in 2 Timothy 1:7 tells us that You have not given us a spirit of fear, but of power, and of love, and of a sound mind. Empower this reader to live out their faith fearlessly, lovingly, and wisely. May they be agents of change in their communities, reflecting Your light and leading others to the truth of the Gospel.

I also pray for a heart of worship that seeks You above all else. Let their worship be in spirit and in truth, as John 4:24 instructs. May their adoration go beyond songs and rituals, becoming a reflection of their everyday lives, where every action and thought is an offering pleasing to You.

Father, in their quest for spiritual depth, let them not be swayed by the shallow currents of contemporary Christianity. Instill in them a hunger for Your deep truths, and satisfy them with the richness of Your teachings that go beyond the milk of the Word to the solid food meant for the mature (Hebrews 5:14).

As they walk the path of righteousness, protect them from the snares of the enemy. Let them wear the full armor of God, that they may be able to stand against the wiles of the devil, having girded their loins with truth, and having put on the breastplate of righteousness (Ephesians 6:11-14).

In their journey towards holiness, remind them that they are not striving in their strength but in the power of the Holy Spirit. May they find rest in Your promise that Your grace is sufficient for them, for Your power is made perfect in weakness (2 Corinthians 12:9).

Let this prayer serve as a catalyst for an inward examination and a deliberate step towards repentance where needed. May they echo the heart of David in Psalm 51, seeking Your mercy, asking for a clean heart, and renewing a steadfast spirit within them.

Lord, as they engage with the community of believers, let them remember the importance of fellowship as outlined in Acts 2:42-47. Foster in them a spirit of unity and collaboration, that they may bear one another's burdens and so fulfill the law of Christ (Galatians 6:2).

May this reader rise as a beacon of hope and a testament to Your transformative power. As they put into practice the divine insights gleaned from these pages, may their life be a living epistle, known and read by all men (2 Corinthians 3:2-3), demonstrating the beautiful work of Your hands.

Finally, Lord, I pray that Your peace, which surpasses all understanding, will guard their hearts and minds in Christ Jesus (Philippians 4:7). Let this peace rule in their hearts, to which also they are called in one body; and be thankful (Colossians 3:15).

Thank You, Father, for hearing this prayer. I trust in Your unfailing love and believe that You are at work in this reader's life, crafting a story of renewal and restoration that glorifies Your name. In Jesus' precious name, Amen.

About The Author

Bishop Al Cheeks is a respected spiritual leader and apostolic visionary, renowned for his profound commitment to restoring biblical foundations within the church. As the founder and apostolic head of Call To Glory Ministries, Bishop Cheeks has dedicated over three decades to church planting and Christian leadership development, emphasizing the need for doctrinal purity and spiritual renewal, themes central to his book, "Church Gone Wild: A Call to Renewal and Restoration."

Under his leadership, Call To Glory Ministries has flourished, making significant impacts across Sub-Saharan Africa, the Caribbean, and South America. His ministry is committed to developing strong Christian leaders and establishing vibrant local churches, a mission that Bishop Cheeks passionately advances through his writings, global conferences, and personal mentorship of emerging leaders.

Beyond his ecclesiastical endeavors, Bishop Cheeks is a vocal advocate for ethical leadership and Christian engagement in societal realms, driven by a belief in holistic community upliftment through initiatives in healthcare, education, and economic development. His entrepreneurial ventures span diverse industries, where he applies biblical principles such as those from Ecclesiastes to foster sustainable practices and community empowerment.

Bishop Cheeks champions the concept that prosperity should fuel kingdom-building and social betterment, especially in underserved communities. His life's work and teachings inspire many to integrate faith actively into all areas of life, making a tangible impact in the world.

Connect with Bishop Al Cheeks on Social Media:

Threads: @BishopAlCheeks

X (formerly Twitter): @BishopAlCheeks

Facebook: https://www.facebook.com/@BishopAlCheeks

Instagram: @BishopAlCheeks

YouTube: @BishopAlCheeks

Visit www.BishopAlCheeks.com to learn more about his writings, leadership philosophy, and speaking engagements.

Connect with Call To Glory Ministries on Social Media:

Threads: @HisCallToGlory

X (formerly Twitter): @HisCallToGlory

Facebook: https://www.facebook.com/@HisCallToGlory

Instagram: @HisCallToGlory

YouTube: @HisCallToGlory

Visit www.CallToGlory.org to learn more about our global impact in church planting and Christian leadership development.

www.ingramcontent.com/pod-product-compliance
Lightning Source LLC
Chambersburg PA
CBHW062005180426
43198CB00037B/2399